LOVE LETTERS

FROM

THE FRONT

Published in 2000 by Marino Books
An imprint of Mercier Press
16 Hume Street Dublin 2
Tel: (01) 661 5299; Fax: (01) 661 8583
E-mail: books@marino.ie

Trade enquiries to CMD Distribution
55A Spruce Avenue
Stillorgan Industrial Park
Blackrock County Dublin
Tel: (01) 294 2556; Fax: (01) 294 2564
E-mail: cmd@columba.ie

Foreword   © Myles Dungan 2000
Introduction   © Jean Kelly 2000
Letters   © R. T. and P. H. Kelly

ISBN 1 86023

10 9 8 7 6 5 4 3 2 1

A CIP record for this title is available from
the British Library

Cover design by SPACE
Typset by *Deirdre's Desktop*
Printed in Ireland by ColourBooks,
Baldoyle Industrial Estate, Dublin 13

LOVE LETTERS

FROM

THE FRONT

EDITED BY

JEAN KELLY

I would like to thank Phyllis's family,
my brother-in-law, Patrick, and his wife, Margaret,
and especially Tom, Jane and Robert
for their encouragement and help.

CONTENTS

FOREWORD

One of the frustrations for Irish historians working on World War I is the phenomenon of the 'clear out'. It is the great intangible – it may even be part of historiographical mythology – but it leaves a feeling of unfinished business in the consciousness of the researcher. It goes something like this. It is the 1970s or 1980s and Grandfather has just died. The mottled contents of the chest in the attic can finally be destroyed. Old letters to Grandmother are tossed out on the rubbish heap with no regard for their possible significance.

It may never have happened, certainly not on any vast or premeditated scale. But such was the lack of awareness in this country of the extent of Irish participation in the Great War that it is difficult to believe it did not occur in some cases. Even one is one too many. Fortunately, the letters of Eric Appleby to Phyllis Kelly did not meet such a fate and survive to tell their story.

One of the other frustrations for the historian in dealing with letters like those that form this collection is the omnipresence of the military censor. Correspondence was required to be long on sentiment and short on detail, which is how the soldiers themselves probably preferred it anyway. But it can be galling to read a literate, detailed account of an event from the war and not know exactly where it happened, either because the correspondent knows not to exclude such information or because an officer has excised the reference. Contemporary diaries, kept away from the eyes of authority, are far more useful for those little details which help us to build up a picture of the war. Letters are rather better on atmosphere and emotion.

Much correspondence from the front tended to be personal and anodyne. Its very blandness acted as a protection. By maintaining a neutral or even upbeat tone, the soldier could convince himself that things were really quite normal (albeit in an abnormal world) and his loved ones could maintain their own sense of his relative security and well-being. The most interesting correspondence was usually from officers, and officers in extremis at that. The commissioned officers were the censors of the private soldiers; their own letters home were not always subjected to such vigorous scrutiny. Furthermore, 1914-1918 was a period in which literacy was not universal. The officer was likely to be better educated than the men under his command, and letter-writing was still an art which had not been lost among the middle classes. The letters which have survived to the present day reveal much about the true nature of war, and the effects on those who endure it.

Lieutenant Guy Nightingale was an officer in extremis when he wrote an extraordinary series of letters to his family in the aftermath of the disastrous Gallipoli landings of April, 1915. He made no attempt to disguise the incompetence and bungling which had characterised the assault on 'V' Beach by the 29th Division. Nor did he spare his family the gory details of the days and weeks that followed. His correspondence, which is on file in the Imperial War Museum in London, offers a fascinating and realistic insight into the mind of a soldier under severe pressure and in constant jeopardy.

Rowland Feilding's letters, collected and published as War Letters to a Wife, present us with a picture of the burdens of command, the process of decision-making which the commanding officer of a battalion knows will cost the lives of some of his men.

Sgt William O'Reilly's letters, collected by his family, to which this writer was allowed access in 1994, allow us to see the torment of a man whose wife has died in childbirth, just a few weeks after he had been taken prisoner. He sat out the war in German prison camps, agonising over the child he had never seen and who was growing up every month in his imagination, courtesy of letters from his sister-in-law. But there was to be no happy ending for William O'Reilly. Days after his release from POW camp he died in London, a bare twenty-four hours before his four-year-old child was to have been brought to him for a rapturous first meeting.

Such are the treasures of correspondence from the front. Letters, both straightforward and complex, have the power to inspire great emotion in the reader. For a researcher, there is nothing quite like the feeling evoked when confronted with a pile of old, yellowing letters – the fruits of a correspondence between soldier and loved ones. Furthermore, there is nothing quite like the sinking feeling when it becomes clear as you go through the pile that the correspondence does not last until November 1918. It is like looking at someone's life in 'forward' mode and realising that they are going to die sooner rather than later.

Eric Appleby and Phyllis Kelly did not live happily ever after. When Phyllis fell in love with her 'Englishman' in 1915, nationality didn't matter. By the time of his death in 1916, it was becoming a more significant division. Had he survived and come to claim her in 1918, it might have been an unbridgeable gap, so much had happened to poison Anglo-Irish relations in the interim. As with so much of the correspondence between the mud of Flanders and Picardy and the 'Home Front', we will never know.

Myles Dungan

INTRODUCTION

These letters tell a love story – that of Eric and Phyllis, during the First World War.

Eric Appleby was born in 1893, near Liverpool. He was an engineering student in Manchester at the start of the war in 1914. He had been in his school Officer Training Corps, and in the Royal Engineers Territorials while at university. He enlisted in the Royal Field Artillery late in 1914 and was sent to Athlone for training, where he met Phyllis. In the spring of 1915, Eric was commissioned Second Lieutenant, and posted to France.

Phyllis Kelly was born in 1892 and brought up in Athlone, on the River Shannon. Her father was a local solicitor. She met Eric at a dance in 1915.

Although his letters have been edited to shorten some of the longer letters, the words are Eric's. They tell of his dependence on Phyllis's love to overcome the horrors of the war.

There are some two hundred letters, field service postcards and telegrams. Phyllis kept the letters all her life, tied in bundles and numbered in chronological order, each bundle corresponding to Eric's times at the front.

In addition to Eric's letters, I have used his 1916 diary. Quotes from it are in italics. The diary gives details that the censor would not have allowed in his letters, thus we are able to track where he was in France.

Although there is only one letter from Phyllis, Eric refers to her letters constantly, so the correspondence does not appear one-sided. He recounts for her the four leaves he spent with her in England and Ireland because Phyllis asked him to write about 'their love days together.'

Before she died, Phyllis gave the letters to her family. She felt that the letters might be of interest to a wider audience, as first-hand memories of those times were getting fewer and fewer. This book is an attempt to fulfil her wish and to tell one soldier's story of the war.

Jean Kelly

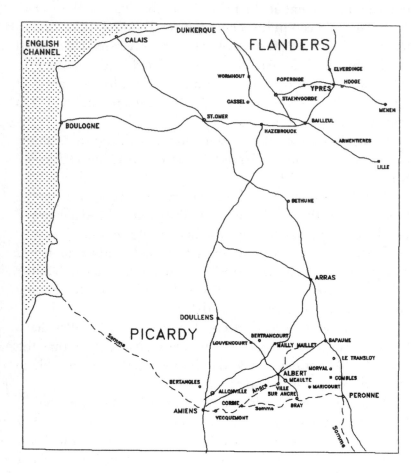

Map of North-West France and Southern Belgium

GLOSSARY

BEF	British Expeditionary Force
DA	Damn all, a family joke meaning small gift
FSPC	Field Service postcard
HQ	Headquarters
MG	Machine-gun
OC	Officer Commanding
OS	Observing Station
OTC	Officers Training Corps
RAMC	Royal Army Medical Corps
RFA	Royal Field Artillery
RE (Terr.)	Royal Engineers Territorial
SR	Special Reserve

1915

25 March

Dear Phyllis

I am writing this in the music room at home and I would like to hear you singing in it some time. I wish you were here now. My father is playing the angelus (like a pianola).

You have no idea how wretched I felt when I left you, and especially when I was in the train. I saw someone waving in the dining room but could not make out who it was. They want to know why I am so quiet here. I said I didn't know, but I guess I do. I believe I could have nearly cried when I was looking at some shamrock my sister was growing. I started looking for a four-leaved bit and found one nearly immediately.

We had a very smooth crossing and arrived at Lime Street Station at 4.45 am. Since I came home I have been trying to get my kit together. I have not received any orders yet but am expecting them at any hour now.

I am having an RFA button made into a brooch for you and will send it on as soon as it is ready. The ring is quite safe and will bring me good luck, I am sure. I shall put it on the string with my identification disc, and I am sure it will be safe there.

If you have a moment to spare, I would like a few lines to tell me about yourself.

Goodbye now. My dearest love is sent with this.

Eric

27 March

Dear Phyllis

Here is the button. I hope you will like it enough to wear it. I would like to have sent you something more valuable as a souvenir, but unfortunately my cash is rather low at present, owing to having to shell out so much for kit. I kept finding myself thinking of all that I had done at Athlone.

I received a wire from the Adjutant today to say that my orders are following, so I suppose I shall be off on Monday.

Well, bye-bye, Phyllis, for the present and remember that I do love you really and truly.

Will you write to me sometimes.

Yours always,

Eric

FRANCE

1 APRIL
ARMY POST OFFICE, HAVRE

Dear Phyllis
We have arrived safely and are enjoying the most glorious weather. The crossing was quite choppy and several were ill.

We have quite an easy time here, and we are allowed into Havre in the afternoon and return to camp when we like. Yesterday, a whole crowd of us went in, and I came back in a huge six-cylinder Daimler belonging, so the chauffeur said, to Sir John French.

Did you receive the button and letter? How did you get on with your singing? I wish I could have heard you. I had to cut that photo of you down to a smaller size because I could not get it in my breast pocket. It is often looked at by me.

If I remain here in France for very long I shall be able to speak the language like a native. All the French are very amusing. We have not seen any of the people who came over before us but may be sent to Batteries where they are at present.

Please remember me kindly to your mother and father and all the family. Send any letters here until I give you my final address.

With much love from
Eric

WEDNESDAY 7 APRIL
ON ACTIVE SERVICE
6TH DIVISION, ARTILLERY HEADQUARTERS

My dearest
I have just received your letter today. I have been away from the Base Depot for the last four days taking a draft to a railhead and it takes a long time to get there and back. We could hear the guns firing when we were up there, about five miles behind the line.

Will you always date your letters, giving the day of the week?

I want to see how long they take to come. I am glad you got the button safely and am so glad that you will wear it for my sake. I was rather hurt when you refused my ring, but in a way I am glad because I don't want to cause any ill feeling between you and your parents. Your ring and photo are with me always as my talisman. You have no idea, sweetheart, how I treasure the only two things I have that were yours at one time. Why you should really love me, God alone knows; you seemed to try and make me dislike you. But I never thought it would end – or should I say begin – as it did.

The weather is appalling. It is simply teeming for the last five days. Everything is soaking. I go up to the line tomorrow. I will write as soon as I can and try and explain what I am doing. I do, do, do love your letters, and tell me everything, and the longest letter is most acceptable. I hope you will get to like my name. If not, give me a pet name of your own.

We have got 'The Sunshine of Your Smile' here in the mess and it always will remind me of the last night I had with you whenever I hear it. If you would really like the ring, I will get Mother to send it to you.

Bye-bye now, Phyl, and God bless you. Yours for always,
Eric

MONDAY 12 APRIL
FIELD POST OFFICE
21ST BATTERY, 2ND BRIGADE

At last I have arrived at the front, and at present I am having quite a gentle breaking in. Of course the test may come all at once, well sufficient unto the day, etc. All the officers in this Battery seem to be very nice men, especially the Major and the Captain. We have very comfortable quarters in a large house, part of which has been shelled at some time, but at present seems to be fairly safe. Yesterday both our own artillery and the Germans seemed to get rather excited and shelled one another all afternoon and evening. We were busy making gun emplacements between two lines of shell fires, and shells were whizzing over our heads, but nobody here seems to take any notice of them at all.

I did not like your second letter nearly as well as the first; you seemed to have been so reserved at the time you wrote. Do let me have a letter as often as you can.

Tons of love for you. Yours for always,
Eric

FRIDAY 16 APRIL

My very own Irish lassie
I received your letter yesterday, so it took five days to get here. I don't call that at all bad. I can't make out why you were so angry over my letter. Please tell me what offended you. I never want to have any more rows. It was at the second dance we had after I arrived at Athlone that I began to have a queer feeling in my heart. But at the first dance, when I met you, I spotted the people that I liked immediately. Tell me whether you reciprocate the feeling in the least way.

They are potting at two aeroplanes with anti-aircraft guns. It is very interesting watching the puffs of smoke suddenly come in the sky as the shells burst. They are fairly blazing away at them; I can see them from the window just beside me.

Tea has just been brought in. By Jove, I often think of the afternoon teas I had at your house.

I have just received another letter from you, posted April 14, so that was quick work. I am writing to my mother to ask her to send you my signet ring. I always used to wear it on the little finger of my left hand. It was given to me for my twenty-first. I think it was awfully nasty of you to mention anything about me getting a swelled head. Also, kindly stop talking about your being 'the cat who walked by himself'. Please forgive me for breaking my promise and showing my mother your photo; I can't keep anything from you. She said she was sure you would not mind if you knew. She particularly asked to see it and she

25

said 'she looks a very nice girl'. You are a real darling for writing such long letters. I read them over and over again. I think I can stand a great deal of the 'horrid me' as you put it, in order to get a little of the 'nice one' and I know you can be nice and have been already to me. I have just got your photo out but I do wish the real person was here in its place. I am very proud of you for singing well and am only afraid a whole crowd of fellows will fall in love with you when they hear you. I am very, very jealous.

Now bye-bye, my dear, dear love. Your own Englishman,
Eric

SUNDAY 18 APRIL

My dearest
I think you will be tired of my letters if I write so often. Every day last week we have had a course of instruction under one of the majors. It has kept us occupied all day. As today is Sunday, I have some free time, so I am sitting in our billet writing this. There has to be always one officer in the billet in case of an emergency, and the subalterns take it in turns. The weather is simply glorious here. This morning I got up early and went for a ride. We went over the frontier into Belgium for a very short visit. I have not got my own horse yet, so I had to borrow one. Sunday here is like every other day, except that the French people are togged up in their best clothes.

Several men in the Battery come from Athlone and it seems very funny to see the letters addressed to Athlone when we are censoring them. We did quite a lot of firing this afternoon and, am glad to say, received no replies.

Have you been up the river at all? I should think it would be lovely on the lake if you are having as beautiful weather as we are here. Now I must write to my sister, so au revoir, love.

Always yours,
Eric

My dearest
I received the muffler on Monday; it is a beautiful thing and an absolute work of art. It is beautifully knitted and seems really too good to wear out here. It is so nice and long and wide. Many, many thanks to you, dear, dear girl. I was disappointed that no letter came with it.

Last night we had a little bit of excitement taking a gun to a position, and this afternoon the Major allowed me to give the necessary orders and observe for fire of the gun. It was quite good fun and we got some beauties into the German trenches. Tomorrow I am going into the trenches to have a look around and then I shall take my turn as Forward Observing Officer once every four days. It has been chilly but fine.

Did you have your photo taken? If so, was it a success? Tell me if you receive the ring and, if so, how you like it and what finger it fits.

With fondest love, always yours,
Eric

SUNDAY 25 APRIL

My dearest Phyl
Your letter (April 21) arrived today.

I went down to the trenches on Thursday afternoon, stayed the night and all day Friday. On Thursday night I was walking along a communication trench when suddenly there was a fizz-z-z-z-crack and a bullet landed in the parapet of the trench, in line with my shoulder and not two yards away. It is weird in the trenches at night. The Boche shoot things like rockets into the air which give a very bright light for a few seconds. While the light is burning they fire at our men. The latter watch for the flashes of their rifles and fire at them. There is a continual intermittent (that's Irish, isn't it!) rifle fire going on all night and all day. Funnily enough, Brinkley came down, and it was his first night down there. This afternoon I took a party of men to the baths and was going to have one myself, only the place was full up so had to go without.

Please send me one of the photos if you like them better than the one I have at present. I wonder what would have happened to our friendship if I had not been able to dance a bit. Do you remember, at one of the dances I put my head close to yours and you pressed yours against mine? I wonder whether you noticed it. It made me very happy at the time. I wonder do you really mean 'because it belongs to the dearest person in all the world', because it means a very great deal to me.

There is an awful row going on down in the trenches, it sounds like another attack. It is a funny thing, warfare. I often wonder why we are here killing each other by every means possible. As yet I haven't even seen a German, except some prisoners we saw down at Havre. Well, I wonder when it will all be over and what I shall do when it is. I am thinking Athlone will be like a very big magnet to me. Tomorrow we are going to do some driving drill with the wagons as we used to do at Athlone.

Night-night now my dear, dear love. I hope your next letter will come soon.

Always your own Eric

THURSDAY 29 APRIL

Very many thanks for yours received last night. The muffler is beautifully soft. I took it down to the trenches as a covering for my air pillow. Yesterday was boiling hot down in the trenches. I had to try and spot where a German Battery was and where a German aeroplane had landed. Last night Harvey and I went church-breaking. We had to take a trapdoor off its hinges up in the clock tower. It was weird, climbing into the church by a shell hole in the wall and then climbing up innumerable steps and ladders. The clock was non est owing to German shellfire.

We had a glorious view from the top because it was brilliant moonlight. All along the line we could see the flares shooting up into the air.

I forgot to tell you, I was going up to our observing station, which is a very battered house, when the Germans put three shells, one after another, into one corner of it, just below where we sit. I thanked my stars I wasn't up in it at the time. I am trying to decide which horse to take for my own charger. I have my eye on a very nice dark chestnut mare and I shall call her Phyl. If I get a second horse I shall call him Tommy after the one at Athlone.

The Captain and yours have been round to our church this evening. The Boche shelled it this morning and have made an awful mess of it. They were about six-inch shells. A figure of the Virgin was badly damaged. Several houses round the church are badly damaged; one is a total wreck, blown inside out. In one place in the tower, a shell has pierced a wall at least four feet thick, and another has gone clean through the tower, piercing two walls, each at least two feet thick. Most of the ladders we went up are smashed to atoms.

> So here's to the girl with hazel eyes,
> She's always nice-looking and very wise.

Bye-bye, my sweetheart.
Always yours,
Eric

SUNDAY 2 MAY 1915
IN THE TRENCHES

My own dear love
I wonder if there will be a letter waiting for me when I get back to the Battery. I do hope so. I used the muffler to cover my pillow again and will do so always when I am down here. It is beautifully soft, and makes me sleep like a top.

We have got another dugout. It is quite a palatial place. There are two rooms in it: a mess room and a smoking room combined, and the other room is the bedroom. The total length is about sixteen feet by eight to nine feet in width and about five feet ten inches in height. It is made of wooden planks and is dug out of a bank of clay. The roof is wood with corrugated iron on top and then about one and a half feet of clay on top. In the bedroom there are two bunks raised about two feet from the ground and made of planks. For a mattress we have straw. On top of this we put a groundsheet and then we have two blankets. Of course, we sleep in our clothes, just taking our boots and tunics off.

The front of the mess room faces away from the line of trenches. A lamp is hanging on the wall just above a table. Above the lamp is a shelf on which we put plates, cups, knives, forks etc. Further along the shelf we keep condensed milk, jam, bread and general eatables. Lower down the wall on the other side there is another shelf with papers and a mirror, tobacco and other oddments. We have several pictures on the wall, one of which is called 'Arfa the Kaiser'! and is a British Tommy in full kit with a rifle slung over his shoulder, busy lighting his pipe. We have a small coal stove with a chimney going up through the roof. There is room for a medium-sized saucepan to go on the fire. Above the stove is a small glass window, about two feet by eighteen inches. There is a line of clothes hooks on which we hang our coats and straps. We have three chairs and two tables, one a small wickerwork table. It is very comfortable and I hope you will be able to imagine it from this lengthy description.

I have been trying to find out the positions of German machine guns and a Battery. My servant has just brought my lunch in so I will finish afterwards.

After lunch

I would give a lot to be able to give you a good hug and heaps of kisses. Crack-siss-s-s-s a bullet has just come along quite close to the hut. You may be sure I take double care of myself, knowing that you want me to.

All my love to you, Phyl, from your Englishman,
Eric

My sweetheart

I got your letter posted May 1 yesterday. Somehow your letters seem to get nicer each time, and I notice the changes in them very much. First you say something which makes me feel as though I could kiss the very ground you walk on, and then you say something which acts like a bucketful of cold water being poured over my head. I am so glad you have got the ring, and am more glad still that you like it. I did not think it was horrid of you to say nothing and I was pleasantly surprised that you allowed me to be rather familiar in the car. But that incident and one or two other small things that happened before and after kindled my love for you.

I suppose your brother will have gone by now to England. I wish I had seen him while I was at Athlone. It will be an experience going to the Dardanelles, won't it? I hope you have a good time when Joan is over, but don't forget me quite.

I had a nice long letter from Dad yesterday. He gave me some fatherly advice as to what I ought to do out here and says, in connection with the Huns, shoot first and talk afterwards.

We are being served out with these asphyxiating gas protectors – sounds lively, doesn't it? Yesterday morning the Boche shelled this place very heavily and did a certain amount of damage, e.g. set some houses on fire and killed some horses, wounded several civilians and soldiers. I was safely out of the way in the trenches.

How is the ring feeling now? Has anyone made any remarks about it? I am sure your mum must feel your brother going, but she must just remember he is 'doing his little bit' as any decent fellow ought to. I was looking through my notebook the other day and found the piece of shamrock you gave me pressed between two pages. It has kept its colour wonderfully. Now please tell me, are you twenty-two or twenty-three this June? I want to know. Now please remember, in future you are to write as much as you can in your letters and try and tell me everything you think of, no matter how 'silly' it may 'think' to you.

We have just heard the Lusitania has been torpedoed and • sunk. Only 500 saved out of 2,000.

I do wish I had been with you the other night to give you the kisses. Well, I send hundreds more with this and my fondest love.

Always your Eric

WEDNESDAY 12 MAY

My own sweetheart
I received your letter written on Sunday. It seems ages since your last one arrived and yet it was only last Saturday.

The Boche shelled us this morning just before lunch. One shell burst fairly close to the guns – no damage done – and another came close to this place and wounded eleven men and killed one of the Leinsters. Seven or eight shells came over altogether.

I shall soon be quite hardened to my cold baths but at present they are liable to give me a shock. And now for what I used to think of you. I thought you were a girl who would make a real friend. But I found you rather hard to understand and at times I thought I bored you. Your funny feelings were quite unfounded because I didn't disapprove of you at any time. I wonder will you want me when the war is over. I am afraid it is only a case of absence makes love grow stronger. I am absolutely certain I look out for your letters much more than you do for mine. The post usually comes in after lunch and there is a horrid suspense while the man hands us each our letters and parcels.

I have just received some ammunition from home for my automatic and am going to have some practice in order to be sure of hitting these d—d Huns when I get the chance. I think the danger from these gases is being overcome now. We heard they had failed to act on some of the men in our trenches to the south.

Now my dear, dear love, please write soon and a nice long letter, never tear them up but send everything you write to me.

With my very fondest love.

Always your Eric

TUESDAY 18 MAY

Dear Phyllis

I have just received your note this evening. Why have your letters changed so suddenly? The whole of the last one was a brute. I have had a bath this afternoon and although I feel nice and clean I also feel exceedingly bad-tempered, cross, and in general fed up.

Let me know all the songs you sing at the concerts and how you get on at them. I should think it will be quite strange for you at home again after being in Dublin for so long. I am extremely sorry to hear you can't care for anybody just because he or she is ten days younger than yourself.

I am glad to say 'Miss Phyl' is already showing great improvement in her behaviour, and after a little more riding will understand my ways perfectly. I have got a brand new set of harness for her, and have also got a good groom. Yesterday the Boche shelled the communication trench that goes along down to the trenches. Several burst about fifty yards away from our huts. They were kind enough to stop shelling just before I went up the trench on the way home.

Please remember me kindly to your parents.

Yours,

Eric

THURSDAY 20 MAY

Dear Phyl
What am I going to say in this letter? Oh! I wish I could get an hour's talk with you and I am certain that I could put matters right in a very short time. Really, I am afraid of sending a letter to you in case you misunderstand me again. You can't imagine how I long to have again some of the nice letters you have sent me. But each time it has been cold and yet polite in the extreme. No, Phyl, I cannot climb on to my side of the 'ditch' (as you call it). You may be able to do so, but I must remain in the ditch until I can persuade you to take up the thread – of something stronger than ordinary friendship – where it was dropped. I was conceited enough to think you had a little bit of love for me; at least, you have sent me your love in your letters. I feel horribly lonely and wretched out here now that your letters have altered, and the worst of all is that I have to bring myself to think it is my own silly fault.
Goodbye and my love to you,
Eric

THURSDAY 20 MAY

Sweetheart
You can't possibly imagine how glad I was to get your letter this afternoon. Thank heaven, it was like the old ones again. I could nearly have cried when I read it. You don't know what a great weight you have lifted off my mind. Please don't be offended with the old heading again. If you don't want me to call you that, just say so, but you will always be that to me.
I am going to change Batteries this afternoon, from the 21st to 42nd. Please write there in future. I shall now be in the same Battery as Brinkley. Yes, Phyl, dear old Layle is dead. Brinkley was very upset the other night about it.
I hope you had a fine day to go to Galway and I hope you had a good run. My sister is going into one of the Military Hospitals.

She has got in through the St John's Ambulance and as yet does not know where she will be sent. I may have to lose my mascot, 'Phyl', but I shall have a good try to keep her. I am riding over to the 42nd on her this afternoon. So bye-bye for the present, my dear, dear Phyl, from your much happier Eric

SATURDAY 29 MAY
42ND BATTERY

Sweetheart
Forgive me for not having written, it is impossible to find a moment. We are really in it now. There is a fearful din going on at present and shells are falling all round us. Quite close to our guns, about thirty yards behind, there is an enormous seventeen-inch shell hole, forty feet in diameter and twenty to thirty feet deep. Really, it is appalling to look at it, and makes one shudder to think of the explosion there must have been to cause such a huge hole. The whole country round here is one mess of shell holes, wire and dead horses.

I got your two letters, and as for the photos, I think they are beautiful; really, I mean it. I will send the photo I have got which you don't like back, as soon as possible. You ask me which – of the two that you have just sent – I like best. I love both of them: they are both the image of you. Oh! why can't I have the real person though, instead? Oh! I wish this cursed war was over and I could be with you again. I have been really frightened this afternoon; it's horrible to have to say so, but it is true. No one has any idea, until they have been in this part of the line, of the frightfulness of the whole thing. We shall want thousands more men and thousands and thousands of rounds to end this ghastly business.

I wanted to send you very, very many happy returns of your birthday on June 1. I looked for something to send you, but there was nothing. Well, here are hundreds of kisses for you, sweetheart, and remember it is a wish from the bottom of my heart, and God bless you. I simply can't think; this place is damnable. Just now we counted seven aeroplanes up, both Boche and our own. There is not a moment that you can't hear shells flying through the air, some screaming, some whistling, some humming, some roaring and some hissing. I can think of nothing but these cursed shells. I will write as often as I possibly can, but you must be prepared for a drop in numbers. So goodbye, and write as often as you possibly can, as you can see your letters mean everything to me.

Your very own Englishman,
Eric

1 JUNE 1915

Sweetheart
I am enclosing the photo of you that I promised to return to you.

I was working till 2 am this morning, getting dugouts made and cover for the guns. We are about twelve miles further north and we see a town blazing each night; in fact, it never ceases. The guns are firing continually and at times the row is appalling. Petill, the Captain out of the 21st, was hit, but not badly. Ellison, I hear, has been seriously wounded. Thank heaven, the weather is lovely. We have to live in dugouts and they are not boarded. I can just manage to get into the one I sleep in and that is all.

I do wish I could have been with you today, and I hope it is a fine day for you. Tell me what you did. There are only two things I seem to be able to think of now: this appalling warfare and your dear, sweet self.

All my love to you, sweetheart.
Your own Eric

WEDNESDAY 2 JUNE

Sweetheart
I sent off the photo yesterday, and already miss it, because it was

the first thing you gave me and therefore I treasured it. Although I love both the photos you sent, I think I like the serious one more than the other. I have just got into bed and kissed them both. Afterwards I will blow out the candle and go to sleep.

They have been shelling like blazes today and have knocked crowds of houses and buildings to smithereens. Tonight I have to take a digging party out to make some dugouts and a communication trench for our observation station and am informed it is a beautiful night for the Boche to gas us. Lively, isn't it? All the grass round here is turned yellow owing to the effect of the gas. As I am writing this, the Boche shells are whizzing over and one of our aeroplanes is making a fiendish din. The row this afternoon was simply awful and some of the shells came unpleasantly close.

THURSDAY 3 JUNE
Back here safe and sound. I am writing this in my little wee dugout. I have a very comfy bed with a lovely soft mattress which my servant got out of a smashed-up house. I just take my boots, socks, tunic and collar off. We never know when we may have to fire, especially at night. Major Boyd, my old major, has just come along and I have been talking to him. This Battery is all right. I have got a section, two guns of my own now, and so it is promotion. Brinkley has the right section 1 and 2 guns, and Burrows has the centre 3 and 4 guns. Although I haven't been in the Battery so long, I am senior to Brinkley. I am very sorry to say I had to give up 'Phyl'.

You know I am head over heels in love with you. All my love to you, darling.

Your own Englishman,
Eric

My own sweetheart

I will try and write a few lines up here; it is hard because I have to keep jumping up to watch where the shells are falling and to watch the German trenches with the glasses. It is a glorious morning, hot, but a nice cool breeze from the west. Luckily it is in the wrong direction for gases.

I had a talk with the Major of the 21st before I left. He advised me not to go into the regulars unless I had a comfortable income of my own. When I explained exactly how things stood, he advised me not to join under the circumstances. Also, I have started an engineering career, and it would be time and money wasted if I did not go on with it. Also, Phyl, I think I shall have had enough of the army before I arrive back in England. I do hope you are not disappointed with me. It is the same with everyone when they come out here: before they come across, they are simply eating away their hearts to get to the front. But after a very short time they cool down and soon want to get back home again. I must say I would like to get back home now.

I am at the Battery now as the Captain came up to relieve me. Have you ever heard a song called 'Harvest' by Del Rego? I heard it on a gramophone and thought it was awfully pretty. I love those two photos – they are absolutely lovely, but not half as good as the real person. I can't get this out of my head: 'Why does she like me at all?' I wish I was with you now – we would have lots of bathing. I often long for a good long swim to cool me. I do get so hot this weather. Another thing I often long for is another good long ride in the car with you. I shall want to put my arms around you and cover you with kisses.

Goodbye now, my sweetheart, with more love than you can possibly imagine.

From your very own Eric

My very own sweetheart
I was so glad to get your letter because I hadn't had one for three whole days. It is frightfully hot here. Everybody is getting as brown as berries and I am sure we shall all be like niggers if the hot weather continues. I had to go to the wagon line to pay the men. I had a very good ride – quite a change to be on horseback again. I have to pay the gunners tonight. I felt rather important, riding down, because I had 4,610 francs in my pockets.

There is a thunderstorm on at present and we are having our first rain since we came here. The number of livestock in the Battery is increasing. We have, now, two kittens, one goat and three cows. We shall soon be keeping hens and pigs.

It is the kindest thing you could possibly do for me to remember me in your prayers. Oh! I would do anything for you, Phyl, absolutely anything now. And now I shall tell you what I never meant to: I also ask for your safety and love each night.

Bye-bye, my dear, dear love, and God bless you forever.

Your Eric

Friday 11 June

My very very own sweetheart
Thank you for your letter, handkerchiefs and cake for my birthday. I could not resist opening the former yesterday because I thought there might be a letter inside. Oh! you dear sweet darling, I can't thank you enough for the presents. The handkerchiefs are awfully nice. But the best present any human being could send me, your 'real, real love'. It mean everything to me, whether I survive this war or not. When I opened the cake, I found the note and notepaper, which I shall keep specially for writing to you.

I have already had sixteen Little Willies (field gun shells) very unpleasantly close this morning. A birthday present from the Germans. Four of them burst right over us, but no one was hurt, thank heaven. The weather is beastly now. It has rained the last two nights, and everywhere is inches deep in mud. At present my dugout is perfectly dry, but all the others are sopping. My servant is busy making new improvements in drainage, to cope with the water supply. It is my turn for the trenches tomorrow night. It is absolutely beastly: thick, sticky mud, inches deep, in which one slithers about like a drunk man. But I do not mind so long as we are not shelled.

I am so glad the daisies told you that 'he loves you' because if they hadn't they would have been daisies that tell falsehoods. Yes, sweetheart, of course I have still got the little ring; it is fastened to my identification disc. Oh! love, I do want you today, more than I have ever done before. Nobody here knows it is my birthday, and although there are crowds of fellows about, I feel most awfully lonely.

The general is coming round here today, so I hope he behaves himself. Two of my men have just been wounded. They were getting wood and found an unexploded German shell. One picked it up and then threw it gently down, the thing exploded, and it caught them both in the legs. One has both legs broken, and the other may lose his foot. Oh! dear, it nearly turned me over when I saw them. I thought I had more guts in me, but it was a nasty sight.

Now, my dear, dear little lady, I must really stop. With this is sent all my love for all time.

Your own Eric

MONDAY 14 JUNE

Your last letter, written 9 June, was brought up to me at the trenches. It was absolutely too sweet for words. I have read it over and over again. I just absolutely long to be with you.

I packed a fuse and some cartridge cases up today for Buzz. Let me know when it comes. It is the fuse of the shell that wounded those two men of mine. We have heard since that one of the poor fellows is dead. My servant and I had a near squeak the night before last, going up to the trenches. We were walking across an open field when we heard the boom of a gun. Quite the usual thing in the distance, and then hor-r-r-r-dud, it landed about ten yards in front of us, and didn't explode. We walked on, thinking it was only an occasional one coming over. Then there was another boom, again came the hor-r-r-dud, and the second one landed only five yards behind us. We had both knelt down when we heard the second one coming, and as soon as it landed again without exploding, we hooked it as fast as our legs would carry us. If either of them had exploded, Eric would only have seen twenty-two years by a day. I was really frightened. It was the nearest squeak I have had yet.

I thought I had told you I was going in for civil engineering. I have another year to finish at the university and then I expect to get out to the Canadian Pacific Railway. That will take me out to Canada soon after I have finished at the university in Liverpool. Well, love, I would then have a year in which I could come and see you or you could come to stay with us. Perhaps then it would be goodbye again for a little time and then – well, it would depend on you then! But it all seems to be far, far away.

The cake was awfully good; everyone liked it and it went like wildfire. I had the first and last bit and thought hard of you all the time I was eating it. We have all got to have our hair cropped like the Germans now, because so many people are dying of wounds in the head, and they say it is due to having the hair long and getting dust into it which gets into the wounds. I shall look a fright with all mine off, and it will be cold.

Now, darling, I must go to the observing station, so bye-bye, and my dear, dear love to you, always and forever.

Your Eric

My real, real sweetheart

I am so tired that I hardly know what to do with myself. I have been up since 7.30 am this morning and it is simply baking hot. I was up in the trenches last night and I noticed the new moon. I wished that you might always love me and that I might always love you.

The night before last the Huns simply plastered all the roads round here with heavy shells. The brutes are shelling us now with Little Willies and it's not at all pleasant. Brinkley was wounded this morning in the foot by a splinter from a shell which burst about 400 yards away. It was rather a nasty wound, I believe, and so he will get home all right, lucky bloke. Look out for what is in the papers about this part. I watched the whole business this morning and it was an awful sight.

I have put the rose you sent me in the photograph case behind the 'smiling' photo. It was not at all withered when it arrived. It was awfully good of your mother to ask if I would like any cigarettes. At present I am well off for them but, as soon as I get low, please may I write and ask her for some? The men are all coming round here now for their beer. We have a barrel sent up each day for them and they can have a pint which they pay for.

I am afraid I don't agree with you at all on the question of marriage – why on earth a girl should lose her liberty any more than a man. However, I am afraid it will be some time before I am able to marry. Now, sweetheart, I must stop. My very, very fondest love to my Lady Phyl, and in ten years hence, if I am married, it will be to her or no one.

Your very, very own Eric

My own sweetheart

Here is the hundreth anniversary of the Battle of Waterloo. How very different, though, the people who worked the guns at Waterloo would find their Battery now. I doubt whether they would find it now: the guns are so well hidden that infantry and transport that pass along the track don't know there is a Battery here at all.

I told you that Brinkley had been wounded in the foot. Consequently we are short-handed and it is real hard work. We have to go to the trenches every other night and do extra time at the observation station. One of the subalterns in the 112th Battery was killed yesterday. A shell came right into their observing station dugout. He was an awfully nice fellow and I had been observing with him several times. The Major is going home on leave. He gets three days clear.

My name has been sent in and in a few weeks' time I may get leave. Of course, I shall have to go home, and I am going to rack my brains to devise some means of seeing you, the one person in all the world that I really want to see. I could ask Mother to ask you to come and stay with us, or maybe you could stay with Joan in London. I would let you know when I was coming and what day I could meet you.

I have got some more cartridges with bullets in them for Buzz. There are four English and one German. I have taken the charges out so they are quite safe, although they have not been fired.

Now, darling, bye-bye for the present.

Your very own and nobody else's Englishman

Eric

My darling

I received your Tuesday letter on Friday. I am enclosing your recital programme; many thanks, my love, for sending it. I am awfully glad it was a success, and I wish I could have been there to hear you sing, especially 'Softly Awakes My Heart'. It is one of my favourite waltzes. I don't know any of the others, except of course 'Home Sweet Home'.

I was up in the trenches again last night and it was beastly cold and uncomfortable. I am sure you can't imagine how miserable I get at times, wishing and wishing this war was over and I was on the way back home to my people and my own dear lovely sweetheart. Yes, I am gone from Athlone nearly as long as I was there. Time goes, in spite of the fact that each day is so much the same. The shelling is the same, the work the same, the weather the same; in fact, everything is the same from one day to another. I often long to be in the drawing room of your house, having my tea and passing hot cakes round. I used to call so very often and usually had only one reason.

Boche shells keep whistling over the whole time I am writing this, going into the poor old town. This morning I saw one of our planes which had been chasing a Boche plane get on fire. It came down quite close to us and the pilot and observer were badly burnt. It was marvellous that they were not killed and the pilot's pluck was magnificent. He landed quite gently although the flames were licking all round him. The machine was an absolute wreck. I was going to our observing station at the time with a telephonist and as soon as we saw the plane coming down all right, we both ran to the spot in time to help.

Oceans of love to you and hundreds of real nice kisses but Oh!!! for one real one.

Your Eric

Phyl, my darling,
I do hope you are all right. I can't make out why I have not heard from you for six days. Each night I have looked eagerly for a letter from you, and each time I have been disappointed. I think it is an ill omen, and I do so hope you are well and that it is no fault of mine.

I have to go up to the trenches every other night now and it is beastly cold. I got a slight chill on the liver and had quite a lot of pain at times but it is passing off now. The last three nights that I have been up in the trenches we have had gas scares but as yet we have not had a gas attack. If some sentry reports gas it is all over the country in five minutes. Everyone has to turn out and put their smoke helmet on.

The Major has just arrived back and is full of everything at home. He says people are far too optimistic over there and he did his best to flatten them out by telling them his views. My old major, Major Boyd, has gone away on leave, and one of my sergeants, lucky man.

I wonder if you will mind me asking if you will send a book out occasionally. One of these 7d editions or paperbacked ones. I am simply sick of reading papers: it is the same thing, day after day. I like any good love stories like Rider Haggard or Leton Merriman.

I do so hope there will be a nice long letter for me tonight. All my love to you, my sweetheart, and do write soon, please.

Always your Eric
XXX and hundreds more

Sunday 27 June

My darling
I received your letters last night. You can't realise how glad I am to have heard from you again, Phyl, although part of the letters are too cruel for words. I knew something must be wrong. Phyl,

my love, do try and see two sides of anything I write that seems doubtful to you. I like anyone as long as the person likes me; I love a person as long as that person loves me. My love for you will not slacken unless yours for me does. I shall never say anything in my letters about the future again. The present is quite enough for me. All I want – and it is a very great treasure – is your love. I also wish that I could have a talk with you. This letter-writing seems to cause all sorts of horridness between us.

We have a fairly respectable dugout here now, made by the infantry. Now, about leave. Of course, it will be some time yet, but I hope to get one eventually. If you can persuade your people to let you come over to my home, I can get my mother to ask you, I am quite sure. She is very broad-minded and would let all conventions go to the wall under the circumstances. It would be heaven to see you and talk to you once again, and it would have been cruel to have to go home and know you were longing to see me and just a few silly conventions stood in the way.

I was not far off eternity yesterday. As we were walking straight towards the guns from our observation station, one of the guns had a premature burst, due to a weak shell. All the ground round me was peppered with shrapnel, bullets and bits of shell, and the fuse went past me like a thunderbolt. I had no time to even lie down. It would have been hard lines to get put out of action by our own gun. One of the bits of shell knocked a rifle out of one of the Leinsters' hands and cut his hand slightly.

The day before yesterday a German shell came right over our guns, struck the earth eight yards behind one gun and ricocheted over the top of our dugouts. It came over with a horrid burr-r-r-r-ring noise. A six-inch shell landed just in front of the guns without bursting the other day; it is a nasty-looking thing too.

Your own real real Eric sends all, every atom of his love to you.

Your Eric

Phyl, you darling

What an absolutely sweet letter I got tonight. I couldn't possibly ever do anything but love you. Oh! you can't imagine how happy I feel at present. It seemed to bring you quite close to me, especially when you wrote about the sofa and the cushion. The mosquitoes are fairly humming round my face, neck and arms as I write. We are simply pestered with flies, ants, mosquitoes and all kinds of insects; it is beastly.

The telephonist and myself have been here since six this morning and those brutes across the way have been shelling our poor fellows in the trenches at one place all the time. Unfortunately it was not on our zone so we were not allowed to retaliate. We had eight big gas shells in front of the Battery the other night: seven of them burst, and one that landed just in front of No. 3 gun was a dud. Luckily the wind was blowing quite strongly away from us and so we did not get any of it.

I am sorry to hear your brother is going to the Dardanelles because I shall not have a chance of meeting him, although I think it is a better place than this. I hope the dance was a success and that you all enjoyed it. You don't know how much I envy all the fellows you danced with. It would be nice to have another dance with you.

I have two gees now, Phyl, but neither are as nice as 'Phyl' was, and they are both gentlemen. I don't get much chance of riding them up here, but I have to go down to the wagon line tomorrow to get a well dug for water, so I shall get a bit of a ride after all. He is an excellent jumper and shies at no jumps. I call him 'Tommy', although he is nothing like the Tommy of Athlone. I wonder if that was Tommy you saw when you were going up to Dublin that day. I remember that afternoon you were talking about. You were wearing 'my' things and I simply couldn't keep my eyes off you. I was simply drinking you in – in other words, I was loving you.

Our new subaltern came up with me this afternoon. He comes from Dublin: Weldon by name, and he was in training near Cork. He is a good deal older than 'your Englishman' but seems quite a nice fellow. I shan't get leave for another month, I believe. One has to be out here four months before getting leave, so that will be the beginning of August.

AT THE BATTERY

I got my daily shelling on the way down from the observing station. Two really big ones landed about 150 yards away and sent bits flying all round, so I subsided into the bottom of the communication trench until they drew further away. A German plane has just been flying over the Battery at not more than a thousand feet. The men are an awful nuisance; they will not get under cover and we have to yell at them. I expect we are spotted now through their curiosity. They really are idiots. I have been busy all day making electric light fittings for the guns so that we can see the sights etc. at night. It is rather a nice diversion from the usual run of things.

I have got to go out and cut brushwood now, so must say bye-bye. All my love to you, Phyl dear.

Always your Eric

SUNDAY 4 JULY

My own sweetheart
I got your letter and parcel of books last night. Thank you most awfully for them both. I am going to read A Deal with the Devil first: it sounds rather exciting. I will send them all back when we have finished reading them.

Burrows goes on leave on Tuesday, lucky blighter, and he is going to some friends in Dublin. He went home the last leave he had in November. Nothing eventful happened this evening. The Boche gave us the usual shelling and wasted many rounds on a poor old church, already battered down (St Jean). They sent some huge shells over into the town – they must have been about twelve-inch ones. They made a regular rumbling noise as they came over. We were troubled with gas for the last two nights. Each time we had to put our smoke-helmets on. The gas came from shells they sent over and it goes for the eyes, making them smart and water like blazes. The smoke-helmets are very hot because you are absolutely closed in and have a little window to peep out of, which gets all steamy. It made my eyes very sore last night.

Why did you say you were getting too silly for words? You do make me love you when you are in a 'silly' mood, and I want the silliness to make me happy out here. It isn't much of a compliment to me to say that when you do fall in love you do it in 'such a very bad form'. But I don't think you have done it in a bad form. You are a real nice sweetheart and one that shall be loved forever, by your lover. Yes, I am English and you are Irish, but what does that matter? We are of the same race now, and I don't think it matters what nationality we are as long as we love each other.

All my love, and heaps of hugs and kisses, and many thanks for the books.

Your Englishman, Eric

TUESDAY 6 JULY

My own darling
You have simply no idea how I loved your last Thursday's letter. It was too sweet for words. As soon as I had read it, I wrote a long letter to Mum and asked her to ask you to come and stay at home when I was going there on leave. It will be simply heavenly if you can come, and you must do so now. I will take you for a row on our 'lake' if I get there and you come.

It is raining hard at present and blowing like the very devil. I hit a Boche yesterday. He was showing himself well up above the parapet and I fired at a working party which happened to be just behind him. The shell burst right in front of him and over he went. I stopped them working in three places that morning and they didn't attempt any more that day. The other evening, when I was getting brushwood to conceal the guns, I wandered off from the party of men and found a lovely little garden, or what had been one. It has a large pond in the centre and a little Japanese bridge across a kind of watercourse. There were some roses on one side of the pond and I brought some back. If I find a really nice 'Lancashire' rose there when I go again I will send it to you. I like the old red rose for its scent, its colour and its meaning.

The little agate ring is safe, and I think that, as long as I have it, I shall be also. It is my talisman. As far as I can make out from the Captain's servant, who comes from Liverpool, when I do come on leave I shall arrive at four in the morning and don't have to leave Folkestone until 7.15 on the fourth day, so that gives three absolute clear days. I hope I am not counting my chickens before they are hatched.

WEDNESDAY NIGHT

I have been awfully busy all today. This afternoon I was out laying a wire to fire trenches and then fired at a road-barrier of the Boche and got five direct hits out of nine shots. And what is more, the first round was a direct hit for the old eighteen-pounder. The infantry were simply dancing about, they were so delighted with seeing the d—d Boche's road-barrier going in the air.

Look here, love, you must not object to my 'toothbrush' – I beg its pardon, moustache I mean. Because, you know, I am in the army and it is a regulation, so one has to make an effort. I don't think it will get in the way much. Is your sister still keen on her hospital work? Kathleen is still waiting for them to tell her where she is to go. She has all her uniform ready so that she can go immediately she hears.

All my real, real, true love for you, from your very very own Englishman,
Eric

My own sweet lady
You really are a dear, darling girl to write such a divine letter; it is the sweetest letter I have ever had. Fancy you refusing to go to a dance because you knew I was having a rotten time. I call that self-sacrifice and yet I don't think you ought to forgo your pleasures, because I am only doing what any English, Irish or Scottish man ought to do.

This afternoon I was looking at two graves, one of a second lieutenant and one of a lance corporal of the Essex Regiment. They are about twenty yards from my dugout, along the line of trees. The graves have both been tidied up by our men, and flowers planted in them. I stood by them for a long time and thought, 'Those two poor fellows are in happier surroundings now.' I wondered if their people would ever come out to look at their graves. Just two mounds of earth with a little wooden cross. It's a fine way of dying, and if it's to be my fate to be 'killed in action' I hope I shall be buried where I fall. However, this is a morbid subject to talk about, especially when one wants to live for years and enjoy my Lady's love. If anything does happen to me, you will know that he loved you on this earth and loves you beyond it.

I forgot to tell you, they put eight seventeen-inch shells into the town the other day. They make a most terrific rumbling noise going through the air and the explosion is more of a roar than a bang.

Phyl, you don't know how glad I was you came in by yourself that last night. Do you remember, we had just made friends in the afternoon, after the Sunday's row. I saw you evidently did care a bit about me and it made me love you. Sometimes I think to myself, 'Why didn't I tell her before that I loved her?' I have often thought since that it was time wasted, especially as it turned out to be the last motor ride we had together. When I came round after dinner and told you I was going, I had nothing to say, so I kissed you. It was a token of my real, true love and came from my very soul.

This will be the last night we are in this dugout. We are clearing out of the trenches as the infantry are moving their headquarters and are going to make new ones. So we are moving as well. Mum said in her letter that she will write and invite you to come to be with us when I get my leave home. I will send word when I have any idea when I will be leaving.

My fondest love, Phyl, my darling. Always and forever your Englishman,

Eric

WEDNESDAY 14 JULY

Sweetheart

It is raining quite hard now, for a change. I have been busy all day. This morning Burrows and I went down to our new observing station to discuss what work had to be done tonight. We crawled about the country on our hands and knees, then we came back here and did a bit of looting on the way, for which efforts we got reprimanded by the Major. We were a couple of fools to walk in with the things in broad daylight, because there are strict orders about looting. As a matter of fact we had only got a couple of flycatchers, three saucers and a strainer. The Major told me afterwards that if we wanted to go looting, we must do it when it's dark. This afternoon I have been busy with the electric lights for our aiming posts.

We are doing twenty-four hours in the trenches now because our new observing station and the place where we go for the night are quite close. Yesterday I had to go down to the Sixth Division headquarters to get a map. I had a good ride and called at the wagon line on the way back. The headquarters is a big chateau, a huge place in lovely grounds. Of course, the latter are much the worse for the war, owing to horses being picketed all over the place.

Well, my love, how are you? All right, I do hope. What kind of a singing lesson did you have the other day? Are you sure you don't want the books back? Otherwise I will give them to the men. There was no letter tonight and I was and am disappointed. Oh! Phyl, I am getting spoilt. If two days go without getting a letter from you I get cross and grumpy. The weather does not tend to improve my state of mind. If I have to stay the winter in this place, it will be pretty awful. Thank goodness I had not to go out digging tonight. We would have got soaked to the skin, as it's simply raining in torrents, and muggy as well.

Heaps and heaps of love for your dear, dear self.

Forever your own Englishman,

Eric

SATURDAY 17 JULY

Sweetheart

I just got your letter tonight: what a lovely long one, too, but it's horribly doleful again. I must try to cheer you up. You are horrid about the toothbrush. Nobody hates the thing more than I do, and I curse every time I shave. I do not fancy myself with it on in the least. However, your wishes are my commands, and if I do see you, I shall have it off on the first possible occasion. I have had a devil of a struggle with the Major today. An order has come round, for the second time, that everybody has to have their hair clipped short. I protested, as I may be going on leave, and at last managed to persuade him to let me have mine cut short round the sides and back but not clipped.

It has simply teemed all day, and everywhere is in a most appalling mess. Mud inches deep and rain blowing in everywhere. There is a howling gale on at present, and a little rain, and it's beastly chilly.

I quite realise at times what our people may think about the leave. But they never had to undergo the same circumstances as we have at present. When all is said and done there is no harm in us loving one another and I know it does me an unthinkable amount of good to know that you do love me, especially at this time. Also, love, there is no harm in your coming to stay at home. It is purely a matter of d—d silly conventions, and the world would be a far sight happier without them. Phyl, do promise me that you will do your best to come. Sweetheart, don't think of the distant future at a time like this. God knows, there may never be one for me, and now you will understand why you really must come home when I go.

Au revoir for the present, my sweet lady. My love to you for all time.

Your Eric

MONDAY 19 JULY

Phyl, you darling

How absolutely heavenly to think that you can go. Oh! my love, I feel as though I could jump over a house. I can't imagine how simply lovely it will be. You know the window that you dreamed about? It is a remarkable coincidence, but your description is identical to what you see out of one of the windows in our music room. This room is at the top of the house and runs across the width of the house. This window is at the front of the house and overlooks the tennis lawn and drive. Nearly all round the tennis lawn are flower beds. Your dream seems to hold up a great amount of hope.

The weather is fine again now and, thank heaven, everywhere dries up wonderfully quickly out here. The Boche put some big crumps quite close to our observing station this afternoon while I was up there. They are wanting observers for the flying corps but the Major doesn't want any of us to go. I shouldn't mind it; rather exciting work, I think.

I have just started a 'Wishing Gate' cigarette and it reminds me that I will put a note in with this for your mum, as I find I am getting near the end of my fags. Are you quite sure she won't mind me asking her for some? It really does seem a cheek. If you think it is, just tear the note up.

Fancy your daring to suggest such a thing as doubt as to whether I want you to come or not. Good heavens! I call that scandalous. Want you! Why, my love, it is all that is worth living for now, you and nothing else.

Night-night, my own sweetheart, and God bless you.

Forever your lover,

Eric

FRIDAY 23 JULY

My own White Lady

I got your letter this morning. What a dear, nice, lovely thing it is. I couldn't help counting the pages – fourteen whole lovely pages, and I know I can never answer it as it deserves to be answered.

I must tell you about yesterday first. It was my twenty-four hours down in the trenches and the liveliest I have ever spent, I think. The Boche started shelling the communication trench we use at about 5.30 in the morning, and kept it up at intervals of an hour to two hours all day long. Soon after lunch they started again. I had just put some shells into one of their trenches when they started shelling ours with 4-inch gun shells and 4.2 howitzer shells. They were dropping very unpleasantly close all the time, until one of the howitzer shells landed right on the parapet of the little trench that connects our observing station with the communication trench. There were three of us in the observing station at the time: the observer, my servant and myself. The observer was in the doorway crouching down, and I was sitting facing the door. I saw the brute burst, and it was only fifteen feet away and barely that. It was marvellous that none of us were hit. The concussion was awful. It blew part of the hedge away in front, cut to shreds over a dozen sandbags filled with earth, lifted seven or eight of them some six or seven yards and knocked the whole of the parapet in, where it landed. Later on in the evening they shelled us again with Little Willies and one hit directly behind us, some four or five yards away. It must have only missed the roof by a foot or less. I was heartily thankful to get away from there last night.

Ah! sweetheart, you are real kind to send me such a dear, dear letter. I can't thank you enough, my darling, for it. Fancy you, love, writing till 2 am and missing your sleep for me. Oh! I do love you for it, Phyl. To think that any girl on this earth could have such love for me is wonderful. If ever anything does happen to me and I am taken from this world, you will, I feel sure, be the first to know it, because my thoughts are always with you, and my soul would naturally seek yours when it leaves its worldly home. But there I am, doing what I said I would not do again, talk of the future. Far from disapproving of you on Buzz's birthday, I couldn't help admiring you. You were so energetic, and I was truly thankful in the heat of the game that you had got a fairly tight skirt on, when you chased me to the bottom of the garden. And then, you little villain, you made me 'it' after our making a truce.

Dear love, I shall be able to say nothing but 'I love you' when I do see you. Oh! the hours will simply fly, I am sure, far too fast, and then another age before I see you again. Well, three days of the nearest possible approach to heaven have to come yet. It is good of your people to let you go. I shall not forget that I owe them a great deal if I do get leave.

Our Captain Robertson was saying that he is getting a gramophone sent out by some of his people. It will be nice to have one here. Weldon, Robertson and I have been discussing the war, and many other things, since mess-time. The Major usually retires early and we sit and gas for ages. It is a lovely moonlit night, but there is a strong chilly wind. I have got to have a bath or rather wash all over tonight (as we don't get baths here) and it's beastly cold work, washing outside. It makes me feel like nothing on earth at the time, but you get a fine 'glow' on afterwards. What it will be like here in the winter I don't like to imagine. I am sure I shall lie and shiver each night.

Now my own real darling, I must stop writing. All my love to you, sweetheart, forever and ever.

Your Eric

Here goes for another letter, my Lady Love

You really are a dear kind soul. I have got another letter tonight; that is three nights running. Oh! it is a dear, dear thing to do. Phyl, dear, somehow my love for you seems to be my sole object in life now. Really, I can think of nothing else but your dear, darling self. Have you got any new songs lately? You must take a lot with you when you go to my home, as we all love singing, especially Mum and Dad. I think you will like the music room for singing in.

Phyl, my love, do you, can you really mean what you say in this letter? Oh! it does seem far, far too good to be really and truly meant. Listen to what you say: 'It makes me tremble all over and feel that I just adore you.' Oh! I simply can't ever realise it, until I see you and feel you, and then perhaps I shall. Sweetheart, I nearly cried tonight. I was reading your letter, and the gramophone was playing Madame Butterfly. My soul felt just as though it had left my body and was very near to yours, and I loved you, adored you and, though I shame to say it, idolised you.

This place is simply alive with mosquitoes. We did quite a lot of firing early on this morning. The Boche shelled our trenches hard so we bombed away at theirs. It's rather chilly at present and is inclined to rain. I am going down to our new wagon line this morning, so I have only a short time to finish this.

As yet I have heard nothing about leave but will try to find out today. Oh! I do long for those three days to come. Yes, four months is a long time, but I hope we never have to wait for one another's company for longer than that.

Every little wee bit of my love to you forever.

Your Englishman

PS Please thank your mother for her nice letter; I will write to her soon. By the way, this paper is running short.

My very own sweetheart

I got another lovely letter last night. Oh! My love, I did feel happy with a nice letter and some music at last. Robertson, our captain, has had a gramophone sent out. It is a beauty and you can't possibly imagine how it brightens us up. We have only got a very few records at present but are getting a lot sent out and I am going to get some when I go home. I am afraid I shall not get home until August now. But it will come soon, I am sure, so cheer up, my dear love.

On last Saturday afternoon, the Boche began shelling a working party just behind us and dropped a round short. It burst in among some ammunition under one of our timbers and alongside No. 3 gun. Of course, the rounds caught fire and began going off. We all had to rush for our dugouts and leave it, as no one could go near with the shells bursting. We kept poking our heads out to see how it was going on, and withdrew jolly quickly when a round went off. It was awfully lucky there were no aeroplanes up at the time or we would have been spotted, I am sure. All the woodwork was burnt, and the gun damaged very slightly. It was bad luck, being an absolute chance shot and the last they fired. Thank heaven, no one was hurt.

The weather has turned nice again here, and my spirits always revive when it comes fine again. The wet weather is quite enough to give anyone the 'pip' out here.

A Boche plane was brought down last evening by one of our machines. I was watching the flight and saw our man suddenly swoop out of the clouds above the Boche plane. The latter caught fire, turned upside down and rushed to the earth, falling behind our lines from a height of at least 6,000 feet. Terrific cheers went up from all round. But what an awful death. One fellow fell out when the machine was coming down, and the other was still alive when the machine had struck the ground. It made me shudder as I watched it all the way down.

I used to always carry all your letters in my coat pocket, but they grew so in number that lately I have had to only keep the latest ones on me. But they are all safe, and I wouldn't lose one of them for worlds. Oh! I do, do wish the time would go and I was sure of getting my leave. I shall be simply mad with delight when I hear I am going, yes, going to my own one dear darling little lady.

I must stop now, dear one, as I want this to go today. My love (every atom of it) and my everything to you, Lady Phyl. Always and forever,

Your Eric

THURSDAY 29 JULY

Dear love of mine

Just a short note to let you know about the leave. I ought to leave here on the eighth of August (Sunday) and get home about lunchtime on the ninth. I shall have from then till Thursday morning. I have to catch the 5.40 from Victoria (London) on that day. This holds good unless you hear otherwise from me. I have written to Mum today to tell her the same, so I expect she will write to you. I am the last officer in the Brigade to go on leave, as the others have only come out a short while since.

Oh! My dear, dear love, just think, only ten more days and then . . . It does seem far too lovely to ever come true. But I do pray that it will do. I must fly and have some lunch now.

All my love, sweetheart.

Your own Eric

SATURDAY 31 JULY

My own darling

I am writing this in the trenches and at present there is a terrific bombardment going on over to the right. It has been fairly peaceful down here this morning; they put about eight fairly big shells over, but we stopped them. Later there was a terrible din going on. The Boche were shelling all over the place and some big ones were going past, or rather over us, and landing in a village just behind. The row they made was terrible and the bits were flying all round us. Last night I was woken up three times by the telephonist on account of rifle fire or shelling and did not get to sleep finally till 2.45 am. Then I was wakened again at six. It was a very stuffy night and a fearful din had been going on over on our right. We thought we would have to take part in it, but no.

I do wish the time would hurry up and go. As I lay awake last night I was thinking of you at my home and pictured you just getting there and Mother meeting you for the first time. I was wondering what your feelings would be; whether you would like my mum and dad and the family as I do yours. I think you will and I do hope so. The idea of getting home and seeing you seems to be much too good to ever come true and I don't believe I shall ever believe I am going till I am actually on the way.

Our captain is leaving us and going as major to the — Bty. We are all most awfully sorry to lose him, and of course our gramophone goes as well. That is a fearful loss to us. At any rate, we are going to get another of the same kind, so we shall soon be all right again. I am sorry if I don't write for a few days, as it depends on what the Major wants me to do. You may be quite sure I do write as often as I possibly can. Oh! I do want you to talk to and kiss and hug, even if it's only for three days. And I will chase any doubts away from your mind, if there are any, but I pray to God that there aren't.

Sweetheart, I have only two more sheets of this paper, but I have seventeen envelopes left though. I am fed up tonight because the mail has not turned up. Your letters are the one pleasure I have to look forward to, and by Jove, I do that.

The Boche had the cheek to begin shelling us again, so I have just reminded them that two can play at that game. I must write the operation report, so bye-bye, my sweetheart.

All my real, real love to you forever,
Your own Eric

Sunday 1 August

My very own sweet love

I got your absolutely sweet letter this morning and the books as well. Oh! Phyl, love, I can't thank you enough for both. The last piece of your paper is used so I have to write on this now. I haven't used 'yours' for anything but writing to you.

It is exciting here at present: there are attacks on at all ungodly hours and we have to 'Be Prepared'. There is a devil of a din going on outside again. I hope the Boche get all they deserve. The brutes, they have started this blazing liquid again now, petrol I suppose it is. If ever I have a German within my power he won't stand a dog's chance: mercy or no mercy, I choose the latter.

I got a letter from my sister tonight and she says they want to have Phyllis over before I arrive, and she is quite looking forward to seeing you. I am sure you will like her. Sweetheart, please don't talk about the parting after three days. It will be quite bad enough to bear when it comes. You are always in my thought and prayers. I am going to chop the toothbrush again tomorrow; it is getting too visible again, so must make it less so. Yes, you shan't be bothered with anything that would mar my kisses.

God bless you, and remember, I am thinking of you and loving always,

Always, your Eric

Wednesday 4 August

My own dear Lady Love

I have just heard all leave was suspended. Just my luck! Oh! Sweetheart, we are really in it this time, there is no getting out of it, I can't tell you more than this. I got to bed at 5.30 am yesterday morning and now it is 3.50 am this morning and I am still up. The place we are in is stiff with Batteries, watch the papers. I am so tired, Phyl, I don't want to sleep and yet my feet ache like anything. In fact I feel thoroughly fed up.

I tried to get a wire through to Mum telling her about leave being cancelled, but I don't expect it ever got through. Of course, I don't know how long leave has been postponed for, but I shall just have to wait. At any rate I am the next to go when it does start again. It's teeming now, weeping for me because I should have been on my way home today, instead of being in for this ghastly business.

I got the cigarettes from your mum the night before last, and last night I got two letters and this paper from you. I have just been smoking a cigarette of those your mum sent, and they are very nice ones. Oh! Phyl, I can't write this morning; my mind is too full of this disappointment. I would have been seeing you tomorrow. I will write as often as I possibly can.

All my love forever, dearest.

Your own Eric

MONDAY 9 AUGUST
SENT TO PHYLLIS AT ERIC'S HOME IN LIVERPOOL

Dear Love
Today is Monday and I should have been with you by now. Well, I hope you are enjoying yourself at any rate with my family. I am longing to hear all about your thoughts on getting home. Really, I want the candid ones. Have you been into the music room yet? Is the window anything like that in your dream? I got two nice letters, one the night before last and one on Friday night after I got back from the trenches. They are both dear things. This is the first chance I have had since Wednesday of writing to you.

I went down to the trenches on Wednesday night, down all day Thursday and Friday: that is forty-eight hours altogether. We got shelled intermittently all day long and bombarded at night. The infantry headquarters where I stayed at night were in a wood, one corner of which was devoid of leaves owing to shell-fire. Where we were was fairly safe. I get shelled wherever I go now and it is rotten. One observing station we were in, the shells came so close that we had to move. One landed four feet behind the dugout, and a large splinter of another one just missed my arm. We had all to be up at 2 am this morning and for about four hours the din and smoke was awful. Up to the present the situation is satisfactory.

I hope you are happy there, dear, and can stay till I come. Bye-bye, my sweet love for all time.

Your own Englishman,

Eric

MONDAY 9 AUGUST

Phyl, sweetheart

I got an awfully nice letter from your mum today; she really is a dear to write to me. She wanted to know if I was not going to get leave at all. I shall get it as soon as things have quietened down here, I am sure. It does seem wonderful to think that you are really, actually at my own home with my people about you. Oh! how I envy each one of them. I am so glad you like Mum, because I love her myself and was conceited enough to think that because I love her, you would at least like her. How funny you think I am like Dad in looks. As for the laugh, well, I dare say you are right, because several people have told me the same thing.

Our telephonist sergeant has just come to me. He has a piece of shrapnel in his side, which he got a short while ago – the Boche. And yet, love, I have one thing to thank them for indirectly and that is the one thing in all the world that matters now, our love for each other. Had it not been for the Boche starting this war, Phyllis would have remained an unknown person to me. No, I can't thank these human-devils for anything. I managed to get a bath this evening. At this position we have our cookhouse in a disused house and have got a bath in there. I feel much fresher and comfortable now.

ON WATCH 11.10 PM

I am on till 3 am. The Captain (our new one, rather a nice

chap) was going to do the first half-watch and me the second, but I told him I would do the whole, for the simple reason that I know I could never keep awake if I slept first and then had to come on watch. We are only a very short way from the other place here, perhaps twenty minutes' walk, just the other side of —. We have a fairly respectable time of it down here, but the trenches are a nightmare. One place our infantry had to go over was one mess of upturned earth and shell holes. Tomorrow I have to go up to the trenches again for twenty-four hours. Well, it is a post of honour in a way, and a lot depends on the man who is out there. This will be my third whole day out there in a week. Burrows was out there all yesterday and came back safely; I pray to God that I may do the same.

Thank you, my dear, dear love with all my heart for your prayers; I do need them all so much at present. I will write again as soon as ever I can, but until then, au revoir, my sweet Lady Love. Every atom of my real, real love to you, forever and for all time.

Your very own Eric

THURSDAY 12 AUGUST

Sweetheart
I am safe and sound still, touch wood, and feeling quite fit, but very, very much that I want to be with my Lady. Oh! I do wish they would start leave again. Tomorrow I have to go down to the wagon line and it will be the first time since we came to this place. I shall go to 6th Division Headquarters and try and find out about leave.

Try and enjoy yourself while you are at my home, just as I hope you will when I come to you. It makes me feel happy to know you do like my home and my people. Somehow, I seem to be able to see you now, sitting on one of the large humpties (as we call them) by the fireplace in the morning room, talking to my sister. I am simply longing for those three short days to come, just because I want you. I feel most horribly jealous of everybody at home.

I got such a fright just then. I thought I heard another 'Rumbling Mary' (17-inch shell) coming over. They have been dropping fairly close to us all day. It was a motor ambulance going along the supply track on low gear. It sounded just like a 17-inch shell in the distance. The Major is leaving us, worse luck, and we are getting our old captain in his stead. This is all right, but we are all dreadfully sorry the Major is going, and so is he.

There are two things you can do for me at a time like this, sweetheart: you can pray for me at night before you go to sleep, and the other thing you can do is to write to me as often as you can. I can't get too many. All my love to you again, sweetheart, and forever and ever.

Your Eric

SATURDAY 14 AUGUST

My very own darling
Each day seems to be so much the same that I forget what day it is. I got your two letters this afternoon; one is a lovely long one. I am glad you like my two younger brothers. We are all down here in the mess dugout for dinner and the gramophone has been put on. We have got a fine selection of records now. Last night we had it going till 1.40 am. Our mess servant was hit just a minute or two ago on the shoulder. Luckily, only a bruise. The Boche put some shells close to here and he was standing outside; a piece evidently hit him a glancing blow. Burrows just says a small one landed close to my dugout up by the Battery. There will be a row if the blessed thing has gone in. Later I discovered it landed just four yards away, just outside, the devils!

In today's letter you mentioned something about news from the front. Well, my dear love, that's about us. We are at, or firing at, the place you mention. It's a lively hole, too, I can assure you. You see, we moved to here nearly fourteen days since. Robertson is our new major, so we got his gramophone again. Yesterday I rode down to the wagon line with the Major, and as I was coming back, the Boche were shelling the road we had to go along. We were galloping down the stretch where they were shelling, and as we got halfway along, a shell landed a little way to one side of us, and the bits fairly flew about. One piece came at me, and it hit the road under my horse, bounced off and hit a tree. It was a lucky one!

Well, my love, I think I am in the midst of 'things sensible and practical' as much as anyone, but I long for some (a lot of) real, real 'silliness' with you. I didn't find out about leave yesterday because the 6th Division have moved nearer here, but will do so as soon as I possibly can. I shall just have two hours' sleep, so I must really stop now. Give my love to everybody, please. All, all, all my real love to you, my darling sweetheart, for all time.

Your Eric

TUESDAY 17 AUGUST

My very own dear, sweet love
I got a lovely letter from you last evening; really, it is the nearest approach to the divine that a letter could possibly be. Oh! it did make me feel happy, and cheered me up more than anything else could do, except your own dear self. I had a ghastly night a few nights ago. I have evidently got a chill on my liver and I simply lay and groaned all night long. Luckily it has more or less passed off, leaving me so cross and grumpy. You mustn't worry your head about it and just remember there are hundreds who are worse than your lover, and who say nothing about it.

Listen now, we have a certain amount of work to get done here in a week, and then I hope for a present of seeing you. I pray to God that we may do it in that time. Well, my sweetheart, I must have my 'lunch' now – it consists of a jam sandwich and some cold tea.

LATER

How was it you didn't have a bathe the other day down at Southport? I wonder you didn't take the opportunity. Do you know about the dooshes I had in the lake? We used to have great fun making a canoe of canvas for the ponds, but it was difficult to balance and we often fell in. After that, we made the wooden punt which still exists, I hope. There are lots and lots of stories to tell you about home, and my one great wish now is that I may be allowed to do so.

Dear love, you mustn't go and make yourself ill on my account. If you can't find time to write during the day or evening, you mustn't wear yourself out by sitting up late writing to me. I shall just have to be content with fewer letters, but you are not to make yourself ill. And now, bye-bye, my sweetheart through all worlds and ages.

I am your lover and your Eric

FRIDAY 20 AUGUST
AT THE OBSERVING STATION

My everything

How can I possibly thank you for your last letter? It is really a dear. I was up at 4 am this morning to come up here. Ugh! It is rotten getting up at that hour.

Now here's some news to cheer you up. Leave has started again and yours truly ought to be home as soon if not sooner than this letter. Provided all goes well and the d—d Boche keep quiet, I shall get away from this hole on Sunday, and arrive on Monday morning. I shall send a telegram either from Folkestone or London so you will know in time. Imagine, it is not two days now and I shall be on my way to my own true love. Then again, it seems impossible to realise that I am going to get out of this appalling hell for five whole days: away from the sounds of these beastly guns and rifles, away from all these beastly rabbit burrows and broken-up houses, and last but not least, away from the horrible smells.

The Boche put at least 200 large crumps within an uncomfortable distance of us yesterday afternoon – no damage done, though. Our 'heavies' have been firing on the Boche trenches and so they are firing back like blazes now. There is a fearful din going on – they don't half put them over when they start. One does get heartily sick of the din that is going on. At present, my clothes are simply clogged with clay, and the slightest tap I give my leg sends out clouds of dust.

I know I shall want to stay up all night and talk to you and love you. This will be the last letter I write before coming to the arms of my Sweetheart.

Her own Englishman, Eric

MONDAY 30 AUGUST 1915
FROM THE HOTEL DU NORD, HAZEBROUCK

My sweetheart, my love, my darling, my everything
It is now 5.30 am. We arrived here at 4.30 am and have wandered round the place trying to find a hotel. The whole town was asleep, and we happened to find this place, and the door was open and not a soul about. We walked in and dumped ourselves down in this little room where we found this writing paper.

I wrote to you on the train as soon as I got outside Central Station, but the train was shaking so I will now copy out what I wrote – I made up my mind long ago that I would do this, just so that you should know my deep down thoughts after leaving you. Among all the mixture of thoughts in my mind now, there is just one outstanding one. In spite of all you say, I have some of your love, and that some loves me with a great love. Oh! I could feel it was so when I had you clasped to me, over and over again. Just think, we have had four happy days together, thanks to your love and my people. Four days of real happiness and forgetting all trouble for a while. Oh! sweetheart, they were far, far beyond what I had expected. It has been a taste of heaven on earth. And yet there is a feeling growing in me which makes me think, 'Why should you love her with all your heart and she only with a portion?' But dear, dear heart, this is far overcome by my love for you. As I said this morning, what must all your love be like? At present I only seem to see the petals of my white lily, and pray that in years to come I may see the pure, untouched, loveliness of the centre of the flower and your love.

Do you know, sweetheart, I feel as I used to do when I was going back to boarding school. It is a form of homesickness, but now for you, dear love. For your dear arms to be round my neck, and those dear lips pressed so hard against mine. Four short days and then as many months in Flanders. Thank heaven when the war is over. It is nearly seven o'clock now and our train does not leave till 9.55 am. I am so sleepy, I can hardly keep my eyes open, so we are going to have some breakfast now.

TUESDAY
I arrived safely yesterday and had a good look round. We had a great evening last night. My love, I will write again as soon as possible.

Forever your Eric

SUNDAY 5 SEPTEMBER

Phyl, my own very dear lady
It is now 11.55. I was dragged to a men's concert at the 21st Battery and so I am late starting this. I had intended spending the evening in writing to you. Burrows is busy writing as well. Somehow we both choose this time when all is quiet.

Thank goodness it has been fine today, because I have been on duty; also, thank goodness I have no guard to turn out tonight. Yes, dearest person on earth, I got your dear, lovely letters. My love, it is even dearer to me still, just because it expresses your own deep-down thoughts about our three and a half 'love days'.

I am most awfully sorry to hear about your dad and I do, do hope the operation will be quite successful in every respect. I can't grasp what you mean when you say 'the family is going to have a tough time'. Do always tell me anything that troubles you, if you can, in the future. Dear heart, your troubles are mine and your joys are mine, and I may be able to help you, even by letter. I have been thinking of you on your journey home, just waiting at Chester, then going on to the boat at Holyhead, and then calling a cab to take you to your aunt's in Dublin. I just wish I had been with you.

Do you know, I was dreaming today about my first visit to Athlone, when I went to get my commission. It will always remain clear in my memory now. I remember seeing the Shannon for the first time as I crossed in the train over the bridge. It was a bright, cold, frosty morning and I was feeling very excited about the interview with the Colonel. I walked up through the town while I waited. Oh! sweetheart, not for one moment did I think that Athlone held such a priceless treasure to me.

Dear, dear, dear Phyl.

Forever your Eric

SUNDAY 26 SEPTEMBER
IN THE OBSERVING STATION AT 8.05 PM

My own very dear sweetheart
I am just recovering from awful palpitations of the heart. About a quarter of an hour ago, the Boche started a most terrific roar of rifle fire in front of us here. I told the Battery by means of the telephone, and they opened fire immediately. The bullets were fairly whistling over my head, a regular rain of them. Of course, I thought the Boche were going to attack us. However, it turned out that they had spotted some of our men by means of one of their flares and opened fire on them. All is quiet again.

I haven't heard from you since Wednesday. Sweetheart, do please tell me why your last three letters have been so very different to the others before them. My heart has the same awful ache as it had when I came away from leave. I want a letter so very, very much. I was talking to the Colonel last night, and he was telling me that he was stationed at Athlone for three years. I told him I was in training there and he knew a lot of the people I knew. He said he knew Major Hancock very well. You will have heard the news of our people and the French down south. It sounds very good tonight. I wonder if it is true that they have broken through and captured 21,000 prisoners. Somehow it doesn't seem possible, and yet it is supposed to be official.

My candle has nearly burnt away, so I must hurry up and turn in before it goes out and leaves me in the dark.

MONDAY 27 SEPTEMBER – 11 AM

I had been asleep about an hour last night when the Boche started firing again like the very dickens, but this time it was gunfire as well as rifle fire and some way over to our right. I believed they were going to attack, but our guns began firing nearly immediately. There was a terrific battle for about an hour, then things quietened down.

Have you any more news from your brother? I was reading Sir Ian Hamilton's latest account of the fighting at the Dardanelles. It must have been pretty awful, especially at first when they were landing under fire. Everyone is getting very excited up here at present over the news and everyone has great hopes of course, quite a change to the usual pessimism that flies about.

AT THE BATTERY – 9.25 PM

I found the apples waiting for me when I arrived back. The parcel was badly knocked about but the apples were all right. I am sorry to say they have all gone soft on the way and so we shall have to use them for cooking; it does seem a pity, because they look so lovely. Thank you very much for them. There was a letter waiting for me too; you don't know how glad I was, and it is so very different from the last three. No, love, my section did not go into action at E—. We are a little in rear of our first position in this part of the world. We live in a fairly respectable farmhouse, rather draughty but dry. How I wish you had been present at that argument we had with Weldon. I am afraid I

71

don't agree with you about one Irishman being equal to two Englishmen in arguing. I think it is just the other way round.

Don't worry too much about your dad; I am sure he will soon be all right again and I shall be jolly glad when I hear he is, for his own sake and also because I shall know you won't worry then about his health.

I pray to God that He will keep me safe just for you. So I am going to bed now and I will have a really good think about you before I go to sleep. All my very deepest love to you, my darling lady, forever your Englishman,

Eric

THURSDAY 30 SEPTEMBER
IN THE TRENCHES

Phyl, my very, very dearest,

I got this absolutely dear letter this morning, brought here by my servant. The remainder of the Battery came to where my section is last night – the other Battery going to rest. This is my fourth day in the trenches since the week began. Well, although it is so uncomfortable, especially at present when everywhere is simply soaking wet after two days' heavy rain, I can write to you much better up here with no one bothering me.

This morning after breakfast I went for my usual walk down to a company of infantry in some support trenches just in front of this place. Some of them were working, repairing a part of the trench that had been blown in by an 8-inch shell fired by the Boche the day before yesterday – luckily, not a soul was hurt. Evidently the Huns had spotted them working, because all at once there was a swish and a bang and a Little Willie landed some distance behind. The men stopped working and got down on either side. Over came another, nearer this time, but behind again. On my way back here I was stuck in the trench with about seven of the infantry all crouching in the bottom of it. Over came another and landed just in front of the parapet, simply covering us all with dirt. What a bag the Boche would have had if the thing had fallen five yards further.

I managed to get past the men and along the trench. Over came another with a terrific bang; down I ducked with the others in the trench. It landed somewhere near. I hurried down the communication trench to this place, which is all knocked in in places and as slippery as the — and muddy water all along. Some more rounds came over but fell behind me somewhere.

I shall have to go down to the infantry headquarters in a few minutes to have my powwow with the Colonel. Last night he invited me to dinner. I was only too glad to have something warm, because we couldn't cook anything up here all yesterday.

My darling, how you make my heart thump with your daydream of the picnic up the lake. I wonder and I hope we may some day go on a picnic like that all by ourselves. But to say that I would be more or less ornamental when getting lunch ready offends my sense of usefulness. For instance, I could light the fire, fetch the water, make the lemonade or tea or peel the potatoes, if we had them.

9.35 PM

I have been down to the headquarters. It is a pitch-black night and the track across country which one can walk down at night is terribly muddy. I stumbled and slopped along, nearly falling flat over a dozen times. I arrived back here splashed from head to foot with mud, feeling fearfully fed up. Now these cursed Boche are making a beastly din firing at our transport on the roads behind. Also, it is now teeming with rain. Ugh! Phyl, you have no idea how one gets into the dumps when the weather is bad, and it is fiendishly cold at nights now. Even sleeping in all one's clothes and a thick overcoat on, I can't keep warm.

Phyl, my darling, how could you even think, let alone write, asking me if I would rather not 'turn back'. What must you think of me. But you must know I love you, adore you and you are my own sweetheart for now and for always. Turn back will I never do. It would break my heart if I lost your love now.

FRIDAY 1 OCTOBER

Weldon comes to relieve me after lunch today. He has just rung up to know if there is any means of having a wash up here. I told him that we don't go in for washing here, it is infra dig. It is a nice bright day again now, although everywhere is still very wet after last night's rain. Thank goodness, my cold has disappeared now. Weldon is late after lunch, which means this letter will miss today's post, confound it. I did so want it to go because you will be nearly four days without one.

I wonder if you were shown our family crest when you were at home. It is rather a nice one and a good motto. It consists of a shield with six gold martins on a 'field azure'. Above the shield is an apple on a small branch, and below is the scroll with the motto, in English, 'Prepared for good or evil'.

And now, sweetheart, I must stop and get 'packed up'. All my very, very deepest love to you, my own darling, forever.

Your Englishman

TUESDAY 5 OCTOBER

My sweetheart

I am up in the trenches again with my usual luck: beastly wet. I wonder how your poor dad is now. I suppose he will be up in Dublin, and your mum as well, and you, my Lady, in charge of the house again. When do you expect to go to Dublin? How often I wish I could be by you to try and chase away all your troubles, if only for one short hour. Your last letter seemed much more cheerful than the one before. But please, don't force yourself to be cheerful for me. I have just reread your letter where you asked me if I would rather 'turn back'. Sweetheart, did you for one second think that I ever could? There is one thing that worries me: I don't want to turn back, but do you?

This morning I was up at 5.30 am and have only just got back from a long walk to a certain part of the trenches, which I had to go to to register, or shoot at a place we can't see from here.

It is now 3.45 pm and when I got back here, what do you think I found? A message waiting for me to say I was the next for leave. That means if there is nothing that crops up to stop

74

me, I should leave here on Monday the eleventh, that is next Monday. Oh! sweetheart, just think of it, four more days, and I shall in all probability not be able to see you. I knew I would be getting another leave now soon, but did not expect it as soon as this. Well, I suppose we can't grumble, because we have had one four days together, but oh! the longing, longing for another is awful. I suppose there is no possible chance of you being in Dublin by then, and even if you were, with your poor dad in his present state, it is no time to bring any more worry to the family, but it is hard luck.

Oh! why do you live in Ireland and I in England? Well, it is no use bemoaning my fate. I must write to the family now, and tell them the news. Bye-bye my very own sweetheart.

Your Eric

SATURDAY 9 OCTOBER

My own very dear lady

How I am longing for a letter to come tonight. Fancy, I ought to leave here the day after tomorrow for home again, but the one person in all the world will be just as far away as she is here. My darling, you don't know how hard I prayed for your dad's safety last night. Surely my prayers will be heard, for your sake and therefore for mine as well.

An order has just come in saying that I have to be in charge of men going on leave. It is a — job and so, of course, falls on a subaltern. I was going to try and get away by an early train, but that is now out of the question.

Yes, love, I do remember something in connection with the 'funny wee stool'. You were sitting on the stool the night I had heard that I was 'going': to what, I did not know, but that was why I had originally come to Athlone. By offering to do my 'bit', I had found my love. I came to tell you my news because I loved you. I knew you did care a bit, so I came to you and, kneeling down, kissed you. I am telling you this because it seemed – and always will do – so wonderful. Then, I remember you sitting there once while I held the silk for you to wind up, and you would not speak more than a monosyllable. Also, I remember sitting there myself several times, once especially when you scolded me for attending badly at teatime. How happy I was then, so long as I was with you.

All my soul's love to you now and forever.

From your Englishman

TUESDAY 12 OCTOBER
FROM THE EUSTON HOTEL, LONDON
REDIRECTED TO PHYLLIS FROM ATHLONE TO DUBLIN

My Phyl

Here I am on the way home again. It is just 2.45 am and I have to wait until five for my train. There is not the same excited feeling in my heart this time as there was last. Although I know there is my dear mum, dad and sister waiting for me, I also know there is not the dearest person in all the world, waiting and longing to see me as I am to see her. I know when I get home I shall do nothing but think about you and your awful trouble. Thank God I have got away from that place, if only for a few days. My brain has got absolutely fuddled lately and I have no more been able to think of one thing at a time than fly.

TUESDAY NIGHT

Here I am at home in my own cosy bed. Coming back home seems to have brought back the four wonderful 'love days' we had here together so very clearly, until I imagine you are here. Tonight, Mum has been playing a lot of songs, and among them 'Irish Eyes' and 'The Sunshine of Your Smile', also the duet out of The Tales of Hoffman. I can see you now on that last night I had with you, singing by the piano each of these songs. You were wearing the frock I told you I liked. Then I thought of you now, with troubles heaped on you and no one to tell them all to and I can't think, dear heart, why I have heard nothing for so long. Mum gave me your letter you had written to her, to tell her about your dad being operated on today, and yet I didn't know anything about it. My love, how my whole heart goes out towards you now; every single atom of me and my love is lying at your feet for you. I think your dad has everything in his favour – you say he has never hardly been ill up to now. He must have plenty of strength stored up in him. But his own wish to get better for your sakes is the one thing in my mind that will help him most to pull through.

My darling, I am most awfully lonely tonight. Although I am in among my own people, there is the same aching feel nagging at my heart that there was the day I left you. This afternoon when I went into the music room a lump rose in my throat. I was thinking of all the happy, happy hours I had spent in it with your arms round my neck and your dear, fierce, love kisses burning on my lips.

WEDNESDAY 13 OCTOBER

Sweetheart, I got your letter this morning and I am coming to see you. I gave Mum your note as soon as I had read your letter, and asked her whether she would mind. She said she had been wondering whether I could have seen you or not, because she said she knew I must want to. My love, just think of it: a whole day with you and I hadn't expected to see you at all. Thank God your dear dad is all right so far. Now, my darling, I shall come by the 11.10 from Lime Street tomorrow night. I arrive in Dublin either at Westland Row or Broadstones. I will meet you wherever it suits you best and whatever time. Let me know if you can.

I must simply rush into town now, so bye-bye for a short time, my own sweetheart.

Forever your Englishman

SUNDAY 17 OCTOBER

Dear, dear one

Here I am back at this beastly place, feeling at present just about as wretched and down in the mouth as it is possible for anyone to feel. The journey back from Boulogne was simply beastly: the carriages were all full and I had to sleep sitting practically bolt upright. We got to H— (you know the place) at 4.30 am and the train did not go on till nearly eight. Connell and I went and had some breakfast when we got to P— and rode along here afterwards.

Sweetheart, I hope you did get home all right. I felt awfully worried about you. What a glorious night it was, the water was like a mirror and the light from the moon was reflected in a long, clear, silver band, twisting and twirling like a snake. As soon as you were out of sight, I felt the horrible lonely feeling creeping into my heart. On going to the north side of the boat as she moved out, I noticed all the people staring at the sky, and when I looked, I saw the Northern Lights or aurora. It was a wonderful sight, just for all the world like hundreds of searchlights shooting up into the sky. I have seen it once before, but it was not nearly as distinct.

I managed to get a bed on the sleeping car and slept like a top till seven o'clock. A man from the Euston Hotel came and told me Mum and my sister were waiting for me. I was glad they had come, and we had a great day. At breakfast they wanted to know all about my visit and they were awfully pleased that I had been allowed to see your dad. My darling, I do hope he is still improving. We went to the Regent Palace, where they were staying, and then went to do some shopping at the Army and Navy and Gamages, where I bought a Primus stove and some electric light bulbs. I tried to get a special kind of candle lamp for the mess but was not successful. I purchased a leather coat in an outfitters in High Holborn.

We had lunch in the Regent Palace dining room; it is huge and there was hardly a table unfilled. After lunch we took a taxi to the Gaiety to see Tonight's the Night and all had a jolly good laugh. It was over by 5.15 and we arrived at Victoria in plenty of time. Connell told me he went to Ireland by the Rosslare route so naturally I would not see him on the boat. I did enjoy the day and would have been simply lost without them. But my own dear, dear Phyl, I would have given a lot to have been able to stay over Friday night in Dublin. I did realise how great a trouble was yours and every one of my senses seemed to say, 'Love her with all the deepest love you have, she wants every atom you can give.' My Phyl, that afternoon I gave you my whole, whole love, and will you ask God that someday you may hold this gift, the greatest that any human being can give to another?

It is now 12.45 and I am so tired. Forever, oh! yes, may God grant it forever.

Your lover,
Eric

TUESDAY 19 OCTOBER

My own darling

I am just going to write a few lines before I go down to the infantry headquarters. It is beastly chilly but it is fine. Last night it fairly froze, and I kept waking up as cold as ice. My silk muffler wrapped round my pillow made me think of you and your dear, dear love for me, and that there is even more of it to be won.

Last night, we had just finished dinner and the gramophone was playing while we sat talking. All at once, without the slightest warning, there was an awful bang; the house fairly shook and the glass crashed on the floor from one of the windows. We knew it was a shell but nobody was hurt, and only one of the windows smashed. It had landed fifteen feet from the house. No others came anywhere near us. Robertson said he hoped the Boche gunner that laid the gun got two months' hard labour for laying the gun badly.

The brutes have turned us out of here already this morning. They shelled us with Little Willies and got so close that the whole place was one mass of smoke and dirt, so we subsided into the bombproof (up the trench) for a while. The bombproof is a dugout lined with wood, the top being about five feet below the ground. The roof is about five to six feet thick and consists of earth, sandbags, bricks, corrugated iron and wood, and as you enter it looks something like this:

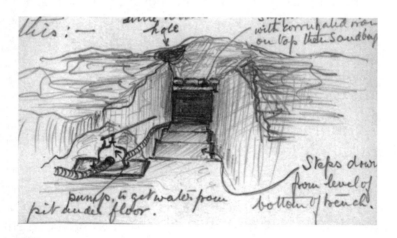

A Little Willie landed on the side some time ago and made a small crater.

Oh! Phyl, my Lady, it does seem just ages and ages since I left you last Friday night, and yet it is not a week yet. What a dear, dear day that was, but it went so horribly quickly. Do you know, I was worried I didn't give you a last kiss before going on board, as I did when the train was moving off the time before. I was sure you would notice it and now I feel so sorry. Have you heard anything about our visit to Mitchells for lunch? Perhaps the lady hasn't returned home yet, I wonder! Has anything been decided about letting your house? I do hope you manage to do so because you are bound to feel much happier in Dublin near your dad. Phyl, do you remember asking me if I wanted anything you could make? Well, I wonder if you can make me good, thick socks. I can see I shall want them. If you can, I take 7 in boots, as I can see I shall suffer more from cold feet than anything this winter.

I did so want to finish this off last night, but of course they wanted to play bridge and there were only four of us and now it is getting jolly late. It was a relief to know that you had arrived back safely and that your dad was all right.

    Bye-bye dear, dear Phyl, forever and forever
    Your Eric

FRIDAY 22 OCTOBER

My own very dearest darling
I got your letter yesterday and I was just dying for one. I discovered quite by chance that I never gave you a letter Mum had given me for you when I came over to Dublin last Thursday. I really am a sieve-brained owl and I am most awfully sorry about it. Phyl, I think it must have been the excitement of seeing and being with you, my own very dearest person, that made me forget it.

    My dear, I want your letters much, much, more than I ever have done before but I am going to practise what you and I said we would do: I mean the 'give-and-take-a-bit-more' resolution we made, and so this time I was just going to wait until your letter came. Oh Phyl, dear love, I am so sorry that you got the flu. I hope you didn't catch it on Friday last (fancy, it's just a week today and it seems ages and ages). You don't know how much I do care about your letters and I read them over and over again. It is awful to think that you imagined I only half-read them. That one last love day – I wouldn't have missed it for anything. Last Friday I broke down and cried like a child, for really no reason except the awful emotions caused by my love for you.

I am sure you will all be very thankful when your brother is back safe and I can very well imagine it would be a piece of very cheering news to your dad and mum to hear he was on his way home. I am glad you think your dad is really getting stronger. I wrote to your mum this evening to thank her for being so kind to me last Friday.

With all my love I have in me for my darling Lady, forever her

Eric

SUNDAY 24 OCTOBER

My very, very own darling

Everybody is out at present, so here goes for a letter. I go up to the trenches tomorrow. At present I am feeling beastly chilly, because the stove we are getting has not turned up yet. How is your poor dad? How awful the time must have been for you, when I think what it would mean to me if my dad was so dangerously ill. I used to think my dad was hard on me at times, but now when I look back I can see very plainly how very wrong I was.

I have been wondering a good deal lately what will become of me after the war is over. I think it will be fearfully hard to settle down to university life again and finish off my engineering training. What can I do? Stay in the army? No, no, I am not going to do that. I might go into an office, but that is a more hateful idea than staying in the army. I might go in for cattle-rearing or horse-breeding: it has always interested me, but they both need a great deal of experience and the only way to get that is to go to a ranch in Canada or a station in Australia. But if I have lost the knowledge I had of engineering, I have found something much dearer to any human being: I have found real, true, strong love.

MONDAY MORNING

I stopped writing last night when your letter arrived, and

sweetheart, what a dear, dear thing it is. Do please be careful of your dear self, for my sake as well as your own. How awfully glad I am to hear about your dad being better and being able to eat solid food so soon after his operation. I thank God I wrote that letter to you when I got home – it is awful to imagine if I had not seen you. It didn't feel quite like home at first; it must have been because you were not there. Every room I went into reminded me of you. You had sat on the chesterfield beside me making me so very, very happy and I longed and longed for you, my everything.

Confound the post, it has to go, so I must stop, Phyl. All, all my fiercest love for you, darling.

Forever, your Eric

THURSDAY 28 OCTOBER

Phyl, you dear, dear person
What a simply beautiful letter this one is that came last night. Darling, I simply adored you when I was in bed after reading this letter for the second time. I just absolutely yearn to crush you to me in my arms and kiss you.

Really, I am going to get a fit of the blues before this winter is over. It is simply d—ble, teeming all day and every day, everywhere inches deep in mud, and cold. It is beastly, but what is the good of growling? I suppose we might be much worse off. I spent a wretched two days up at that beastly observing station of ours. My feet were like ice the whole time and everywhere was soaking; I simply couldn't keep warm.

On Tuesday morning I was down with the infantry, just in front of us, and the Boche were shelling one of our planes at the time and it was flying right over our heads. The bits were whistling down and falling all round us from the shells, and by Jove, all of a sudden there was a fizzz-wump, and a shrapnel bullet hit the trench in line with my head and just two feet away. It gave me a jolly old fright because it had landed before I actually realised it was coming. On Tuesday night I climbed out of the trench and made a tour of inspection all over the ground in front of the station, it was quite exciting, what with bullets flying about and Boche flare lights going up all the time. I nearly trod on two huge rats, and finally managed to fall headlong in an old trench about six feet deep, getting covered with wet sticky clay. Yesterday the Boche covered the trench with dirt from one of their shells and sent a whole heap flying in at the door.

I am at present at the Battery but the gramophone has not been turned on because it is out of action again, owing to the spring having broken again. It is rotten without it, too. But to go back to your letter, you wanted 'our own love day' bringing back to you. Well, shall I go over it all again now? How very, very much I like to think of it myself.

When I arrived at Chester, I sent a telegram to the chief steward of the boat for a berth to be kept for me and so I don't remember anything after getting into bed, until 5 o'clock. Up I jumped and had a wash and shave. I took great care over the latter, and yet you told me in as many words that I had not shaved. I tried to brush my hair into something like shape, but owing to its terrific length it wouldn't go any way, so I just said to myself, 'Phyl will have to forgive that.' I went onto the quay and your train ought to have got into Kingstown by then and so I walked up and down in high spirits. Five minutes passed, then ten, and no Phyl arrived. After waiting a quarter of an hour and seeing another train arrive without you, I decided to wait on the boat. So I had made up my mind to sit tight and wait where I was. Then all at once my angel appeared at my side and I was surprised to see you. I felt all silly and awkward, with the 'How shall I begin?' kind of feeling. We got on all right over breakfast, but afterwards, when we were walking up through the town, we almost seemed inclined to quarrel, and talked about things that I am quite sure didn't matter to either of us. But all that seemed to melt away after we had found that seat and the ice began to thaw. How often while we were sitting there I longed to draw you to me and give you my first kiss. Of course, I did kiss your dear hands while we were there.

It was a happy morning just because I was with you, and had you by me. Then when we were in the train together, I couldn't keep back my feelings any longer. I just had to kiss you and you seemed nearly frightened of me. Do you remember saying, as I drew you to me to kiss you a second time, 'Eric, don't.' I know I wondered at the time why you said it.

Phyl, dear, I shall have to stop as I am simply racked with toothache. The filling came out of a tooth up at the observing station and it is giving me just h— now. But I know you will not mind.

Just simply all my very, very dearest love to you, my Lady, forever and for all time

I am just your Englishman

SUNDAY 31 OCTOBER

My Lady

I am up in the observing station again, and as usual it is raining for all it is worth. Fancy, it is All Saints' Eve, and this time last year I was miles away from here up in old Fort Dunree. Then I didn't know what was to happen in one year. How my life was to be changed and how I was to find my Lady and my love. When I applied for my commission, I did so to Preston RFA Depot, because I thought I might have a good chance of getting home now and then. But owing to an army order, I had to apply to the nearest depot, which, of course, was Athlone. Even when I had been to see the Colonel at the barracks I hoped and prayed that I would get sent to Preston. Well, I thank God with all my heart now that I did not get sent to Preston. Phyl, I wonder, are you a fatalist at all?

Now for this dear, dear letter which I got on Friday night. Of course I still carry your letters wherever I go; they are far too precious to leave about. I do so wish you could let the house. I can quite understand you would feel much happier with your dad in Dublin, where there is first-class aid if anything did go wrong. I am absolutely a believer in will-power in connection with many ailments and there has been many a life saved by a person making up his mind that he is not going to die.

Four infantrymen have just come wandering about on top here. They have got lost, and I don't wonder. It is a simply pitch black night, so dark that I couldn't see my hand at arm's length in front of me. I put them on the right track at any rate, poor beggars.

MONDAY – 12.45 PM
My dearest, really what a lovely surprise it was to get another of your dear letters this morning. With your letter arrived one from your mum. She says your dad is getting on very well. I am so glad, but I hope he can be persuaded to stay at Elpis until he is really fit to go home.

It is simply pelting and I am already covered with mud. I must send this letter down by my servant tonight. Yes, sweetheart, you are really spoiling me with your letters, but I do want them so very, very much. I am so glad my ring does bring such dear thoughts to you. Darling, your ring is never away from me; it always hangs on the silver chain round my neck next to my skin. I remember you said, 'It is just a plain Irish handmade ring of no money value', but it is a token of your love for me, and I know all the money in this world could not buy it, and therefore it is very precious to me.

Phyl, thank you for sending me the cake and sweets and notepaper. It was an awful shame, that last block getting pinched. Yes, my love, I do like ginger cake, but not nearly as well as chocolate cake.

Phyl, you darling, your Englishman sends you just all, all his very deepest-down love forever.

My very own dearest, darlingest Lady Phyl

Just before starting this letter, I picked up your muffler and had a good look at the stitches and then buried my face in it and kissed it. I am going to make a proposal, which if you don't think is too silly, I would love you to do. I am going to kiss the first word of each of my letters, 'My' in this case, and will you now do the same with each of yours? Then I can kiss the same spot where your lips have touched. Now, Phyl, about the socks: can you make them of nearly stocking length, to just below the knee?

Burrows has just rung up to say the gramophone spring has arrived, so I shall hear my new records tomorrow night.

Well, my sweetheart, I must journey off over mud and slosh and slime to the infantry. It is simply teeming down.

TUESDAY NIGHT – 11.20 PM

AT THE BATTERY. THANK HEAVEN!!!

Phyl, you dear Phyl

I have got another letter tonight; how absolutely lovely, and they are all so very, very dear to me. It is hard to feel I am 'doing my bit' when one feels absolutely wretched, as I have all day. I sat in that beastly dugout with the rain dripping in, in every conceivable place, and then, to give a final touch to everything, the beastly stuff began dropping down my neck. I am just going to put my back into things and make the best of things at present. We are having a taste of this awful winter now, and there doesn't seem to be a break in the clouds of war anywhere.

Night-night, my darling, darling lady, forever and for always

Your Englishman

FRIDAY 5 NOVEMBER

Phyl, dear

The parcel arrived last night, and so here is the first letter on this paper. Thank you, my love, very much for everything in the parcel; it was excellently packed and arrived in perfect order. I am munching one of the sweets at the present time; they are awfully good. We have not sampled the cake, but it looks luscious and the book looks very exciting. We are suffering from wateritis here. It's a case of 'water, water everywhere' etc. Some of the men seem to think that if we get much more, then their huts will be floating to Berlin. Weldon went on leave yesterday, and by now will be in Dublin, the lucky blighter.

LATER, AFTER TEA

The gramophone has just been playing some very good records from La Bohème sung by Melba. My darling, here is a letter from you. Phyl, I am glad there is a really good chance of your letting the house. I do hope everything will be satisfactory. You will have an awful lot of work getting everything put away, but then you will be much, much better with your dad in Dublin. Eddie being in London will be a great piece of news for you all. I am sure your mum will be awfully glad to have him back safely out of that mess-up. We will be going into 'rest' again now, soon. None of us are looking forward to it. The amount of work we have been doing lately is enormous, and yet there is always more and more to be done.

SATURDAY MORNING

I am frozen this morning, and have the delightful prospect of going to the observing station before me. I have just been censoring letters. Some of them who have come back from leave are very doleful. One said, 'Now it is all over, it is worse than ever out here.' I have now got to go round the guns, putting the electric lights in order, so I must run.

Bye-bye, you dear, dear lady, forever, your
Eric

Phyl, my very own darling
Here I am, enjoying my weekend holiday! I came up yesterday;
I have never had such a walk in my life. It usually takes us about
forty-five minutes to get from the Battery to here, but yesterday
it took us an hour and a half. Just as I was leaving the Battery,
Robinson said, 'You had better put a pair of waders on, or you
will get soaked.' So I got a pair from the telephonists, and by
Jove, I'm glad I did. One part of the trench was in mud up to my
knees, and a bit further on I was walking through water up to
halfway up my thighs. In fact, it nearly came over the tops of the
waders. In one part I got onto the parapet, and was scrambling
along, but soon got into the trench again when a bullet hit the
parapet a foot in front of me, knocking the mud into my face. I
eventually arrived here sweating like a pig and covered with
mud. This morning there was a very thick mist up to ten o'clock.
I walked from here across country to the trench in front, but had
to come back by the trench because the mist had lifted. Per
usual, my feet are simply aching with cold.

Phyl, my darling, I do hope you have settled about the house
and that the doctor man is going to take it. If so, you will be as
busy as a bee. I am glad you will be able to go on with your
singing. I shall expect you to have an even better voice than you
have now (if it is possible) the next time I hear you sing. I just
long to sit and listen to you again.

LATER – 5 PM
We (the observer, telephonist and myself) have just been
pumping the water out of the trench, thereby making ourselves
more or less warm. This afternoon I fairly knocked part of one
of the Huns' trenches about for them; one round sent up a whole
pile of planks and stakes into the air. I must go down to the
infantry now, so au revoir for the present, my love.

WITH THE INFANTRY
I will finish our love day off in this letter but I can't write any more tonight.

MONDAY MORNING – 9.35
Good morning, Lady Phyl. So you have managed to let the house; I am glad and now you will have some work if you are to be out by a week today. Will you be taking the doctor's house in Dublin, do you think? So the lady has returned, and the cat is out of the bag! I wonder what kind of a tale she made of it. Some people are meddling idiots and want a sound kicking to make them mind their own business. The worst of it is you have to bear all the brunt of their meddling, but then I know you don't care a toss of a button for the lot of them. I pray that our love may be a lifelong one, but not only that, I want it to be one that will last after this life just forever and ever.

And now I must go on with our love day. I wished over and over again that the train had been an express: although it would have taken a shorter time, it would not have been broken by stopping at every beastly station. When we got out of the train, I quite thought our day was over. I had no idea that the most wonderful hours of my life were yet to come.

We walked from Westland Row until we got the car (tram) in that square off which the road runs that 'Elpis' is in. Just while we were waiting for the tram, you asked me for the second time whether I was tired. When we got out at Pembroke Road I felt very excited at the idea of seeing your mum and I didn't know for the life of me what I was going to say to her. I was astonished how wonderfully bright your mum was. Then, do you remember, you went out and changed your dress; I wonder why? I liked the navy-blue costume so much, and better than the lighter blue one you put on.

Phyl, you don't know how very, very glad I was that I was allowed to see your dad. I wonder whether he really wanted to see me. (Here is my lunch. To be continued later.) Do you remember, on our way there I sent a telegram home. I must say,

I did get a shock when I first saw your dad. He did look so thin and haggard, but he seemed wonderfully bright, much more so than I had expected he would be. Well, after our visit to Elpis we walked to Grafton Street and from then begins the most wonderful part of the day. I can't explain how most awfully proud I felt at having lunch with you, just you and I together. It was the first meal we have ever had alone and I felt just as happy as a king. Do you remember us spotting the lady from Athlone, and how I kept dodging behind your hat to prevent her from seeing me? One thing my feelings were rather hurt over, and that was you wanting to pay for the lunch out of that pound note you gave me. I did not realise what it was when you gave it me, and of course I wanted to pay for it out of my own money. But you seemed to be hurt when I refused to use it at first, so I did it to please you. At any rate, you dear, dear lady, you will know in future that when you are out with me alone, and I hope you will be often and often, I pay for things.

When we were discussing what to do after lunch, I didn't know what to suggest. I just wanted to be with you, alone, and when you suggested going back to the house, I thought there would be no possible chance of it. However, I thought very much wrong, didn't I? When we got back there, your mum was in the front drawing room, and after talking for a little she said she had to write to your sister, so off she went. I think that letter must have been yards and yards long because she didn't come back till teatime. Oh! The feelings that I experienced in that hour or so before tea. I wanted to make you feel the awful passion that seemed to fill me for you, by kissing you over and over again, as hard as I could. And yet, at the time, my love seemed to change, the fierceness disappeared and I absolutely idolised you. You seemed to be 'the treasure' itself and yet somehow it was only a glimpse and I had yet many a hard fight before I held 'the treasure' forever. I felt I had lost my heart, my soul, my body, in fact my whole self; you seemed to have taken every atom of love I ever held in my body. All of a sudden we were brought back to earth by your mum entering with the tea.

After we had finished, your mum said she had to go to see

your dad, so off she went and we were left alone again. But to tell you the honest truth, Phyl, I am rather muddled how things did go then. I know one of your cousins came, and when a man came, you bundled me behind the screen into the other room. My brain was in an absolute whirl. Then your mum came back and we were together in the back room. I felt most awfully sleepy then, and sat in the chair, resting half on yours. How I just wished I had not to go away that night. I began to realise our dear love day was nearly done. I did not want to waste the time in sleeping. Then I wanted you to come and sit by me on the sofa, and at first you refused, but then you did come in the end and that last half-hour was wonderful. I just wanted to have you as close to me as possible: it was just a real taste of heaven on earth. Phyl, I pray to God we may have many, many more hours like it. Why couldn't that last half-hour have gone on forever? Instead of that, we had to suddenly make a bolt for the train, which we didn't get. I had to say a very hurried goodbye to all. I was really a thoughtless brute to bring you with me at that time of night. But, Phyl, I did want to be with you till the last possible minute.

What a fine horse that was we had in the car; we fairly tore along. I had a vision of us having to get a taxi to Kingstown when no train came and before you thought of taking a tramcar. When we were walking up and down the quay, I thought of how different my feelings had been in the morning. Then I was full of longing to see you and now I was just longing to remain with you. I remember watching the number of mailbags that had to go in, because I knew when they were aboard I had to go and leave you and although my body was going away my soul remained in the care of the dear person that I hope will always be its guardian. So for me, there ends our wonderful, beautiful love day, except that the memory of it will last forever – our first whole day together. It ended in a beautiful night with the bright moon casting a shimmering silver band across the water and the black silhouette of the land that holds all that is nearest and dearest to my heart.

And so, my darling, your lover sends every atom of his love

to you with this letter, and he is for all time your Englishman and your

Eric

Phyl, my sweetheart
I wonder how you are getting on with the house-moving. Well, I hope everything goes through without a hitch, and I think it ought to, with my Lady at the head of affairs. I wonder if your brother has arrived back yet; I can imagine the joy in the camp.

Weldon should have got back here two days ago, but he has not arrived yet, worse luck, because I have to go up to the trenches tomorrow instead of him. It's just pelting again now. Robertson has gone to the Brigade for dinner, so your Englishman is in charge. Wenley – who comes from New Zealand – and I have been having a talk about all sorts of things that interest me. He is a decent chap and I can see we are going to get on together. I was telling him about the training I had at Athlone and I just loved going over those days again because – well, you know why. Just because it brought back all the happy time I had with you, and to add to it, we had a lot of waltzes on the gramophone. How I just long for those dances over again, to dance and dance the night through. I just long for you now; perhaps it is because I first got to know you through dancing, and afterwards got to like you, and then love you. Do you remember, at that first dance your mum asked me to come to tea sometime. I just longed to be asked, and she didn't repeat the invitation at the other dances. Then one afternoon, about three weeks later, Langham had to go to your house for something and he asked me if I cared for a walk. Phyl, you don't know how I jumped at the idea when I knew where he was going. At any rate, I went with him and your mum asked us to stay for tea, and afterwards, when we were going, she asked me to come again.

I remember, I went away just as happy as I could be, and I

don't think I was very long in taking advantage of her invitation. Then all the motor rides and visits and afternoon teas and the concert at the hall. They are all just lovely times to think about, and I am just going to do so tonight when I am in bed. But before I go, I must thank you very much for the apples; they are just lovely. I am sorry to say a lot have gone soft, but the remainder are beautiful.

Night-night now, you dear, darling lady. All the love of your Englishman is yours forever.

MONDAY 15 NOVEMBER

Phyl

I am sure you must think I am an awful rotter for not writing, but I have been murdered with toothache. On Saturday it poured and blew a gale. In the trench we observe from, I was up to my knees in water and had to stand there nearly all day. My feet and hands were hurting with cold and my tooth was awful. That night it froze, so I leave you to imagine what kind of a time I had, with my tooth much worse and the water colder than the day before. It was absolute h—!! The pump got buried under three foot of earth and sandbags, and when we did get it out, it was broken. It is just awful up there now, and I dread going up each time more than the last. Well, I am going to the dentist tomorrow, so I suppose he will either do away with one cause of bodily discomfort or make it worse.

My sweetheart, I got your letter on Saturday and it was the one thing that gave me any pleasure that day. So your brother has arrived back safely at last. How fine it must be for him, after his rough time. Under his sister's supervision, I should think he will soon be as strong as a lion again. And now about your letter. My kisses are tokens of my love whether they are given before the 'world and his wife' or when we are by ourselves. It never entered my head at the time that you would feel 'disgusted' – that word does sting – with me for kissing you at the end of the pier. But I am just going to do my bit of 'give and take more' and ask you, my Lady Phyl, to forgive me for doing it. I would much rather you had told me at the time that you felt offended.

I thought I had a pretty bad time last winter but I have started off with one ten times as bad this year. Again the dear old silk muffler was a very great comfort to me up in the observing station. I had it wound over my head and round my neck. I couldn't wear a coat because it trailed in the water, which in places came to halfway up my thighs and in one part would have come over the tops of my waders if I had not clambered along the sides of the trench. Well, there, I have told you nothing but my troubles.

Night-night now, you dear, darling lady, forever your
Eric

FRIDAY 19 NOVEMBER

Phyl, dear love
I go up to the OS today and I don't expect I shall be able to write because we have to do a lot of alterations and general work. On Tuesday I went to the dentist. It was a long ride, and rained nearly the whole time on the way there. He said the nerve was exposed and proceeded to put a filling in to kill it. Of course, he gave me gyp. I have not had any trouble with it after that night. I have got to pay him another visit a week today and I hope he puts it right.

The news about Booth Mill was the first I had heard. I hope to goodness it is not as bad as it sounds: it will be a nasty shock to the firm. I suppose you are at Northumberland Road. I wonder where it is and how you will like it? Have you got your dad with you yet? I am so glad you will be able to go on with your singing; I do love it so very much and I know you do too. Phyl, the cake is lovely; everybody likes it, your lover especially. It looked simply lovely when I took it out of the paper. All the shamrocks survived the carrying, but part of the remainder of the pattern was broken.

At present my hands are so cold that they will hardly form

the letters properly. There is a heavy frost each night, and it usually manages to rain during the day. We go into rest in a day or two: right back for about ten days and somewhere else for a fortnight. Well, as long as we get away from that OS for a while, I feel I don't mind what happens. It is awful up there, and I do sympathise with the infantry in the trenches. The water in our trench the other day got so high, it came over the top of the waders. However, I shall have to put in some work to try to keep warm.

For the last two days I have been busy making drawings to scale of the electric light fittings on the guns, for Robertson to send to the Major of a Horse Artillery Battery. It was a bit of a job, but I did enjoy doing it because it was going back to my own real work.

Yesterday Robertson and I walked down to the wagon line and it simply teemed the whole way down. It came through my Burberry in every conceivable place, and I was soaked to the skin when we arrived back here. But it was good exercise and made us both nice and warm for once.

We had a great 'strafe' the other night: everybody was firing like the dickens. In fact, it was rather like Hooge over again. The Boche had been making a nuisance of themselves on previous nights, so they had to be severely smacked. A few days ago several of our men were wounded by a shell which pitched right in among them while they were working down here. The wounds were only mere scratches, except for one man who got two small bits of shell in his forearm. We are kept continually on the go here from morning till night with different working jobs and I never seem to get a nice long think to myself. I only manage to read a page or two at a time, but it is awfully nice to have a book that you can turn to for a few minutes. I never have a room to myself now. You see, two of us sleep in what was the kitchen of this house, the other subaltern always being up at the OS. Burrows is now acting as captain, so he has finished with the observing station. Thank heaven it is a lovely afternoon now, so with a bit of luck, I shan't have such a bad time up there.

Please tell me all about your new house. Just for always and always, I am your own, very, very own Englishman.

My dearest
I got a letter tonight, and it seems just ages since I had one last.
Perhaps it is because these last three days have been a regular
scramble. Thank heaven, I did not have any trouble with my
tooth up in the OS this time but there was plenty of other
trouble. The trench was in a most appalling state, and the
dugout, when I arrived, had four inches of water on the floor.
All the store grub that we had up there had been pinched by the
infantry the night before, and the telephone lines were working
very badly. The following morning when I got up there, I found
the water was about seven inches high on the floor and the
pump would not work. Later on, the Boche shelled heavily, and
when we tried to get through to the Battery, we discovered that
all the wires were broken. After about an hour we got into
communication again and let the Huns have some back. Then
an officer arrived to take over the OS because we had to fire on
another part of the line. Just as we were starting lunch, the side
of the old dugout fell in: it had been gradually eaten away by the
water.

TUESDAY 7PM
Here we are at our old rest place, but we are only stopping the
night here. We go on, further back, tomorrow. We are supposed
to be out of action for a month. The Captain is on leave, so
Burrows is in command. The Battery got here at 1.30 after a
twelve-mile march. I had to come along in the rear with a GS
wagon and did not arrive till 5 pm. We did not start until two
and a half hours after the Battery. The wagon got stuck in heavy
ground four times and had to be half unloaded each time before
we got away finally from the old wagon line. I thought my gee
had gone for good and all this morning while we were loading
one of the wagons. I left him to graze, and when I went to him
to mount, he galloped off. Luckily, he went into the farmyard

and was caught by one of the men. When we finally moved off, three packages were shed in the first 300 yards. However, they were soon replaced, and all went swimmingly after that.

We spent Sunday and Monday nights at the wagon line, and we ought to get to our destination – some twenty-five miles behind the line – tomorrow night. This place is full of troops at present, there being a whole crowd of infantry here as well as ourselves.

An order has just come in about parcels and letters being sent for Christmas. The latest date of posting is the seventeenth of December – this applies to us, out here, sending letters home. It is in order to prevent congestion in the mail. But I wonder what you will think I have been doing lately – my letters are so few and far between, and goodness knows when you will get this one, because owing to this removal there has been no chance of sending letters for three days now.

WEDNESDAY 8.30
We have arrived at B— at last. This is a fairly big village that we are in. We have all got really top hole billets, and by the time we go away, I ought to be a linguist. I had to do all the finding of them, and one old lady that Burrows is billeted with has no roof to her house, so you can imagine how I got on.

LATER
Here I am now in a most cosy bed with beautiful white sheets and a kind of curtain arrangement over my head. I shall never want to get up in the morning, I know. I feel most awfully tired and sleepy. I am not going to attempt to answer the last dear letter I got from you tonight. I am going to read your last letter over again, and then go to sleep thinking of you, my own dear, dear Lady Phyl.

Forever your
Eric

THURSDAY 26 NOVEMBER

Dearest of all

Another of your letters has just arrived tonight. I have just finished reading it, and I have taken half an hour over it. It really is the very dearest letter you have ever written. I would have liked to have seen your departure. I wonder if it was anything like our start-off from the wagon line – I am sure the language used was nowhere near as choice. Phyl, I just love and love you the more when I think of you really wanting my letters. You have put new thoughts into my head by the way you talk of your singing. Am I to gather from what you say that it is my rival for your love? You loved your singing long before ever I came on the scene. I want you to be just my Phyl with a dear, lovely voice which she will use to sing to me alone, not to a whole crowd of stupid critics.

FRIDAY MORNING

It is nice to hear such good news about your dad, and I am sure he is glad to be able to get about a bit more. Surely he will soon be all right now. Then, with your brother being with you, it will add to the happiness of everybody. I do wish I could go with you to some of the operas, just you and I. What kind of things do they do? I have never seen the Opera Company.

AFTER TEA

Those wretched six weeks after I came back from leave the first time, I never seemed to have one moment to think of the one person in this world. We got chivvied and chased all the time, then we trekked about half Belgium, changing from one position to another. Then your letters seemed to get more cold and newsy. The worst of this game is you never seem to have finished and when I go to sleep there is always the chance of being hauled out of bed at some unearthly hour. I think that is one of the main reasons why I do not like the army life – I always feel as though I was a schoolboy who had to always be doing what he was told. There is too much bowing and scraping for my liking. However, it is good training.

Yes, Phyl, that is what I want: to be to you the very best friend you have in this world, as well as your lover. You darling, I can't thank you enough for your letters.

Now, sweetheart, au revoir for a short time. Every atom of my love to you, forever and forever.

Your Englishman

SUNDAY 28 NOVEMBER

You darling, dear Phyl

I could hardly believe my eyes when I saw another of your dear letters waiting for me tonight. My darling, the very time these letters are written at: 1.15 am, and not finished till 3 am, and the one before was not finished till 1 am, and so on. The thought of you giving up your sleep to write to me is too kind for words, and I just love and love you for it. You did the only possible thing that could relieve my toothache by writing these dear letters. I have been slightly troubled again, so I shall have to go into St Omer and have it fixed up properly. It has been freezing like the devil each night and has never stopped today and I think it is the keen, biting east wind that has started the thing aching again. Well, I hope not to see the trenches again for a month at least.

Phyl, I hardly dared to think they were your happiest hours, those spent together, and yet I longed for you to tell me that they were. Thank God, Phyl, I did make you feel really, really happy. No, Phyl, I didn't kiss any of those letters, except the one I told I would kiss and the next one. I didn't think you agreed with the idea as you did not mention it, but I will do so now with each one. Yes, I did invent one or two things on the electric lights, and made several improvements, but the original invention was made by a fellow called Pettitt. Also, in a way I did find I had not quite forgotten all I learnt about drawing. I do remember the description of the dugout: it was down at Armentière. We always look back on those as happy days now.

Phyl, dear, it doesn't matter how thick those socks are, in fact the thicker the better, as long as I can get another pair inside them. Do you know, I have never seen *Carmen* yet, but that will be one treat in store for me some day when I am with my Lady. I just love the music of it.

You dear, dear lady, how I just long to be with you and never to have to leave you again. Oh! Phyl, may God grant it will be so one happy day. And now, dearest of all, I must go to bed.

Night-night, you darling.

Forever I am your Englishman

THURSDAY 2 DECEMBER

Sweetheart

I am most awfully sleepy tonight because I have been riding a good deal. Lawrence and I went into St Omer to see the dentist. It took a good two and a half hours' ride from here, so we started at 9 am. We went to the dentist, had some lunch, made a tour round the town and rode back. It was a lovely day, and a very nice change to get absolutely clear of the troops. We both have to go in again on the ninth. Now that the frost has gone, the mud is pretty awful, but if today's weather continues it will soon dry up. We have two more subalterns attached for training, making us six in all. Yesterday we had good fun doing gun drill and in the afternoon we were going to harness a team, but three of the others had to go out with the Colonel. Yes, dear lady, as Burrows is acting captain I am senior subaltern, and it does mean a good deal more work for yours truly. However, I may just survive that and the responsibility.

It is a pity we didn't come out a week later; as it is, we will have just got back into action by Christmas. Well, it is just our luck.

FRIDAY 3 DECEMBER

Do you know, I am as stiff as the devil and I ache all over. The reason is we had a game of 'rugby' this afternoon. Burrows was to be captain of our side, but he had to go off to another place today to see about billeting of the brigade, as we move from here in a day or so, worse luck. So at the eleventh hour I had to take on the job as captain, and it was a job, getting a team in about five minutes, but I managed and we had a jolly good game. After the game we were all simply smothered in mud from head to foot. We proceeded to the brewery (our brigade bathhouse) and all had excellent warm baths in huge big wooden tubs.

Well, to give you a little alarming news, we are likely to go nearly straight back into action, at least in a day or two. Really, it is hard lines if we do, this poor old brigade always seems to get done in the eye.

Yes, dear sweetheart, a pair of mittens would be most awfully useful, in the trenches especially. I like to have anything you give me, e.g. the photos, the muffler and your dear, dear letters. I am so very sorry about you not getting a letter for nearly a week, but it was next to impossible to write while the move was taking place, in spite of the fact that I did want to write, most awfully. Oh! Phyl, it is rotten news about your cousin getting the scarlet-fever germ, and may God grant that none of you get it. Poor girl, to have to be by herself for seven whole weeks, and Christmas included.

At present I am lying in my lovely soft bed, propped up by a pillow. This room is a large one – twenty feet by ten feet – with one high window in it at the far end, the bed being across the other end. A candle is burning at my right side on a bedside cupboard. Beyond this is the mantelpiece with a big tall glass mirror standing on it. Up near the window is the washing stand. There is one solitary picture of an old lady on the walls. Weldon sleeps in the next room. The house is a big one, standing well back from the road and on the top of a terrace. From the garden gate to the mess-room is about fifty yards. The latter is on the opposite side of the road and is a much smaller house and more modern kind of a cottage.

I could just do with hour upon hour of your teasing, my love, if only I could be with you. You never tease me now, Phyl, you are always most serious when I am with you. Yes, then when I got tired of being teased, I would draw you to me and kiss you, and tell you how very much I do really love my Lady.

Night-night now sweetheart, darling, everything.

Forever and ever I am your Englishman,

Eric

1916

My own very, very dearest lovely lady

I must write a wee bit before I turn in. The train has not yet started but it soon will. How unkind it seems too, bearing your lover away from his Lady for an unknown time, and to the most cursed part of this earth. There is a howling din going on outside and the station is packed outside the barriers with all sorts of fearful-looking people, all shouting and yelling, singing, crying and smelling. I had an awful job to push my way through them but I managed.

The boy made the poor old nag fairly go and I arrived down four minutes before the train. I thought I wasn't going to make it because my watch was nearly seven minutes fast. Oh! I wish the beastly cab had been run into and I had been badly injured; anything to have kept me somewhere near you. I had ample time at Lime Street and came straight to the train when I got to the station. Then I had to go and get my sleeping-berth ticket and that meant pushing through the crowd of seething humanity twice over.

There – the train is moving away now. Oh! Phyl, dear lady, how your lover longs for you. What a dear, happy time it has been; may the good God grant us many, many more such happy times together. Oh! how beautiful and yet how awful it is to love: the wonderful happiness of being with you. Please think really, really hard of me, dear Phyl, as I am doing now, loving, loving, loving you with all my heart, my soul and my body.

Forever I am your lover and Englishman,

Eric

XXX

POSTED TO NORTHUMBERLAND ROAD, DUBLIN FROM THE GRAND HOTEL
DU LOUVRE ET TERMINUS, BOULOGNE-SUR-MER

My own dear lady

Here we are, hung up at this place for twenty-four hours. We arrived here at about 1.15 yesterday afternoon and go on this evening at seven o'clock. How I wish I could have had the extra time at home with you instead of wasting it here. I met Grant (the doctor) and Hill (the vet) on the boat and we all retired early and didn't get up till 9.40 this morning. I do hope you got the letter I wrote in the train as I had to ask the taxi driver that took me to Victoria from Euston to post it for me because I only had five minutes to get the train, and the station was absolutely packed with people.

I still feel a peculiar 'come-what-may' kind of feeling. Darling, I feel I don't care what happens to me, because I have left all that I love behind me. I wonder how many long, dreary months it will be before I kiss those dear red lips again; it seems as though I was looking down an endless valley with no goal in sight.

Phyl, what a happy time it has been, but why couldn't it have lasted for always and always? Did you really enjoy Saturday? I would have given a great deal to have had all the other days to ourselves. When all is said and done, we only had the mornings to ourselves, and then only three of those. I must go and have something to eat now before we go to the train.

WEDNESDAY 12 JANUARY – 11 PM

BACK AT THE CHATEAU

The train was packed: we had six in our carriage, but I managed to sleep most of the way. We got to P— [Poperinge] at 1.45 and I went to Talbot House for bed and breakfast and turned in feeling pretty rotten. I started off for here on foot – no horses were sent down for me. However, I got on a motor lorry and had a lift as far as V— [Vlamertinge], then I walked to where our horses were kept and found they had been moved to another place. I was going to trek up here – about three miles – with my saddlebags and oilskin when an idea came into my head that the officers of the Battery in action at this farm might lend me one of their horses, and sure enough, they did. So I arrived up here in time for lunch, feeling anything but happy. Burrows has got his three stars and will command here. At present we have an officer attached for instruction, but he goes soon.

Being back in this place makes my leave seem just like a dream, and yet what a dear, lovely reality it has been. I like to think of the very beginning of it – I mean Monday night, when I came into town to stay at Lime Street, to meet you in the morning. How very happy I was when I caught sight of you as you got onto the platform from the train. My heart jumped nearly out of the top of my head as soon as I saw you really, really there. Did the first kiss I gave you seem to start it all over again?

Phyl, I have got a dreadfully sore throat; it came on after leaving the boat at Boulogne and is rotten now. I wonder if you have got one – I do hope not. What kind of a journey did you have home? Was it as rough a crossing? I shall always sympathise with people who are ill, after my dose coming home. I wonder if you will be able to follow the way we go to the OS and back on your map. I put arrows along the lines to show the direction in which we go.

What did your mum think of the DA? I do hope she really liked it. I wonder how the shoes are – how I wish I could change places with them. Aren't I a silly goose though, my Lady. How did your dad seem, Phyl, when you got back, and did he say anything about your coming over to stay with us?

Well, bye-bye now, my darling, darling lady, for always and always,

Your Eric

SATURDAY 15 JANUARY 3.30 PM

Phyl, my dear, dear lady
It is beastly cold at present. We all sit in this room during the

day with our coats on. You see, we can't have a fire on account of the smoke being seen, and as a matter of fact, we have hardly any coal. Oh! it is rotten, coming back to this after the dear, lovely days we had together, with every comfort. However, I mustn't grumble because, God knows, we might be much, much worse off. There was a rumour that we would go out of action again in a few days, but I am afraid it is only a rumour and no more.

Wenley went digging fuses this morning and found the base of a Little Willie. It will look rather nice as an inkpot if I can manage to keep it till I get home again. You see, we are not allowed to send souvenirs home by post now. Yesterday, Wenley and I were up in the OS. It was simply horribly cold. However, we didn't get bombed.

Last night, I thought about 'our day' of the buying of the brooches and of going to Bacons' and then of buying the shoes. How good it was to know you were really pleased with my choice of a present. I just wanted to give you something that you would wear. Phyl, dear, I got your letter, written at home. What a dear, lovely thing it is. But I am so sorry and yet so glad that you felt my going so very, very much. But the dear time we spent together was worth all these horrible feelings, and much much more beside. I could picture you writing, and you had on a white silk blouse with my belt and the navy-blue skirt and I could see the ring on your left hand. The coming-away part was much worse this time, and when you cried in the morning room before supper, I felt as though I was going to give way too.

6.10 PM
We have just finished tea. Weldon has come down from the OS and is very chirpy, as he goes on leave on Monday and hasn't to go up again. How I wish I was going with him – he goes to Dublin. I was thinking about our first whole evening together and by ourselves. It is just a week ago that we were arriving at the State and you had the shoes on. Then we had dinner together and I did feel as proud as punch, just because I was with my Lady. I drank your health and I thought my Lady looked just beautiful in her lover's eyes.

We were all lazy, this morning being Sunday, and as I have to go up to the trenches tonight I thought I was entitled to a longer stay in bed. I am wearing one of the pairs of socks you knitted at present and you just can't know how I love to have them on, because you made them. I think the very dearest part of this letter is the piece you added at the end, about asking God to look down on our love for one another. My love, when will this horrible business end? I want to live in our own little cottage and be miles away from the world and his wife – Phyl, it would be heaven.

Oh! sweetheart, forever, forever and ever I am your Englishman

Eric

WEDNESDAY 19 JANUARY

Dearest lady in the world

You said in this last letter, which I got on Monday night, that you wondered whether you could put up with me for a longer 'dose' than a week. Phyl, I don't like you to think of my time with you as being a 'dose', whether nice or nasty. I wouldn't worry about it until the chance comes, as it won't be for some time. You have no idea how I hate to hear anyone say somebody is a 'charming person'; it is a beastly, sloppy expression, and I hate to think it is ever applied to me. I wonder if you will understand really and truly by all this. I know that I can tell you all my secrets, and I see you as my friend, a real pal, and I do so want you to be my Lady as well. I want to know that you arrived home safely because I always feel so frightened to think of you going across by yourself. You see, it isn't as though it was peacetime and we can never tell what these — Huns will do next.

My darling, I am so very sorry that you were seedy. I expect it was with rushing about: I mean, going to Bolton and then back to L'pool and off to the circus. Phyl, it is awful having to go back to letters; I wonder how long we shall have to exist on letters only.

We have all got our cigars lighted, but it doesn't seem to warm the room much, because my feet are like ice. How I envy old Weldon in Dublin now. But then, it would not matter whether it was Dublin or the North Pole as long as I was with my Lady.

I am so glad your mum does like the brooch; I would have liked to have given her a better one though. And now, Phyl, I must turn in, as I have to get up at 5.30 am.

Night-night, my very own darling lady. I am just your Eric and nobody else's and please don't forget it.

SUNDAY 23 JANUARY – 3.55 PM

Sweetheart, just the one person on this earth that is worth more than everything in the world

Thank heaven you are home again safely. One of the telephonists brought up your letter with him this morning. It was a beautiful surprise, because I did not expect any letters till I got down here again in the evening.

Yesterday morning I thought I was going to have a lively time going from the infantry to the OS I told the telephonist to waken me at 6.15 and when he wakened me it was five past seven and nearly broad daylight. I had to walk across the open too, and quite expected that the Boche snipers would give me a warm time. However, not a shot was fired at me, and I arrived safely. I managed to spot the flashes of two German Batteries yesterday, and so although a 5.9 landed just short of our trench, I felt quite pleased with myself.

EARLY MONDAY MORNING
I was annoyed last night. I wanted to write this letter, but was not allowed to. They wanted me to play bridge. Phyl, dear, I must send this off today; as I haven't written since Thursday last,

I wanted it to be a dear, long letter, but it must go as it is, so bye-bye now, my own darling.

Forever and ever and all time, I am your Englishman.

MONDAY 24 JANUARY
EXAMINED BY BASE CENSOR

My sweetheart

I have been up at the OS all day and we had rather a squashy time, because there were four of us in a space just comfortable for one. Another Battery observes with us at present, as they got shelled out of their own place. I did not fire a round all day, but was busy the whole time.

All morning I was busy making out a report on the enemy's barbed wire. After lunch, they shelled round about us pretty profusely, and made things rather unpleasant for a short time. Then the others fired at a farm and I helped to observe for them. After that, I had to go scrambling about the country behind the OS to try and find an alternative position, in case we ever got shelled out. I am so glad you can follow the marking of the map, and I hope it draws you nearer to me.

Sweetheart, how I wished that night before dinner that we were going to be alone all evening, and that I could have come over with you to this wretched country, by telling you all about what happened at such and such a place, and showing it to you on the map. But perhaps, dear heart, we will come over here together some day, when the years have rolled on. How very, very happy I would feel then, instead of having this horrible lonely, achy feeling which seems to make the world so dark for me at present. But then, my Lady, there is always my bright light shining ahead of me, making me feel life is very, very dear to me. It's just your wonderful love for me and mine for you.

Oh! I am so glad your dad wasn't cross about your coming over when you got back, but I am really sorry I caused him to be angry the night you came. The throat is perfectly all right again now; there is only one ailment now, and that will last as long as

113

ever I am away from my Lady, and now I must turn in: it is already half past one.

TUESDAY 25 JANUARY
Tomorrow I shall have rather an exciting time. I am going out into no man's land before it is light, and we are to remain in a certain place all day. The idea is that I can see a portion of the German trenches which is very bad to observe from anywhere else. It will be jolly exciting, and very interesting if all goes well, but if not then we shall either have a dull day of it or a horrible time. I shall write you a note out there, and you will be able to say you are one of, if not the very first lady to receive a letter from no man's land. You are not to worry, there is very little danger of anything going wrong, and if it does, then, dear, just remember I am in God's keeping. An infantry officer and some men are going with me. The Colonel only told me this morning about it, so at present I feel rather full of the thing. I have to make my own arrangements and it will take a little thought.

I have told you about this because I promised you I would tell you everything about what happens to me out here. It might, with ill luck, turn out a failure, and if it does, dear, then it is God's will and cannot be altered. But your lover has been chosen for the job over at least one other, and he is not the one to try and get out of it. I shall ten to one feel very frightened at first, having never been out between the trenches, but I am sure it will wear off.

I must stop, dear, dear, Phyl, bye-bye for a short time. Just every atom of love that is in me is yours, forever and ever. I am just your own Englishman

Eric

WEDNESDAY 26 JANUARY
FIELD SERVICE POSTCARD. POSTED 27 JANUARY

I am quite well.
I have received your letter.
Letter follows at first opportunity.

WEDNESDAY 26 JANUARY
AT THE INFANTRY HEADQUARTERS – 7.35 PM. POSTED 29 JANUARY

Sweetheart
After all, I didn't get a chance to write to you from no man's land because – well, here is the tale. We were to go out to some disused dugouts near the Boche trenches, just before daylight. First of all, a patrol with an infantry officer was to go to clear the way, or rather to see that no Boche were waiting for us. Then I and my two men were to run out a telephone wire, and meet the patrol at the dugouts. Well, the patrol went out and we followed, laying our wire as we went. We got as far as a road running across our front; there was a hedge running at right angles to it which the patrol had gone down. All at once there was a rifle shot: the bullet whistled past us, so we dropped flat, resting along the bank of the ditch at the side of the road. I watched one side of the hedge, and one of the men the other. I was the only one of the three armed and had my automatic pistol. I suddenly saw a figure running towards us. By this time I was getting jolly jumpy, but, however, managed to keep more or less cool. The man came on, and when he got close to us, I recognised him as one of the patrol. He said one of the men was wounded and they had run into an enemy patrol at the bend in the hedge. So he watched the left hand side of the hedge and I continued to watch the right.

We waited a little while, then I saw first one figure, then two, three and four. At first I thought they were enemy and told the man that had just joined us to cover one, and I covered another. But thank heaven we waited and didn't fire, because they were the remainder of the patrol. The officer was helping the wounded man and they joined us. We sent the wounded man back the remainder of the way and then my two men started reeling the wire in and I returned with them. I was not sorry to get back behind our wire and of course the scheme was upset altogether.

The patrol was reinforced and went out again to recover the wounded man's rifle and I heard this evening that they got it. We returned here after reeling the wire in. Oh! Phyl, I was truly thankful that the Boche didn't let our patrol pass because we would have been scuppered in all probability and possibly the whole lot would have been shot. The one man was only slightly wounded. There was a bright moon shining but the sky was clouded. It was an ideal night for our purpose, but unfortunately the Boche was there first and so had the upper hand of our people.

Tonight my eyes are fearfully sore. I don't know what it is with, but they both are smarting and watering very badly. I wonder if anything out of the ordinary will happen tomorrow. It is the Kaiser's birthday, and my day in the OS. Phyl, it is nice to know your mum really does like the brooch and I feel very pleased indeed that she does wear it. I do hope your sister gets through her exam easily. Is she going into a hospital again? Has your brother heard anything definite as to what is going to happen to him when his leave is up? I suppose he will be in some station for a long time before he is really fit again.

Wenley went on leave yesterday and Burrows and I are still taking alternate days in the OS. It is jolly hard work, and it may be due to staring through the periscope all day that my eyes are so sore at present.

In the OS – 3.30 pm
So far we have had a fairly quiet day up here. A Little Willie arrived somewhere jolly close this morning. All that I heard was a terrific bang and bits of earth were flying about. There was no warning hiss of the shell, and I don't know even yet exactly where it arrived. I am afraid your lover's equilibrium was quite

upset by the excitement of the escapade the night before last and has by no means recovered yet.

I do wish old Weldon would come back; this every-other-day business is a jolly rotten game. You get very little time to do anything, and if it wasn't for the heavy mist I should not be able to write this. There is always plenty to watch up here. This morning I saw the Huns had lit three fires in their trenches and so I proceeded to shell them. All three were soon extinguished – at any rate, no more smoke was seen. I also saw four Boche walking about some way behind the trenches and had some shots at them. Then I saw the smoke of some trains behind the lines etc. etc., and so one is kept busy with firing at things and writing reports.

Sweetheart, the mittens are most awfully useful. I use them nearly every day I am up here and bless my Lady over and over again for them.

At the Battery – 11.55

Phyl, you darling lady, how can I thank you for this letter; I think it is the dearest one you have ever written. At times I think love is cruel, and there is the terrible lonely achy feel that comes on – my Lady, it is hard to bear out here. But when it comes on, I just try and think that I am with you. Then I think the dearest thought of all. I think how wonderfully good God is that He has given me the love of the very dearest, purest, sweetest and loveliest lady on this earth. Phyl, my darling, I bless the very second that I first saw your dear face. During those three precious months, I learnt to love you, though you had no idea of it. I was so pleased that I had bought the shoes I felt you wanted. I wanted to think of something that you would really like without the aid of anybody's suggestions.

Friday 28 January – Lunchtime

We are a full house here now. Weldon got back yesterday. He said he had four days in Dublin, but everybody he knew wanted him to go and see them, so he decided to move back to London for two days so that he could be absolutely with his wife.

This has to go this afternoon and I have two reports to make out yet for the Major, so I must just wind up. All my heart and soul is yours, now and forever, Phyl.

Just your own, own Englishman,
Eric

MONDAY 31 JANUARY
STARTED IN THE OS

My Lady

I am sitting in this place with feet like ice. It is fearfully misty, and although I have been busy all day, everything is quiet now. We go out of action in a day or two. How long we shall remain out, I don't know; however, we are going. It seems simply ages since we came in on the seventeenth of December. The weeks seem months – except for one dear wonderful week, the very best week I have ever spent in my life. Oh! how very short it seemed, and how wonderfully dear as well.

It has been beastly, lately: everybody has been rather worried because the wind has been in an unsafe quarter, but so far, so good. I have been doing a lot of manual labour the last two days. We have been putting up a new gun pit about half a mile from here and about one and a half miles from the Battery. Both nights I was really tired out, and slept like a log. The night before last, I got a jolly decent letter from Dad. He told me about the aviary he has been making since I left. But, my Lady, he said a very nice thing about my coming back here: 'Yes, I can quite understand your feelings on returning to all the business of war for the third time and leaving one you think most of, behind. Well you can take full credit for having done your duty to your country without any hesitation and, though this is but a small recompense for what you are enduring, it is more than many will be able to claim by the way things are going on here.'

I am so happy to know, exactly, some more of your really own thoughts about your Eric. Phyl, I am going to copy out the piece that I didn't understand until this last letter came, and tell you

118

where the explanation doesn't quite clear it all up: 'Do you know that I always feel that "my Eric" is just mine, you are quite a different person to them. I expect they are really right, knowing you best, but nevertheless "my Eric" isn't at all a charming person. In fact, I wonder if I shall be able to put up with a longer dose than a week. Well, I am afraid I am not to get the chance of experimenting.' I still don't like the word 'dose', and I can't see that this means you wish you had the opportunity of trying whether you could stand having me with you for longer than a week.

It is 12.30 now; everybody is in bed and fast asleep. Over on the right there is a lot of sniping going on, and a little while ago the Battery was letting off hard. I am glad you really like the photo, now it has been done as we wanted, and may it tell you many things you want to know while your lover is away from you.

Night-night now, sweetheart.

I am just your

Eric

THURSDAY 3 FEBRUARY
POSTED 6 FEBRUARY

My dear, dear lady

Your letter written on Sunday came tonight. I can see that you have had a dreadfully anxious time, until you found out that it was due to a chill that your dad had caught. May God grant that this treatment he is undergoing will make him really well and free him from pain at once. Phyl, I want the 'dull' letters just as much as the cheerful ones, because they are all written by my Lady. As you said in one of your other letters, they are the only means of lessening the distance between us.

Well, you don't need to worry about the safety of your lover for the present, because he is back at H— [Houtkerque]. I left the line last night after spending the majority of the day in the OS. I have got a cosy wee room for my billet, and my bed is very

119

comfy, and thank heaven, I am by myself too. My eyes are hurting abominably at present and I have to get up at six in the morning, so I must stop, dear.

Friday morning – 8.30 am

It is a beastly wet day, and a horribly cold wind is blowing very hard. It was pitch black this morning, getting out of bed, and yet the bell in the church nearby was tolling away. All the farmer folk go to bed about 9 pm here and get up at about 5.30, even though it is still dark. I am orderly officer today and so I will tell you just what I have to do. Reveille is at 6 am and stables start at 6.30. This morning we had an early exercise. Each man takes two horses, riding one himself and leading the other; an officer is in charge. We walk along the roads, having a trot now and then. This lasts for an hour and a half, and when we get back, the horses are watered right away, harness taken off and then they are fed. The men are then dismissed and they have to clean up and have their breakfast.

At 9.30 there is gun drill for recruits, cleaning up fatigues for drivers and signalling instruction for telephonists and signallers. This lasts for an hour and a half.

At midday, stables begin. The horses are groomed, watered and fed and it takes about an hour and a half. Immediately after stables are over, there are all sorts of little odd jobs to do; men want to speak to an officer or defaulters are to be questioned. When we can get away, we come to the mess here and have lunch. At 2 pm there are harness-cleaning fatigues, and any other jobs are dealt with then. Often the subs have inspections, or prisoners are being dealt with by the Major and they have to attend. The orderly officer has to attend, water and feed at 3.30 pm, which lasts about half an hour. Then he comes and has his tea and turns out again at 6 pm for another feed and hay up. Even after dinner his duties are not over because he has to visit the guard and picket after 10.30 – this takes nearly an hour. So you see, my Lady, we are kept busy when we are in rest.

This afternoon I have to ride about twelve miles to get the pay; it will be delightful if it keeps on like this. Do you know, my new cap was stolen last night. I left it in the passage when I came in to dinner, and when I was going back to my billet I discovered it was gone. It was not to be found anywhere and is an awful nuisance, because the old one is so disreputable. I don't know why all leave was stopped; there was nothing particular going on over here. Perhaps it was on account of the submarines. Weldon told me the Queenstown boat was chased one night while he was on leave, but got away safely.

AFTER DINNER – 9.45 PM
My new boots arrived from Manfields tonight and look jolly nice: I shall try them on tomorrow. I was writing in bed last night at 11.45 pm and I dropped right off to sleep, and when I woke up an hour later, the candle was on its last legs.

Today – Saturday – is a glorious day, as warm as summer, and hardly any wind. Phyl, it is just the same beautiful kind of day we had that happy, happy time together. Now, Phyl, I must stop writing. Try and forgive your lover for feeling in a very dull and fed-up mood when writing part of this letter.

Bye-bye my darling, now and forever your
Eric

MONDAY 7 FEBRUARY
POSTED 9 FEBRUARY

Sweetheart
I quite intended writing to you yesterday but unfortunately I was on duty. Last night when I had turned the guard and picket out, I went round the horse lines as usual, looking to see that all the rings were on the horses properly, because they are always getting twisted. The sergeant was straightening the ring on one of my horses when all at once the horse lashed out at him for all it was worth with both hind legs. Luckily, one foot only caught the side of his coat and sent him reeling backwards. I thought he was badly hurt but he wasn't even scratched. He went to put it on again and the horse darted at him and again he caught his

coat just on the chest, but it was a near thing for his face. After that, we spent an hour rounding up four loose horses. Today we have been hard at it all the time. I have been taking the gunners at gun drill and have shouted myself nearly speechless.

I am writing this in my room before dinner. My room is a long narrow one with a good-sized window facing onto the main street of this place. It has a tiled floor, two tables, plenty of chairs and a bed in it. It is really the drawing room or parlour of the house, but the old man and his wife (awfully decent old people they are, too) asked me if I would prefer it to the little one I was sleeping in, which, although it was very comfy, was so very small.

AFTER DINNER – 9.55 PM
Phyl, it is a most beautiful starlit night; the new moon is just getting down to the horizon and everything is perfectly peaceful and quiet, except for a motorbike passing now and then: a dispatch rider on his way to some headquarters, or returning home. As I was coming from the mess, I could see the glow of a flare light going up somewhere on the line, at least sixteen miles away. I wonder what my love is doing, miles and miles away to the north-west. Surely my time with you was real and not imagination, and I know one thing very wonderful and that is your love; everything on this earth is worthless compared with it to your Englishman.

WEDNESDAY 9 FEBRUARY

My love
Although it is very late, I am going to write a little before I turn in. How dreadfully sorry I felt when I read your Saturday letter. But I was so very glad when you said your dad was a lot better, and no sign of pain since then. How simply dreadful it all must be for you. His being free from pain is the very best news possible and I shall not cease praying to God. Phyl, I am the last person to say to you, 'Bow your head and think no more of me';

if anything had happened to me, my Lady would never forget me – she would know I was waiting for her and would wait for all time until she came again to her lover.

THURSDAY – 4.45 PM
Phyl, I wonder how your dad is today. I hope that you are able to put your energy into strengthening him, as you said you would have to do in this last letter, when he came out of Elpis. I wonder if you will be returning to Athlone on the fifteenth. I have been thinking of the morning we spent together in the music room, after the night when I had caused you to feel horribly 'cold' and as though you hated the sight of me. It was the last thing on earth I wanted you to feel, and how wretched I felt that night because I thought I had made my Lady not love me. But the following morning you were just my very own Lady then, and I could speak to you of what I had said. We said then that we would like to live together, if necessary in a log hut somewhere in Canada, somewhere we would be absolutely by ourselves. The hopeless feeling of 'Will this war ever end?' seems to be very much to the fore in me tonight. Do you know that low down in me, I have a horrible idea that it will go on for years and years?

Weldon has gone to a school of instruction for a fortnight. Wenley came back from leave and has been married; for that reason he got four days' extension. Burrows says he is to be married the next time he goes on leave, so that leaves the Major and myself. Do you know Tommy is beginning to look a really nice horse now. He had rather a bad time during the gas attack; the groom got quite a fright and thought he was gassed. Our horses were kept about a mile and a half away from the Battery and so got a fair dose of gas. We are very busy training the new gunners who have joined us. It is an awful job and takes a very long time.

My eyes have been aching a good deal lately in the evenings. I don't want to have to start wearing goggles again, but they feel as though I shall have to at present.

I fell asleep last night while I was writing this, in the chair I am sitting in now. Today has been simply beastly. It has rained incessantly and a keen, cutting east wind has been blowing. My dear, I do hope your dad is all right; somehow I expected a letter from you tonight, but none came. I am going to send this one off tonight, so I must stop now.

My dearest, dearest love to you forever, Phyl.

SATURDAY 12 FEBRUARY 1916
POSTED TO ATHLONE

My Lady Phyl

Another lovely day has gone and tonight it is as clear as could be. I can hear the antiaircraft guns firing a long way behind us. Most likely somewhere in the direction of Calais. We could see the flashes from the shells bursting; they must have been a long way off because the noise was very faint. All day there has been a lot of gunning going on somewhere in the line but tonight it has quietened down.

I got your letter, written on Tuesday. Sweetheart, it does seem hard to have a photograph of you in front of me, and a piece of paper that your own lips have kissed, and yet the one person in all the world is miles and miles away from me. What an awful longing I have that it was your own dear lips I was kissing and not a piece of paper, but nevertheless it seems to bridge the distance between us.

SUNDAY EVENING – 6.30

I have just come in from the mess and what a lovely surprise I had when another letter arrived tonight, and such a dear one it is, too. This afternoon has been beautiful. Wenley, Burrows and I went for a short ride round by the aeroplane sheds and after waiting there a short time, we saw one plane land and two go up. Both of those that went up skimmed just over us, and Tommy objected strongly to them. In fact, the second one made him rear up, and I was standing, holding him by the head-collar; he nearly pulled my arm out of joint. Just before we got to the aerodrome we counted eight planes in the air, all close together. I suppose they were going off to make a reconnaissance; at any rate, they all flew off in the same direction. Then Wenley and I found a rather muddy but soft track, so had a gallop along it. Burrows took it more quietly and walked home along the road.

On Saturdays we always have an inspection of harness, billets and gun park. Yesterday I had to do the inspection, as Burrows had to go to the dentist at P—. The harness in my section was streaks ahead of the others, but it is about time it was. Tomorrow is my day on duty, and I'll bet my boots it's raining when I get up at 5.45.

I am going to answer this dear letter that I got tonight later on. Phyl, I have noticed the last three letters have been different to the ones before. I said to myself it is just because she is worrying about her dad. You see the 'catty' bits don't alter my love for you, they simply make me long and long for my Lady, and they may make me say, 'I will make you love me.'

Just all, all your soldierman's love to you, now and forever, sweetheart.

SUNDAY 13 FEBRUARY

Phyl, dear
Here it is, twelve o'clock, and I am only starting this letter. I wanted to be able to send it off tomorrow. They wanted to play bridge, so I said I would play just one rubber and just my luck, the bally thing took from 8.45 till now.

No, Phyl, I should not get tired of following you round all day; it would go only too quickly and if I had been there last Wednesday, you would have heard an awful noise going on when the clapping began, after you had sung. Phyl, when you wore the grey frock did you wear 'the' shoes too?

When I got up this morning, it was raining hard and I got pretty wet on exercise. The mud in the horse lines is simply awful now; it comes halfway up the calf of one's leg and is just like glue. I have just come in from guard-mounting parade at six, after walking round to see the sick horses. We have to go round the horse lines to see that all the horses are fed and hayed up. It makes quite a long tramp, because the sick horses are kept in two barns some distance away from the lines. I wish old Weldon would come back, as he always livens us all up. Wenley is horribly dumpy at present, but that is only to be expected, poor chap, after just getting married.

10.30 PM

Phyl, my sweetheart, we go back into action on Wednesday. Burrows and Wenley go tomorrow, and I follow on Wednesday. The message came in while we were having dinner. I knew something would happen pretty soon, because we will have been out two weeks by then. I noticed the gun flashes over in the direction of the line. I wonder what is happening. Well, I shall know soon enough, I suppose. We heard today that they are busy up there. Truly one doesn't know from minute to minute what is going to happen next out there. I wonder if we will ever get away from this wretched salient. We have been a longer time in it than any other division, and thoroughly deserve to move out of it now. Well, it remains to be seen; at present there is no sign of it.

Night-night, my sweetheart for always.

FRIDAY 18 FEBRUARY 1916

My Lady

I was jolly glad to see your letter waiting for me on the mess-room table when I came in after having my first walk through — [Ypres], you know. Just imagine, I have been here nearly ten months now, and yesterday was the first time I had ever been really into town. It is a most appalling sight. I only came across one house out of the many I saw which hadn't been actually struck by a shell, and that was a very small one in a row of houses. My main object was to find one or two small requirements (what!) for the mess: e.g. a lamp and some plates and a spring mattress. Well, although I went into at least twenty-five different houses which had been less banged about than others, I didn't find anything that I wanted.

It was a lovely afternoon, and the sparrows and starlings were making a fearful row in the ruins of the cathedral and the cloth hall. Both these places are most terribly knocked about; in fact, they are simply huge heaps of masonry and wreckage. About one quarter of the cathedral tower is standing. All the houses round are absolutely flattened.

I was particularly struck by one big house that I went into. It must have been a beautiful place at one time and even now shows signs of its old beauty. The whole house has been painted white inside, and the facings outside were of a white stone. The living rooms were huge, with big windows, and radiators still in. The only piece of furniture that I saw was a bedstead with a damaged spring mattress on it. The front part of the house was not badly damaged – windows were all gone, of course. The back part, however, was partly destroyed by shells: one had come clean through the roof and burst in the kitchen after going through two storeys. The scullery or back kitchen, I noticed, was all white-tiled, as were the bathrooms (two). The room I found the bed in had evidently been a nursery. It was at the top of the house and the floor was covered with a litter of lesson books, toys, dolls, picture books and clothes. I also noticed two untouched butterfly nets in one corner. I expect the people must have got nearly everything away – at any rate, I hope they did. I wonder if they got themselves away, and if so, where they are now. What a dreadful thing it must be to have to leave one's home like that, knowing that, in all probability, when you see it again it will be a pile of bricks and wreckage. I wonder what size of family, and what the people were like; perhaps some of the elite of the town. I was struck also by the beautiful main staircase. It was wide, about the same as the one at home, and was all oak. The banisters were finely carved, with a flowery pattern.

Another place I went into had evidently been a furniture shop, because in one room I found a huge pile of broken chairs, tables, sideboards and cupboards. The back of the house was out.

I did go beyond the main part of the town, because I was by myself, and it was not a very healthy place, from a shell point of view. On my way back, I came across the little house which had not had a shell into it. There were one or two cupboards in it, and a kiddie's bed in one room. On the floor of this room there was a fearful litter of clothing, bedsheets and footwear. I think the lady of the house must have had a dainty little foot, because I noticed a particularly small lady's boot and my heart gave a peculiar jump as I suddenly thought of another lady who I loved very much and who also had very dainty tootsies. While I was in this house, I noticed the light was failing, and so I made a move for the Battery.

I am writing this at the infantry HQ before going to bed. The dugout is for all the world like a piece of one of the tubes in London: it is a circular shape, being made of thin steel with earth and bricks around it. It is built into a bank. At the inner end is a stove, and the outer end has a window in it, the whole thing being about twenty feet long and at the widest part about nine feet. I have been in the OS all day and have had a quiet time, more or less. We are in quite a different position now, and cover a different part of the line.

Oh! Phyl, I am glad your dad is getting all right again. By now he will be getting properly looked after at home. I wonder are you still in Dublin. My love, you must be wasting away. The ring never used to come off, did it? Would you like to have it made a wee bit smaller, because if so, do please. Do you know what I was wondering the other day when I was in town? I was wondering if you and I would walk down the same streets together, sometime when the war was all over and done, feeling as happy as it was possible for us to feel. I wondered what the place would look like then.

It is a horrible nuisance; we have to sleep two in a room in the present position, because there are only three rooms and five of us. I have just been looking at the army list and I find I am 122nd on it; that isn't much when there are about two thousand second lieutenants. Another letter arrived last night; I did not get it till this morning.

Night-night you dear, darling Phyl. I am just your very own Englishman tonight.

SUNDAY 20 FEBRUARY

Phyl dear

I have been wanting to write this letter all day but I have been in the OS and it was horribly cold; also there was a regular crowd up there all day. You see we share the place (a house) with another Battery.

It was a great surprise to get the letter written on the thirteenth because I had got one the night before, and I have got another tonight. I write just as often as I possibly can. How funny it was, you asking if anybody was getting home on leave while we were in rest, and also how long we were to be in rest. You see, I got this letter after we had got into action here.

This morning, after I had been looking through the telescope and glasses for nearly two hours, I was so cold I had to go downstairs and try and get warm by stamping up and down a room in the bottom of the house we observe from. While I was there, I began daydreaming about my uncle's cottage on the Fells, and as I was eating my breakfast, the door opened and you were standing there, and I kissed you over and over again without saying a word. There are lovely walks to go on together, and there would be the household duties to be done and the dear little garden to look after. It would be a happy time. Why can't the impossible things sometimes happen just as one would want them to be?

This is the last sheet of this paper, love, and I must run off to bed; it is 12.30. Night-night, my Lady Love.

Sweetheart

Here is a coincidence for you. What do you think? I am going on leave with the next lot; that means leaving here on the twenty-fifth, twenty-sixth or twenty-seventh. I am not quite sure which.

Oh! love, what am I to do? Your people won't let you come over again so soon, will they?

And you are not in Dublin now. But I must see you, I really must. Well, I have done something – it's awful cheek, I know, but I have sent my address as c/o your father in Athlone, and thereby ought to get an extra day for travelling to Ireland, and also I can get as far as Dublin without expense. But, Phyl, to tell you the truth, I want to come to Athlone or to Dublin because I think your people don't like the idea of you coming over to us. The only thing is, it means only such a short time with you, instead of having nearly seven days together. I will do anything to be with you, Phyl, for as long as I can, but you must tell me what your people and you yourself would like best. In case your people would object to your coming over so often, then I shall come either to Athlone or Dublin for half my leave, according to which you would rather I did. I just want to come for the whole of it, but I must see my mum. If you have any suggestions to make, write both to here and to home, just to make doubly certain.

I would like to see your brother and dear old Athlone again. What a lot of happy times it would bring back to me. I imagine my coming into tea as of old, and sitting on the small stool by the fire and the hot cakes. Then I should be able to see your dad and form my own opinions as to how he was recovering.

This wretched place is becoming a warm spot again; I wonder if we shall ever get away from it for good. Well, I go up to the OS early tomorrow and so now I must turn in, as it is 11.45. Night-night, my sweetheart, and may this get you quickly.

For all time I am just your Englishman,

Eric

My sweetheart

I feel so excited I don't quite know what I am going to say to you. Phyl, dear, I leave, or should do so, tomorrow afternoon. I would like to see Athlone again, but I can't help worrying about the shortness of the time we would have together if I came. I am afraid I am spoilt after last leave. Oh! Why can't I charter an aeroplane and fly over to you? Wouldn't it be fine? I shall get home late Saturday night – how I would love to find you there waiting for me, but somehow I think you will not be there, and then I shall be so lonely. I am glad you got home without mishap and that your dad is really brightening up.

The row here has been appalling lately. The night before last, on our left, both sides were letting drive at each other for close on three hours; the din was simply terrific. I shall be glad to get out of it for a while. It is very cold, too; last night there was ten degrees of frost, and yesterday we had snow – the first this winter, and the last, I hope.

I am up with the infantry and we have just had dinner. A message came in and what do you think it said? —!! —!! 'All leave is stopped.' Just my luck, isn't it. I feel just as wretched now as I did feel happy before.

This is the third time I have had this disappointment, and by the way, I wasn't looking for this one, Phyl. Well, I must hope it is not to be stopped for long. I have just been to the telephone – Weldon rang up to sympathise with me. Instead of going down early tomorrow to get ready, I shall have a pleasant (???) day in the OS.

Sweetheart, I do want you to keep the photo in your own room. It is awfully nice to know your mum wanted it in the drawing room, but I want you to keep it for just your very own self. I am going to stop, because I don't feel like writing. I will let you know as soon as I can when I am likely to come.

A very disappointed Englishman

FRIDAY 25 FEBRUARY

My love and my Lady
Thank you for this letter that I got tonight. It is really the very dearest letter, and it came at the very best time it could possibly have done. Just think that now, instead of being in this place, I would have been on my way to you. Last night I kept waking up with the cold and so I feel sleepy now. There are about two inches of snow on the ground now and it is bitter outside.

SATURDAY AFTERNOON

This afternoon I had a long walk. The major and I started off directly after lunch. He went to the OS, I visited the advanced gun, which happens to be nearer the trenches in this position. You see, we don't observe from the trenches at present, thank heaven. By the way, four officers were badly wounded in an OS, only a few yards away from the one I marked on the map, yesterday afternoon. A 5.9 pitched practically on the top of the dugout; it is a wonder they were not killed. It was lovely and sunny early on this afternoon, but as I was coming back it began to rain violently. That on top of the snow has made everywhere in an awful mess.

Do you know, the tobacco pouch is most awfully useful. It is a beauty, and is doubly so because Phyl gave it me. I am smoking a pipe much oftener now and they taste doubly nice. I would to God I could be with you for always and all time. No more goodbyes, no more horrible lonely feeling, just heaven on earth. Yes, dear, our love does seem to live in a fairyland when I am out here, but not so when I am with you. But as long as it is your singing and then your Englishman – well, I hate it as I would hate a human being who tried to take you from me.

With this I send every atom of love that is in me to my Lady.

Forever, her soldier and her Englishman

Phyl dear

I am glad to know your dad is showing signs of getting well again. Now that he is home, he must get better. So you are learning to drive the car. I do hope you will be an expert soon, so that you will be able to take me out or teach me. You see, although I know most of the internal organs of the machine, I have never driven one for any distance. I have, however, driven a 15 hp Talbot one-handed, very slowly. I wonder would you take me for a long, long drive, just you and I, the next time I come to Athlone, and provided your dad will let you.

WEDNESDAY AFTERNOON

I will tell you what I have been doing all morning. We have a gas alarm in the form of a klaxon motor horn. You know, the things that make such an awful row, as though some monster was in pain. Well, on Monday night there was a gas alarm and the thing was set off, but went rather feebly and stopped in a few seconds, so I had to put it right. The thing had gone wrong internally, and so had to be taken right to bits. It was a bit of a job but I managed it all right, and now it makes a fine din. It was a big relief when we got word to say it was a false alarm. I had a lively time yesterday afternoon. We had to do some shooting with the gun that is up forward. It had been put in a new position and I had to go up to see that they did not hit some trees which were close in front. We fired over a hundred rounds with it, and I thought one of my eardrums had been broken once. It is not quite right yet and all last night there was a terrible buzzing in it.

Sweetheart, I haven't heard anything yet about leave starting; I wish it would or they would tell us whether it is stopped for good or not. I keep thinking of what I might have been doing had I gone. It must be nice in Athlone today, if it is as fine as it is here. What has happened to the motor boat? Is it still in the land of the living? I expect it has not been launched yet this year.

This place is getting more beastly every day. It is never quiet now; even at nights there is someone firing, and we did at one time have peace then. It is now 10 pm, and I am with the infantry. There is a terrific row on the right this evening; our people started it and we counted eighteen planes up at one time and I am sure there were a lot more. Some were flying at such a height that they could hardly be seen. Everything is quiet at present and it is a glorious night; there are just hundreds of thousands of stars visible.

This evening when I arrived up here there were several officers of the battalion coming into the line. I thought I recognised one of them. He had been at the school I was at in Harrogate and he is the first fellow I have seen from that school since I left in 1907. Fancy coming across him out here, and we had a long talk about the school and the fellows that were there.

Sweetheart, I don't feel like writing more tonight.

Your lover Eric

THURSDAY 2 MARCH 1916

Darling

What a day. I never heard such a row: just as if all the fiends of Hades had been let loose to do their worst. It started at 4.30 this morning and hasn't finished yet at 10 pm. It has been continuous all day, and this afternoon our guns made their share of the noise. I have been in the OS all day and my eyes are hurting tonight. I glared through a telescope from 2 till 4.30 and now I have a most fiendish headache. I spoke to our doctor about my eyes and he says I will have to see a specialist about them if they continue to hurt. I am afraid it is an old trouble coming on again, but I haven't been bothered with it for close on ten years now.

It was a fine sight this morning but it was just like hell being let loose. Of course, it was pitch dark when everything started, but the whole place was alight with gun flashes, shell bursts and rockets. But it is sickening, sickening; it isn't as though we were in it, we're just on the edge, hear no news but always this ghastly din. I'm simply f-e-d u-p, dear.

You dear lady, I have got two letters today. I hate to think how you will have waited patiently, thinking I was going to send a telegram, then, when that did not come, thinking I was going to come and say nothing, perhaps. Phyl, I just love to think that what I wanted to do is just what you were wanting. I shall come to Athlone next leave now. It will remind us of the good old times we had there together. But those times are nothing to be compared with our 'love days'. Do you know, I could simply jump for joy, just because your mum and dad didn't hesitate to say I could come. Do you know what I should like to do when I come? I should like to go on all the same rides in the car as before, without calling on the people. I would want to sit in the same place at teatime and hold the wool or silk for you while you wound it. Play all the silly games we used to and even quarrel as we used to, as long as we made up immediately afterwards. I wonder if you would let me peep into your 'holy of holies' and see where my photo was and what it had to guard. I was wondering what your brother would have to say about me when he saw me, and how we would get on together. Phyl, when I come I want you to be your own dear self; I shall want you to tease me and play with me, make me wild and be as serious and as silly as you like. I would like you to 'take things into your own hands', the lady of that Monday night last year, of the seat on Kingstown pier or of the box at the opera.

FRIDAY AFTERNOON

I am going to answer some of the questions in the other letter – it was nice getting two on the same day. There are no civilians in the town; they all left quite a year ago, when the town was first heavily shelled. The people that we relieved when we first came here told us that a month or two before we arrived, they used to go shopping in the town. Just, I suppose, as we have to go to P— [Poperinge] now to do any shopping. Yes, dear, we are nearer; I shall have to make out new tracks on the map for you. Yes, I wonder what happened to the lady of the shoes – I expect she is either no more or a long way from her home. No, Phyl, I did not go beyond the main part of the town; I left out the 'not'.

About the Army List now. It does mean that there are 121 who are senior to me, but it doesn't say that they all have to be promoted before my turn comes.

Phyl, the wonderful happy feeling when I realised that you did care, when I had to tell you I was coming out here, and at the same time make you understand that I loved you. When you came to say goodbye and buckled on my belt, I liked to think I was your knight and that I was going out to fight for you, but what a different kind of warfare it is now, and how horribly rotten it is compared with that clean kind of fighting.

Bye-bye now, you darling lady. Your strong, solid, silly Englishman sends all his love to his Lady, forever and for aye.

TUESDAY 7 MARCH

My sweetheart
Two letters came for me on Sunday night: a letter from Mum and Dear Heart; I was glad to get them. But what simply horrible news this is about your poor dad, and you really are two dear, strong, brave ladies, you and your mum, to do what you did. I do hope it is not the haemorrhage starting again.

AFTER DINNER
Well, now, about Mum's letter. She said there are two officers living in the house at present from the Thornton camp, and that was why she didn't ask you. She said they wouldn't mind me going over to Dublin or Athlone, as you couldn't come over to us. Oh! Phyl, I do so want to come to your house again, especially because I know you want me. Do you think I can ever forget the real good time I had there? The very name 'Athlone' makes my heart beat faster, if I see it on a Tommy's letter, even. I wonder how often I have seen it there since I came out and have wished I could tuck myself inside the envelope and go to Athlone. Sometimes when I have seen such an address, I have looked to see who the man was and have spoken to him about it. I just can't tell you in words how much I want to be there

with you now, and yet there is no mention of leave starting again. It really is hard luck.

Everywhere is covered with snow here now. Today it has snowed incessantly, and of course it's simply awful walking. We have got to be jolly careful that we don't walk headlong into a shell hole, because many of them are full of water, and have a thin sheet of ice, on the top of which snow collects and makes it level with the ground. I shall in all probability have to go up in front again in two nights' time. Just imagine, it took me two and a quarter hours to walk a distance of about three miles. It was most weird going through the town at dead of night; the old ruins nearly give one the creeps. Then there is the continual drip, drip on every side as the snow melts and the water falls from the houses. Suddenly you get startled by a challenge from the depths of a ruined house where a sentry is standing. I had a lot of pain in my eyes today: they had a wood fire burning in a brazier and the smoke was blowing all through the house and of course it made my eyes hurt awfully. Outside it was cold and damp and snowing like the dickens. A machine-gun was rattling off just then, somewhere over on the left. I wore your mittens the other night and kept thinking of the lady who made them for me, all the way. They kept my hands beautifully warm and dry, but when I arrived back they were literally stiff with mud.

Phyl, sweetheart mine, will you tell me what you wanted to do with our time together in Athlone? I shall come to you last, Phyl; I simply couldn't feel happy at home if I came to you first. The times, I expect, will be just the same as the last leave and so I shall not waste any time in London on my way back.

We had a most terrifying time here the other morning, about 8 am. A horrible naval gun called 'Silent Loo' began plugging at some buildings beyond us, and the majority of the rounds fell short, just missing this house. The awful part about it is that you haven't the slightest chance to get under cover when you hear the gun fire, because the shell arrives at the same instant. Bits of brick and earth were flying about like hailstones, and really it is a wonder this mess-room window wasn't smashed, because it was hit by some large bits. I was having my breakfast at the time and rapidly swallowed down the two boiled eggs I was eating and some tea and toast. I had to ride into P— [Poperinge] that day and was jolly glad to get away from the Battery, but we no sooner got onto the main road than over came two Little Willies, which landed unpleasantly close.

Now, my darling, I must turn in – it's 12.15 am – but before I go there is one thing I want to tell you. We will try and make our time together far, far happier than it has ever been before, and remember, there are to be no misunderstandings of any kind whatever. I am going to ask very hard tonight that I may be allowed to go to my sweetheart now, very soon.

Your Englishman's love to you, now and for always.

9 March   *Saw a fight between a Fokker and a B.9. The latter was brought down outside the Lille gate.*

13 March   *Went to see General Bridgeford and Col. Irving about tonight. Up in the front line all night, raid didn't come off because it came light too soon.*

14 March   *Went up to trenches again tonight. Very black, torpedo was exploded but men turned tail, so had to go out again at 4.30.*

THURSDAY 9 MARCH

My very own darling
I have just got your letter. It is awful, the longing I feel for you; nothing on this earth can stay the feeling except your own sweet self. I want to hug and kiss away the horrible lonely feeling I have. Phyl, when will this cursed war ever end? I feel an awful sick feeling because I also heard yesterday from the Adjutant of our brigade that he didn't think leave would start again till June. The only consolation is the thought that when it does start again, I shall be one of the first to go.

You say in this letter you want to give me everything I want when I come, but I want to give everything I can to you. I want to do simply everything that you want to do. Wenley was saying he thought the greatest pleasure of leave was that he could stay in bed as long as he liked in the morning. Now, I don't think that at all: I would like to never want to go to bed so that I could be with you night and day. It seems such an awful waste of time sleeping. Will you learn to drive the car, so that you can take me out by ourselves when I come?

Do you know, I have had a horrible disappointment. A week ago, the Colonel came into the mess one morning and said that he had recommended two other fellows and myself for two stars. Yesterday he came in again, and told me that the other two had been gazetted and I hadn't.

Everything seems to be going wrong all at once. Of course, the other two are senior to me, but only by a week or two. A day or two since, we heard a beastly rumour that when the division goes out, our Battery may have to stay in. Phyl, I am fed up and have been for days now.

Just at present things seem to have quietened down a bit here, although they are simply d—ble even now. This evening as I was coming up here, I had to beat a hasty retreat for safety and wait about half an hour, because the Boche were shelling right across the path I had to come along. I don't know what they thought they were doing, because they put about fifty 'coal boxes' into an inoffensive green field. Last night there were thirteen degrees of frost; my hat, it was cold outside. However, I kept warm. Do you know what I had on top of me? I had two layers of my sleeping bag (camel hair), four thicknesses of blanket, the canvas cover of my valise, on which I sleep, my Burberry over my feet, my leather coat over the middle part of my body, and my British Warm over my shoulders. At any rate, I managed to keep warm and slept like a top.

I wonder will it be summertime when I do come. There would be lots of things to do outside – we would have to get up very early in the mornings and play tennis, or go for a row. I wonder if you would let me row you up the river to some secluded nook which we would have to find – think of the fun we would have in finding one. Then we would make the boat fast and go for a walk together. Then perhaps we could go for swimming expeditions up the lake. Think how happy we would be. I wonder when it really will come true. I want to feel that wonderful, real, deep-down love fairly making me quiver. I want to have you, my darling, in my arms to love you and kiss you forever.

Night-night, you dear, dear lady.

Your very lovesick Englishman

TUESDAY 14 MARCH

Phyl

I am going to try and write a little, now that I have got the chance. Last night I was out in the front line all night and got to bed at 6.15 this morning; although I was allowed to sleep till lunchtime, I got up with an awful headache and still have it. I have to go out again tonight, as the affair was not successful, and this will be for the third time of asking.

I got your letter, written a week ago. You say about the person who was at Athlone last year: you see, he knows he is just the same person now as then, and you say you were wanting him 'dreadful badly'. I long to be with you and talk to you about what is going to happen to us in our lives, and what has happened. I am most awfully proud that my Lady has been chosen as instructor, and I quite see you have got a ticklish job to keep them all in order. The only way is to not give an inch on any point. I am afraid you are going to be too busy to write.

It's simply pelting now, and I have to go up to those wretched trenches in a few minutes. Well, if I only get soaked I shan't grumble.

Night-night, sweetheart. Your lover's love to you, now and forever.

7.25 AM
Back safely, had an exciting time, am going to bed now.

ST PATRICK'S DAY 1916
POSTED 19 MARCH AND ARRIVED ATHLONE 21 MARCH

Dear Phyl

It's St Patrick's Day, and what a different one to last year's. I can't imagine, somehow, that a whole year has gone since that happy time. Do you remember meeting me near the bridge over the river that morning, and I walked along with you as far as the barrack gate. That evening I came to your house for dinner, and then we went to the St Matthew's Hall, to the concert. You know, it is the only time I have ever heard you sing in public. Oh! I can just see you standing on that platform, singing 'Home Sweet Home', just as plainly now as I did that night. Do you remember how we went down those steps and round the back of the hall, in order to avoid the crowd. Your mum, I remember, had been poorly all day with neuralgia and had to be wrapped up well. What a crowd there was in that place. My dear, how I wish I was there with you now.

I am wearing some of the shamrock, not because I am Irish, but because my Lady is. It has kept beautifully green and fresh, and I love it because my Lady gathered it for me with her own hands. I had quite intended writing this on Wednesday, but my servant, instead of waking me in time for lunch, let me sleep on and I didn't wake until 3 pm. You can imagine my haste, when I had to have some tea and be halfway to the infantry headquarters by 4 pm.

Yesterday was the clearest day we have had for a very long time. I could see miles behind the Boche lines. I was watching transport going along a road with the telescope; of course, we have often seen it before, but it was so clear that I could nearly tell what condition the horses were in. It was a long way out of range, though, and consequently was rather annoying in a way because I couldn't fire at it. However, I fired at a Battery in

141

action behind a ridge and got three direct hits on a house which everybody has had a shoot at and has never hit. It is great fun to see the brick dust flying when you do hit a house.

I wonder, Phyl, what you found out about your lover from the pancakes. How he longs to have been there to eat them with you. Yes, sweetheart, I do remember getting the sixpence and I have got it still; also another sixpence which you gave me. I wonder if you can guess when and where? There is not a word about leave starting again, and to tell you the truth, I don't believe it will start again for some time; I mean a month or even two. As to my turn when leave does start again, I may possibly not go with the first lot, but I ought to get away with the second. I will wire to you as soon as I land, Phyl, if I possibly can. If not, then as soon as I get to Victoria. How my heart will be beating when I write out that wire: just think, I shall be on the way to my Lady. Oh! when will it come?

Well, Miss Instructor, I wonder how the work is going on; I do hope smoothly and that I shall not have to use one of your dressings, or anybody else's for that matter. If I had been on leave and with you at Athlone, would you, if you had the chance, have gone to sing at that concert, or would you have given it up and stayed with me? Phyl, I have told you before, I hate your singing, or rather your love for it, because it seems to be my rival and because I think it might take you away from me. Surely it is far more wonderful to hold the heart and soul of one person, than holding the attention of a large audience – well, I think so.

Night-night, my Lady.

Just forever and forever, I am your Englishman.

17 March   *640 francs for pay.*

18 March   *Went down to see Battery position on Elverdinghe Road on a bicycle. Went up to forward guns tonight.*

Darling

I have got two letters tonight, and really, they are both so very
dear that I hardly know how I can answer them as they deserve
to be answered. We came out of action last night and are
supposed to be out for a long rest (???) It amounts to stables and
my sleeping on a stone floor instead of on a comfy spring
mattress, except, of course, the nights when I am up with the
infantry, and even then I don't sleep on the floor. It is rather a
consideration because there is not a doubt that bed is miles away
the best place out here.

Well, I am going to tell you something: leave has started
again! Now, I hope your heart gave a great big jump. Mine did
when I heard the news last night, just before we came away. I
was wondering, if I leave on a Sunday, I would cross over on the
Wednesday night and have Thursday, Friday, Saturday and
Sunday with you, Phyl, but now when I think of it, that would
be awful because there is no boat on Sunday night, is there? I
can't quite make out where I stand now on the list, because
before, I was right out of my turn, on account of others senior to
me not being able to go. There is even the possibility of it being
the first, but it can't be later than the second or third. Now, my
sweetheart, you must be ready to hear from me at any time.

I am going to tell you about yesterday now. In the morning I
had to go to see a position we might have to use when we go
into action again, so I decided to ride on a bike to the place. It
was a jolly warm day and I had to go along a very unpleasant bit
of road. It is in full view of the German lines and they were
bursting shrapnel over it. The dangerous stretch is about 400
yards long. Well, I fairly pelted along it, and of course just got
bang in the middle when over came a Little Willie; it burst short
of the road and just behind me. I don't know where the bullets
hit, but I simply put every ounce of strength into the bike and I
am sure I beat all cycle records. Well, when I got near to the
position, I found a Battery was being shelled with very heavy
shells close to. Two came over every three minutes, and I had to

wait my chance and make a dart for it past the place they were shelling. I only stayed a very short time to look at the position and then came back. Of course, I had to do the same coming back and had to go along the same stretch of road. Thank heaven, the shells were going beyond it, though, and were bursting harmlessly over a ploughed field.

Then last night I had to go up to where one of my guns was, in a forward position. I had to take the people of the Battery that were relieving us and one of their guns up, and it meant going right through the town. The Boche were firing on all the roads. As we got into the big square, a shell landed right in the middle of the road that we had to go along at the far end of the square. So off we went at a good hard trot and I didn't stop until we were clear of the town. Luckily they were only firing one shell at intervals and we got through before the next one came over. It is an awful feeling when you know you have to go along a road which is being shelled and you are expecting one to arrive any second. Thank goodness, they had stopped by the time I had to come back.

I arrived at the wagon line at 1.40 and got to bed finally at 2.15 am and I am tired out now. But this letter must go tomorrow. Phyl, I have been wanting a letter most terribly badly. It is a week today since I got your last. When will I get away? I feel as though I would go mad if I can't see you soon. Here we are, dumped down in a ploughed field miles away from anywhere, billeted all over the place. I can't get over the disappointment, Phyl, I wanted so terribly badly to be able to come to you this leave and show you that I had got some reward for being out here a year, but no, leave being stopped wasn't enough, and as usual I was odd man out.

I haven't answered either of those dear letters, but I will do so tomorrow. All the love of your Englishman who doesn't quite know whether he stands on his hands or his feet at present: I am all muddled up.

TUESDAY 21 MARCH 1916

Sweetheart

I have come to my room early to write a little to you tonight. Tomorrow I am on duty so have to get up at 5.15 am and I don't look forward to it. Bed is very hard, nowadays: the tiles don't give at all. It has kept up a constant drizzle all day and the whole place is getting like a quagmire already. Well, Phyl, I am not coming with the first leave party after all. They leave here on the twenty-fifth, but Burrows told me that he had heard that two parties were going in every eight days, so it may not be so very long in coming. Dear heart, I feel I am just living for it now. Will you be watching for me as the train comes past the end of the garden? I know I shall be hanging out of the window, ready to catch the very first glimpse of you, and I can just imagine how my heart will be thumping away. Phyl, what will be the very first thing that you will say to me? I really can't tell what I shall say because I know I shall feel nearly too excited and happy to say anything.

You darling, the mittens will be doubly worth having, just because you have worn them. Phyl, can't you understand, I want to come to you for all my leave, because I love you as I can't love anyone else. But at the same time my mum is my mother and I must just see her for a short time. She is so good and kind to me, and so is my dad, but if it had to be either you or they then I would not hesitate to go to the one person on this earth to me. It is all I ask that I may be with my Lady for always. You kind, kind lady, you don't know how you soothed a very tender spot about the promotion. It seems simply heaven to think that you would and will be prouder of the second star, when I get it, than of having sung well. The very fact that you can say that brings your lover nearer to his wonderful treasure. The Colonel said the only reason he could think of for my not getting it was that I had not been out here quite a year. At any rate, it leaves me the senior one-star man in the brigade.

And now, night-night, you darling. I want to love you and to hold you with all my might against me, to hold you as my own; yes, you shall be my own Phyl.

Your lover just adores you.

145

My own dear lady

It's 9.45 pm – think of a year ago at this time. I was with you, perhaps saying the very words which made you show me that you did care. Phyl, I almost feel that, as I write this, there is the same wonderful happiness in me that there was then. Then you bent your head and I thought you were crying and then I was kneeling beside you while you sat on that little stool and I kissed you; yes, I gave you the first kiss. I remember you saying in a very low, quiet voice, 'Eric, you mustn't'; it was the first time you had ever called me by my name when you were speaking to me. Oh! I can never forget that night, never. What a short time it was to be before I knew I would have given anything not to be going, so long as I could have been with you.

THURSDAY NIGHT

Phyl, I had intended the first part of this to go off today, but I found it had not been collected. A year ago today was our last day together. But it was all far, far too short: only a few hours, but how very dear they were. Just think, Phyl, we had barely four hours together, and when I think of the months that followed, what a great deal of love we put into that time. The navy-blue blouse, 'my belt' and navy-blue skirt, Oh! I can see them now, and the agate ring which has never left me since then. 'It is only a handmade Irish ring, but I value it more than any other I have.' And your lover values it more than anything, because it is a token of your love. Do you remember the little luncheon party, and you all drank my health, and I had to finish your glass of champagne and so we drank each other's health out of the same glass. After lunch, you and I retired to the drawing room and stayed there until it was time to go. Then, all far, far too soon, our time had gone, and I was saying goodbye. I simply had to tear about and down to the station, and when I got there, I was sweating like a pig. I got to the window as we crossed the bridge and I thought I saw you waving in the dining room window. Then you seemed to be gone and I sat like somebody knocked on the head, and a very big lump in my throat.

Dear heart, what a really terribly short while we have had together, a mere drop in the ocean. Let us make the very most of this leave when it comes. Listen, there is another leave party going on the twenty-ninth, and if I don't come with that, it will surely be the next one, which perhaps will be about the second of April. I do wish the time would come: it is awful, this wait, wait, wait. Burrows has just come in. We are sleeping together in a farm, some distance from the mess. He has been cheering me up and making out that I am nearly bound to go on leave with the next lot. Oh! I do hope so, Phyl, the longing seems to be terrible this time – nearly more than I can bear. I can think of nothing else now.

I must turn in now, darling. Just forever, your Englishman.

SUNDAY 26 MARCH

Dearest and best lady of all
On Friday I got the letter with the piece of poetry enclosed and today I got another dear wonderful letter. It makes the longing for you terrible to bear and I know I have to do so for a week yet. I had expected to get away about the second of April, but since then, things have altered. Now I have to take command of the Ammunition Column belonging to our brigade, because the man who is at present in charge goes on leave on the twenty-ninth. But it means that I shall not get away until the sixth or seventh of April. Oh! sweetheart, how am I going to wait that long?

Phyl, I am having trouble with my eyes again. The doctor says I must see a specialist and is going to try and take me to somewhere further back. He says he is sure I have strained them.

AFTER DINNER AT THE AMM. COL. MESS
Dear love, I got the parcel today as well as your letter. Thank you very much for the books and the mittens, and I do like to think that you have worn them. Phyl, the cigars are simply

delightful. I do thank your dad so much for them and I shall write to him. I am smoking one now and the smoke is getting blown on to the paper.

At present I have a wee puppy belonging to one of the subalterns here. She is fast asleep, curled up against me with her little wee head resting on my left arm. The little lady is an awful mix of breeds. Her father was a Pekinese and her mother a short-legged kind of fox terrier.

Yes, Phyl, we did manage the job the third time, and I assure you, I wasn't sorry to have done with it. It did not succeed, however, completely, because one of the objects was to get a Boche prisoner and they didn't. At any rate, my revolver is in the German lines now because I lent it to an infantry officer who kindly lost it for me. However, he killed one Hun and wounded another, so it has done its bit.

My Lady, isn't it just dreadful to think that a whole year has gone and that we had only twelve days in it together. May God grant that it shall not be so again this year. I want every day in every year to be ours. Oh! when will this wretched war be finished?

Dear heart, your lover thanks you with all his heart for these two letters; they are both very dear to him.

Night-night, my sweetheart.

TUESDAY 28 MARCH

Dear Phyl

Everyone has gone to bed and so I am going to write to you before I turn in. I am OC Amm. Column now. I have been sleeping over at the Battery each night since I came here on Sunday. Although it is only about a quarter of a mile away, it takes a quarter of an hour at least to walk over. You see, I have to pass the Battery horse lines, and the ground on either side of the road that the horses are standing on is in places nearly eighteen inches deep in mud. It's simply awful; every step one takes it nearly pulls off your boot.

Phyl, just think, in just a few hours over seven days from now, I ought to be on my way home and then to my Lady. At times I get the most horrible doubts and fears that something may happen to stop me.

I wonder what kind of a day you had for your ride to Tudenham, and what were your thoughts on the way back? I remember when your mum asked me if I would go with them to fetch you back, there was no doubt about accepting her invitation. But I couldn't make out when you saw me in the car whether you were glad or sorry I had come. Then, going to the Adamsons', I wonder did you have any breakdown this time. Sweetheart, do you remember telling me when we were playing blind man's buff that I was to let you catch me and then when I did I went sliding down the bank at the side of the lawn. Also, you got top score at shooting that day and I was so pleased that you did. Then do you remember getting me to put a piece of cake in a safe place out of the way when you couldn't manage it all at tea. And playing the fool at hunt the slipper. Phyl, what happy, happy days those were, just because I was with you and saw you nearly every day. Phyl, will you tell me truly, did you ever think for a second in your mind that I did love you then? This letter, written on the twenty-third, makes me love you. The very thought that you kept everything for me and have put your whole trust in me seems far, far too wonderful for your lover to really understand, and I hope I shall be absolutely deserving of such a wonderful love. It makes our love for each other seem a beautiful dream, which is true, true, true, and every feeling I have in me is for you, my Lady.

I am just your Eric

THURSDAY 30 MARCH

Sweetheart

I haven't had a letter for four whole long days. I wonder if anything is the matter, because there has never been over three days in between letters for a long time now. I wrote to your dad yesterday to thank him for the cigars.

I have to get up with the lark in the morning. Tomorrow I am on a court martial again, worse luck. Well, I hope it won't take long. The present life I am leading is rather nice: I mean, being more or less one's own boss and doing what you want. Today has been a lovely bright day and I do hope it will be so again tomorrow. We have had enough rain to last us for months lately. I had expected to go with the doctor today to see about my eyes, but it did not come off, for some unknown reason. He is going to get a motor, as we have to go some twenty to thirty miles, I believe. If it is a fine day when we go, it ought to be jolly nice. At present it feels as though I had got a huge lump of grit in each eye. The worst of it is they are the same each night and morning.

My love, I seem to have got a horrible suspicion that your poor dad is not well again – how I wish I knew. Yesterday I was talking to one of the new subalterns in this brigade who was at the Dardanelles. But he won't say much about it except that he was jolly glad to get out of the business alive. I have not heard definitely yet when I am to get away. The last I heard from the Adjutant was the fifth or sixth; that is next Wednesday or Thursday. I will try and find out definitely tomorrow.

Now, my own darling, I must go to sleep. All the love of your Englishman to you.

XX

SATURDAY 1 APRIL

Phyl
This can't be a long letter because I must go to bed early, as I have to get up early tomorrow. I got a letter yesterday, a very dear one. I feel most horribly cross and grumpy tonight. The men have caused me a great deal of annoyance today, because the farm people at one farm had to complain to me that a ladder had been chopped up for firewood. They really are a lot of dunderheads. Another thing that has annoyed me is that I find,

from another farm, a crucifix has been taken by one of the men. I think this stealing is the limit and it makes me wild. On top of this, this evening we were to have had tinned fruit for dinner and at the last moment the servant discovered that the tin of fruit had been taken.

By Jove, I will make them sit up tomorrow, unless I can find out who has done this. My right eye is particularly sore tonight as well, so altogether I am not in a very amiable mood. How jolly thankful I shall be to get away from all this business for a few days. And now for some news. The first day of my leave is the sixth, next Thursday. That means I have Friday, Saturday and Sunday at home, and cross over Sunday night, arriving in the presence of my Lady on Monday morning. Then I have Monday to Thursday with you, and leave by the mail train on Thursday evening. You see, under the present arrangement, the first and last days of leave are taken up with travelling. It's a beastly shame but there it is. Do you know what is going to happen, too? Weldon is coming at the same time. The Colonel is sending as many as he can before we go back into action.

My Lady, you can't think how I wish it was to be four months or years, not four days, so we must make the very most of what time we have. Now, darling, I must fly; Madame is shouting to lock up this place.

All my love to my Lady, now and forever, your Englishman.

SUNDAY 2 APRIL

Sweetheart

This morning the Colonel knocked every atom of stuffing out of me by telling me I couldn't go on leave. It really is the very hardest lines I have heard of. For the fourth time, now. But I must be jammed on a cursed court martial, which owing to reasons had to be adjourned, and as I am a member, I can't go on leave until it is over. Heaven knows when I shall get away now. My darling, I don't know quite where I am; I haven't the very slightest interest in anything just at present, I am so f-e-d u-p. It's a lovely fine hot day but it doesn't matter a tinker's curse to me whether it's fine or it's snowing; in fact, the latter would be a vast sight better – at any rate, it would be more in keeping with my feelings at present.

I can't write any more, I simply can't, Phyl. So bye-bye, my Lady, your lover's love to you.

WEDNESDAY 5 APRIL

My Lady

I am going to write just a little to let you know I am still alive, although I might just as well not be from all the enjoyment I am getting out of life at present. I can't help thinking of how I ought to be going tomorrow. Why am I such an unlucky bloke? There is no possible chance, as far as I can see, of my getting away for another two weeks at least, and heaven knows what may happen then. There is one consolation and that is in the fact that it doesn't affect the leave next time it comes round and I shall get two leaves very close together. The Colonel told me this.

Do you know, I feel exactly the same way as you say you do in this last letter: 'just as though I were getting along through each day and being glad to get rid of it as it makes my coming to you one day nearer.'

The General came round here today and asked me crowds of questions, all of which I was able to answer, thank heaven. He is awfully nice, and seemed jolly interested in everything. But, my sweetheart, do you know what has happened tonight? We were just going to have dinner, when in rolls an elderly captain, and who do you think he is? Captain Wall from Athlone. He left there last Thursday and took his kiddies to Dublin with him. What a funny old stick he is; he talked like the dickens and kept saying he must go to bed as he was so weary, but still went on talking. Of course, he was full of Athlone and everybody there when I told him I had been trained there. He said he knew your mum and dad very well and said something very nice about you. He seems rather an old gasbag, though.

What heaven it will be to be by you, with you, holding you very close and tight to me and making me feel as happy as a king. I love to imagine I am in the mail train just arriving at Athlone. Then I shall jump out as soon as the train gets into the station. Oh! Phyl, how I just long for that happy, happy time to come.

Night-night, my love, your Englishman forever.

SATURDAY 8 APRIL

My very own sweetheart

Do you know, I have had no letter since Monday; I am so worried and I imagine all sorts of horrible things have happened. Well, I have returned to the Battery. Came back last night after I had been to H— [Hazebrouck] to see the eye man. He said he could find nothing radically wrong with them and thought I must have been trying them too much. But I know they aren't right, and I think I shall go and see our man at home. When I get away.

I told you about Captain Wall coming to the Amm. Column in my last letter. Well, he is a major now. He was promoted, or rather gazetted, about a week ago and of course did not know until he arrived here and was told by someone he knew. This morning we went out for a marching order and thought we were going to be inspected by some general or other 'en route'. But no, we never passed them.

This afternoon I took a long walk, trying to find out when I was going on leave, and the Colonel said I could go with the next lot, and that means leaving here on the fourteenth. The worst of it is, I have to return here on Good Friday night, and do you know, there is no boat across from Dublin that one night; isn't it just my luck? Well, I am going to try and swap days with one of the officers of one of the other brigades and that would mean coming from here on either the thirteenth or the fifteenth. Whatever happens, I am not going to refuse to go, because I want to see you and be near you far too badly to run the risk of having to wait years again.

Wenley and I are going to ride to some place or other tomorrow, if it is fine. My love, I do wish the time would go and that I was really with you again. It has seemed such an awful long time this three months; more like six. I am writing this in bed; I am sleeping in the same room as Wenley. I took Weldon's place, and the mattress is most horribly lumpy, but I sleep very well. I am just going to blow out the light and think of the one lady in all the world.

Night-night, my own darling.

Your lover's love to you, now and for always.

TUESDAY 11 APRIL

Phyl, my very own Lady

I got your two dear letters on Sunday. How they both cheered me up: yes, the good time still has to come. Really, I think it would be almost too hard to bear another disappointment. Just think, I should be with you at this very moment. I wonder what we would have been doing if it was wet, as it is here at present. Perhaps I might be showing you where I am at this moment on the map, or telling you where we are going to. It has been simply glorious here for over a week now, but today it is beastly wet again. I do hope it will be fine when I come. I am so sorry to hear that your brother has gone, because I did want to see him. What a rotter the doctor is, not letting him stay at home and pushing him off to a place like Blackpool. Mum asked me if he would care to come home for a weekend now and then. She said they would all be very glad to have him if he cares to go.

This afternoon I am going to try and find out definitely whether I can get away on either the thirteenth or fifteenth, and will let you know before I close up.

5.30 PM

Well, it's not definitely settled, but I think it will be the fifteenth that I go on; at any rate, I hope so. I must hurry up because the man is waiting to take this letter and I want it to go tonight.

All the love of your Englishman to you, you dear, darling lady.

My darling
I don't know what I am going to say this time, because I feel far too happy at the thought of going, really going, on leave. I have actually got my leave form and leave here on Friday night. Then I cross over on Tuesday night and will be with you, my darling, on Wednesday morning, in time for breakfast. Just a week tonight I shall be with my Lady. I want your real, real love, your own dear wonderful lovely sweet self too, to make all so much more real. Will the time ever come?

It's blowing a whole gale outside and has rained like the devil all day. I went to a horse show which was absolutely spoilt by the wet weather. Sweetheart, I must stop now because I have to be up at 6 am tomorrow.

Until we are together again, know that your lover is loving you terribly much.

My Lady, my own darling Lady
What am I to say? I really don't know. I can't think and haven't been able to since Thursday night, and I couldn't bring myself to write, even to my sweetheart. Phyl, your lover is flattened out. I feel I have no use for anything in this world at present. Dearest heart, I have been stopped again. You would know this, though, when you get no wire tomorrow. Stopped again! Just my luck. I am the most unlucky fellow that ever walked this earth. Never again am I going to write and try and make arrangements.

It's too bad, far, far too bad. Why, why is all leave stopped? I don't know how I am going to live through the weary long hours and days and maybe weeks before I get away.

But I don't know what to say, Phyl, I am simply too fed up.

Night-night, my darling.

TUESDAY 18 APRIL

Darling

I feel I don't know what to tell you except about this beastly leave business. Try as I do to take an interest in my work here, I feel I can't now. The days seem to drag and drag, and there seems to be no ending to this weary road, no house in sight where one could rest. When the Major told me about being stopped again, he was kind, and tried to cheer me up by saying that when we get to this other place (we are not going into action for some time, either, but to a kind of gunnery school, in place of another Battery) I may get away fairly soon. Surely I have been kept long enough away from my Lady. It is hard to bear and turn a smiling face to the outside world.

I keep thinking all the time of what I would have been doing. Tonight I would have been leaving home for Athlone. Tomorrow morning I should have held your own sweet self in these arms of mine and I would have been happy, just for a little while, and that is all four days would be, in the long weeks that would follow. Then there is another big worry. You say in this last letter that you were going to Dublin to sing on Saturday, and I am so very sorry if I have spoiled your week. Well, I shan't write again when I'm coming, because it always seems to make things worse and mess up everything if I don't come in the end. I shall just wire as soon as ever I possibly can on my way. But I must stop writing like this; it's enough to give anyone a 'fit of the blues'.

What has made you suddenly begin to sign yourself 'Phyllis' at the end of these last two letters? This last one was clearly written 'Phyl' and then 'lis' put on the end afterwards. And now, dear love of mine, bye-bye for a little while; we move on Thursday.

Forever and ever and ever, I am your Englishman,
Eric

SATURDAY 22 APRIL

Phyl

I have just got your letter, written a week ago. It has been hung up some time owing to the move, and also, of course, it went home. It nearly makes me cry to think that I missed being able to meet you in Dublin. It would have meant five whole hours more with you, and we could have had a day together in Dublin and then have gone down to Athlone together.

I wonder when I shall get away. We heard a rumour yesterday that leave was soon to start again. Before we left the other place, the Colonel came round and was very decent to me. He said he was awfully sorry to hear I had been stopped again, and told the Major he was to see that I was sent as soon as it was possible.

Well, we are now in the new place, further south and away from the brigade on our own, not in the line. It's not a bad place from a scenery point of view and the billets are good; mine is an awfully nice little room in a wee cottage, wonderfully clean, and an exceedingly nice old couple live there. It's halfway between the Battery and the mess and it's a good mile walk from the mess to the Battery. The latter is on a hill and there are hills to the north and east as well; to the south the country is flat. It's an awful drawback, being away from the Battery down here, and means starting every time a quarter of an hour before parade, as it's all uphill.

The field the horses are in is in an appalling mess: mud and nothing but mud everywhere. Today I am on duty and it has simply teemed all day. My pants are soaking wet at the knees and I have still three journeys to make up there before I turn in tonight, so it means that when one is on duty we have to walk nearly twelve miles a day.

Along with your letter came one from Mum, and in it she said your brother had given them a very nice surprise by suddenly turning up last Saturday afternoon from Churchtown. She says he reminds them of you in looks a little and very much in speaking, so I am sure I shall like him when I see him. Mum says I must hurry up and come home and then they will ask him up while I am at home. I do want to see him very much.

Would it be possible for you to come up with me on my way back when I do come? I feel I want to do any mortal thing to make the time with you a little longer. Dear heart, will that time ever come? It must. I must run off to water and feed now, as it's 4.10 pm.

Bye-bye, my dear, dear love. I am nearly dying for letters now.
Your lover, Eric

20 April	*Real April day. Left Zeggers about 9. Had lunch en route just outside Steenvoorde. Arrived Berthen about 4.30. Jolly nice billet. Battery rotten.*
21 April	*Not nice day. Fatigues all morning and aft'noon. Not a bit like Good Friday. Paid Bradley 20 francs.*
22 April	*On duty today. Rained like hell all day. Got mail today, first since Sunday last. Letters from Phyl and Mum. Wrote to Phyl.*
23 April	*Easter Sun. Lovely day. Went to Abele with Hogg to see engineers. Went to service in school shed.*
24 April	*Lovely day. Gun drill. Laying lecture afternoon and miniature range afterwards. Got letter from Phyl.*

25 April	*On duty, exercise late, stables. Went to Bailleul for men's cash at P. Office. Continued drawing tonight, late to bed, had headache.*
27 April	*Fearfully hot day. Gave drawings of range to fitter. Busy with watering scheme all afternoon. Finished letter to Phyl.*
28 April	*Started building dam for watering place for horses. Had to go into Bailleul with gunner for pipes.*

WEDNESDAY 26 APRIL 1916

Sweetheart

I wonder what you are doing now at 10 pm. Are you wanting your Englishman as he is you? I want to be there to take all the love that is sent to me in this last letter. We heard in a roundabout way that leave had started again, but have heard nothing definite. Try as I may to do my work as though nothing had happened, I can't really put my back into it. It's just the awful 'want, want' feeling which will never leave me. Do you know, we heard that leave was stopped in order to give the railway people a rest over Easter. Now did you ever, in all your days, hear anything like it, if it's true? My Godfather, I'd pack the whole d—d lot off out here and send troops back to take their place and have a rest, if I had the chance. Think of the hundreds of poor devils that were stopped or sent back; it makes me feel hot to think of it.

Phyl, it has been simply glorious weather for the last four days; today has been fearfully hot. And now I will tell you why I haven't written since Saturday. I have been working each night until late on at the drawings for the miniature range, and have only just finished my labours in that direction. It has been jolly nice work and is such a change from the usual Battery game. Of course we are at it all day now and I never get a chance to write except at night.

There is an awful row going on over in the line; there is a terrific low rumble going on and has been all night. Sweetheart, do you know what has happened – Weldon has left us. On Monday night a message came to say he was to proceed to London at once, and with it came his ticket. The only thing we can think of is that his name was sent in some months since for being able to speak Persian. Probably he is off out there on some job, but I am afraid he is gone for good. I am most dreadfully sorry he has gone; he was such a decent fellow. So now Wenley and I are doing day about on duty and it is a sweat.

THURSDAY NIGHT
Another lovely day today. I have been in such a state of moisture all day that I feel about as limp as a piece of string tonight.

Phyl, what are these beastly people up to in Dublin? It really is the limit; the whole lot deserve shooting, in my mind. I hope to God you are clear of the place, or if not, at any rate you are safe, because heaven alone knows what those devils will do: they are not particular who they go for, in my mind. I do hope you are quite safe and away from it all. I try to console myself with the thought that you said you were going back home for Easter. The worst of it is that letters take such a fearful age to get here, and heaven knows when I shall hear that you are all right and safe. Well, I shall just have to wait and wait.

I have had a letter each day from Mum since Tuesday and it has been nice. They seem to be enjoying themselves at Windermere and I wouldn't mind being with them either. She said she was writing to you, so you will know about my sister having been called up at last. I am glad for her sake, but I'm jolly sorry that I shan't get a chance of seeing her now, when I come on leave. I wonder where she'll get to.

Sweetheart, do you know what I would give anything to be doing now? It's a glorious starlit, quiet, warm night – not a sound. I want to be in the garden of your house, with you taking a walk round but really standing, holding you very tight and close to me, as I did the night of our last 'love day' at home. But

Second Lieutenant
Eric Appleby

Eric

22/3/15.

Phyllis
15-8-16

Phyllis Kelly

Phyllis in 1915

A photograph of Phyllis that
she disliked. The reverse reads:
'E. Appleby. Given to me on
March 21st, the day before
leaving Athlone for the front.
Returned on June 1st 1915
from Belgium because you
asked me to do so. Very many
happy returns of your birthday.
From Eric'

Eric in civilian clothes

Phyllis, Eric, Eric's sister, Kathleen, and Mrs Appleby,
Liverpool, 20 August, 1915

Phyllis with Eric's younger brothers, Liverpool, August 1915

Eric mowing Abbey House lawn
(p 204)

Abbey House
from the Shannon

Athlone railway viaduct with Abbey House on the left

Phyllis's father outside Abbey
House, Athlone, 1916

Phyllis's younger brother, Buzz

Dorothy, Edward,
Phyllis and Robert
(Buzz) Kelly c. 1914

St Mark's, near Glassan, County Westmeath

' . . . the view is lovely from there; you look right out over the lake and can see all the islands dotted about . . . ' (p 215)

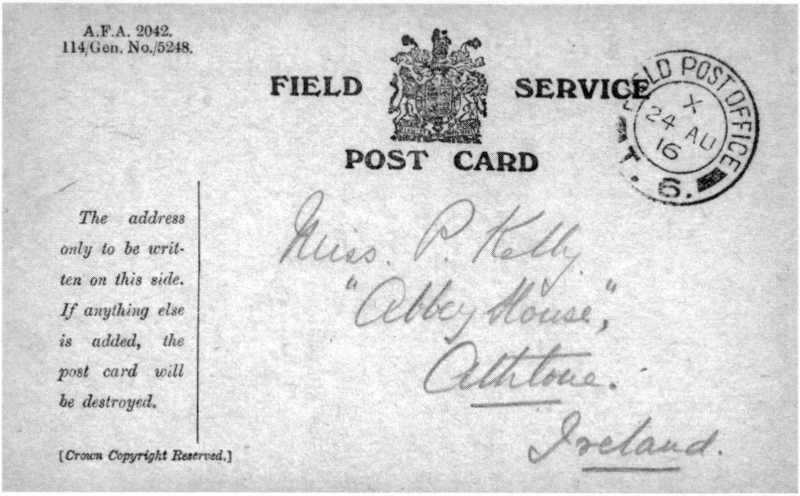

A.F.A. 2042.
114/Gen. No./5248.

FIELD SERVICE
POST CARD

FIELD POST OFFICE X 24 AU 16 T. 6.

The address only to be written on this side. If anything else is added, the post card will be destroyed.

[*Crown Copyright Reserved.*]

Miss. P. Kelly
"Abbey House",
Athlone.
Ireland.

Field Service postcard (front)

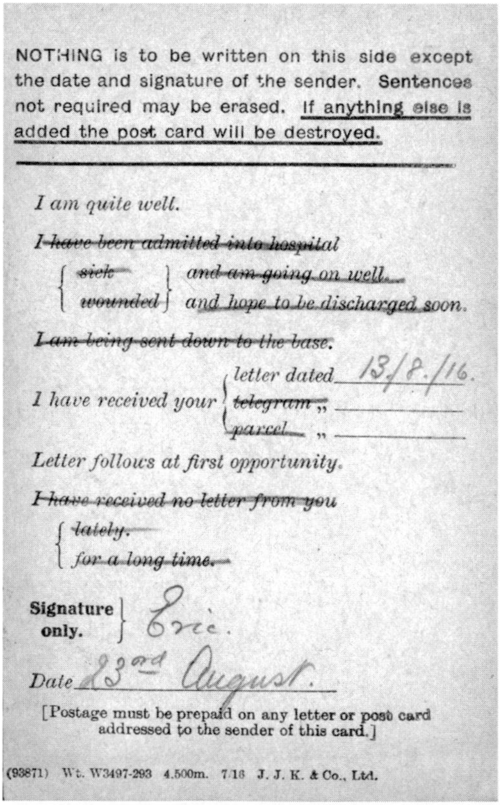

NOTHING is to be written on this side except the date and signature of the sender. Sentences not required may be erased. If anything else is added the post card will be destroyed.

I am quite well.

~~*I have been admitted into hospital*~~

~~*sick*~~ ~~*and am going on well.*~~
~~*wounded*~~ ~~*and hope to be discharged soon.*~~

~~*I am being sent down to the base.*~~

I have received your *letter dated* 13/8/16.
~~*telegram*~~ "
~~*parcel*~~ "

Letter follows at first opportunity.

~~*I have received no letter from you*~~
~~*lately.*~~
~~*for a long time.*~~

Signature only. Eric.

Date 23rd August.

[Postage must be prepaid on any letter or post card addressed to the sender of this card.]

(93871) Wt. W3497-293 4.500m. 7/16 J. J. K. & Co., Ltd.

Field Service postcard (back)

POST OFFICE TELEGRAPHS.

N.B.—This Form must accompany any inquiry respecting this Telegram.

If the Receiver of an Inland Telegram doubts its accuracy, he may have it repeated on payment of half the amount originally paid for its transmission, any fraction of 1d. less than ½d. being reckoned as ½d.: and if it be found that there was any inaccuracy, the amount paid for repetition will be refunded. Special conditions are applicable to the repetition of Foreign Telegrams.

Office of Origin and Service Instructions.

Euston

Handed in at 5·0 p.m. Received here at 6·45 p.m.

TO { Miss P. Kelly "Abbey House" Athlone

London at last. Cheero

Eric

Telegram to Phyllis, May 30 1916

Eric's diary, 31 August – 6 September 1916

TRENCH SCENE AT BATAGLAN 'FOUR DE PARIS'.

Life in the trenches

FRENCH ARTILLERY OBSERVATION POST.

Artillery Observation Post

CAPT. GUYNEMER IN FULL FLIGHT.

'. . . as I am writing this, the Boche shells are whizzing over and one of our aeroplanes is making a fiendish din . . .' (p 37)

Artillery in action

Sur les routes de France : Soldats anglais au repos. — Troupes françaises en mouvement.

On the march. The caption reads: 'On the roads of France: English soldiers resting – French troops moving on.'

Ypres, 1914-1915: Lille Street

Ypres, 1914-1915:
The Cathedral of
St Martin

Ypres, 1919: After the war

Ypres, 1919: Rue d'Elverdinghe (p 142)

Guerre de 1914
Artillerie Anglaise traversant Compiègne

Imprimeries Réunies de Nancy - Cliché Rol

Guns on the move.
The caption reads: '1914 war. English artillery travel through Compiègne.'

Convoi anglais traversant une rivière
sur un pont de bateaux

An English convey crossing a river
by means of a bridge of boats

The wagon lines

Eric;
the picture
Phyllis kept
hanging
above her bed
throughout
her life

The letters, Eric's diary and personal effects as Phyllis kept them

Grovetown Cemetery at Meaulte, near Albert

The gravestone reads:
'Second Lieutenant
Eric Appleby,
Royal Field Artillery.
28th October, 1916'

this time it must be your home, the home where our love for one another was born. Then the time would slip away and we would have to say night-night and then run inside to the others and I should be in a happy, dreamy mood, simply longing for the next day to come when I would be with you only again.

Night-night, dear, dear Lady Phyl. I am just your lover Eric tonight, just an Englishman that loves you with all his very heart and soul.

29 April   *Finished making dam this morning and allowed it to fill this afternoon. Worked well. Played cricket against Mont de Pats, beat them easily. Bad news from Ireland. Dublin Riots started on Monday. Glorious weather all week.*

SUNDAY 30 APRIL

Sweetheart
This is just too awful. I haven't heard from you since Monday, and that letter was written a week ago last Wednesday. Phyl, dear heart, I am most terribly afraid something awful may have happened to you. Heaven knows what those brutes may be doing to you; they are brutes of the worst kind, although they are of your country. This morning I have been reading an account of what has been happening and it's dreadful to think what's going on over there – as though there wasn't enough war already and enough poor innocent civilians being killed out here, without those brutes shooting them right and left at home. Even if I came on leave now, I couldn't get across. I hope to God the whole thing will stop soon.

SUNDAY AFTERNOON
A beautiful hot summer day. All the hedges are fully out now and a good many trees are the same. Some of the little byroads on the hills round here are awfully pretty. The trees meet right

161

across and there is a kind of soft half-light, just like there is in a thick wood on a sunny day. In fact, the whole country round about tries to make one feel happy, but it doesn't succeed with me.

Wenley and I have been for a ride this evening and the country where we went was lovely. We passed right through a lovely wood and down an awfully steep path. Tom got quite excited over it all and so I had to let him let off steam as we were coming back by having a race with Wenley; he fairly leapt along, too.

Phyl, there was no letter again today; why doesn't one come? In today's paper it said that the boats to Dublin from Holyhead were running but were very irregular. I am simply fed up, tired, tired out with this waiting game, it fairly 'plays old Harry' with my temper and I get so grumpy that I don't really know what to do with myself. I must run off to dinner now, my darling.

AFTER DINNER, BACK IN MY LITTLE ROOM

I am going to tell you about my room. The house is a case of three in one; that is, there are three separate houses under the same roof: two in the front facing the road and one at the back. My room is facing the road. In it there is a very comfy bed, with sheets across the window. Two tables – one, on which I am writing, is next to the bed, the other is alongside and is my washing stand. There are three chairs, one of which I am sitting on, and which is a basket armchair. There is an old-fashioned clock hanging on the wall which keeps remarkably good time. The floor is tiled, and the wallpaper has a pattern of a bunch of mauve chrysanthemums on a green ground. The roof of the house is thatched, and it is only about 200 yards outside the village. The bed is cosy and I sleep like a log, and now I am going to get into it as soon as I can. I have to be up early tomorrow.

God keep you safe, my darling, and may he send me to you very soon. Just your Englishman's true love to you, now and forever, you dear, dear lady.

FRIDAY 5 MAY

My very own sweetheart
Thank God you are out of all this beastly mess in Dublin. I was glad, most awfully glad, when your letter came to say you were all right. Fancy, it was started on the twenty-fourth of April, posted on the twenty-seventh, and didn't get here till the fourth of May. Practically everything that you say in this letter about rumours from Dublin was actually happening at the time. You at Athlone were absolutely and entirely cut off by 'phone or telegram, and by rail from the city for some time. Thank God, it never got a hold.

Dear heart, I am most terribly sleepy and tired now, and I am each night. The heat is terrific and simply makes me as limp as a rag. This morning we had Battery gun drill for a solid hour and a quarter. It was fearfully hot and I ended up simply dripping with sweat. This afternoon I tramped round; the whole Battery was on fatigues and I had to keep an eye on over a hundred of them, and it is no light job when they are working in two places at once. The last three or four days I have been most frightfully hard-working and I am sure I am much thinner. I have been making a dam across a brook in order to make a pond for water for the horses. The other place we had was not good water and so I had the job of getting this other place made. The horses were watered there at evening stables last night for the first time and it worked splendidly. It's awfully good water.

Sweetheart, please don't put anything except the name and Battery and BEF on my letters, because they take longer to come if anything else is put. Oh! wouldn't it have been horrible if I had got my leave at the time the trouble was on in Dublin. As you say, I couldn't have let you know anyway that I was even at home, and the thought of my being there and not even able to go across and be with you is horrible. Think, Phyl, seven more days and it's four whole long, dreary months since I arrived back at the Battery, and there isn't a sign of leave, even now. It really is hard lines after being raised to the seventh heaven of delight three times and then being stopped.

I don't know what I shall want to do when I do come; I shall want every single second with you when I do.

Your lover's love to you, my darling.

MONDAY 8 MAY

My own very dearest and naughtiest lady
I am getting your letters all right, but they are taking a dreadful long time to come, and there is a long, long time between one another. And now I expect you are wondering what the 'naughtiest' at the beginning is for. Well, it's just this: how dare you say, 'There is not very much use in writing letters that goodness only knows when you will get.' Of course there is just all the use in the world, even if they are held up for weeks. I shall get them in the end, and God knows, I want them so very, very much. Dear heart, how many times have we said that our letters are the one bit of each other that we have while we are miles away from one another. It's only too true and when they take such a fearful age to come it makes the days just drag.

What a blessing it was that you had no trouble in Athlone. Really, I don't know what to make of the whole thing. It seems so absolutely appalling and yet could so easily have been prevented, as far as I can see from what the papers say. I should think it quite probable that that traitor (Casement) will not be shot. I wonder what the latest news is; we haven't had a paper since Saturday and in that things seemed to be quietening down pretty rapidly – I hope it's true. Yes, they must have knocked old Dublin about a lot with using guns and I see that as far as insurance goes, all damage done is a dead loss, because the policies don't cover damage done by riots. Won't it be awful for some of the people, who have ten to one lost all they had. By now you will have heard it all and perhaps a good deal more, so I'm going to shut up gassing.

I wonder how your dad is now. You have not said anything about him for a long time and so I think he must be better, and I do hope so. Heavens, it's 10.30 now and an early rise for your Englishman in the morning. I have been rereading some of your letters and counting them. I have them all numbered and this last one makes number forty since last leave. Oh! some of them are dear ones too.

June – yes, I said June in one of my letters – would be about the time for leave to start again, and it does seem so very far away now. The glorious first of June. Oh! dear, wouldn't it be lovely if I could be with you on that day. The most blessed day the world has ever seen, just twenty-three years ago. The day the dearest, purest, loveliest lady was born on. Sweetheart, I love to think that that lady was to keep her heart for nearly twenty-two years for this Englishman. Oh! I thank God for the day he sent me to Athlone and to my Lady, and may He let me come to her again soon. My darling, I feel simply mad with love and longing for you tonight. Then and only then can I be happy.

So night-night, my very own darling. XXX

SUNDAY 14 MAY

Phyl, my sweetheart
I wonder if Wenley wrote and told you what happened to your unfortunate lover. I do hope he has, because my last letter was

165

written last Monday. Of course I hadn't the very slightest suspicion of what was going to happen in two days' time from then. Measles! What an ignoble thing to come to hospital with for the first time. The illness is simply nothing, though, compared with the horrible hopeless feeling that getting it just at this time has caused me.

It's simply no use trying to talk about it, though, because it seems to make the time when I shall get home on leave even further away. When will it come, and why should I always be stopped at the last minute? I am the most unlucky devil that ever walked this earth in many ways.

Well, on Tuesday and Wednesday I had a rotten headache all day, but didn't suspect anything. However, when I got up on Thursday morning I discovered I was covered from head to foot with a rash. I thought at once it was possibly measles and so at breakfast I told the Major and he said I must see the doctor at once. When the doctor came he said it most decidedly was German measles and that I would have to go to hospital. So he telephoned for an ambulance and bid me adieu. By that time, everyone had gone out about the day's work and I was left by myself. So I went round to my billet and packed what things I wanted in my saddlebags and returned to the mess to wait for the ambulance that was to bring me here.

I was sitting in the window, trying to read a newspaper, when a motorcyclist came along and stopped in front of the mess. He asked me if the Major was in and I told him 'No', so he asked me to open the envelope that he handed me, in order that he could get back with it signed by the receiver. I opened it and drew out the contents and oh! my dear, dear lady, how my heart seemed to stop, for there, poking out from among other papers, was an officer's leave warrant. Of course, I knew it was mine, and I felt so terribly flattened out that I simply sat and stared vacantly at it, until the motorcyclist asked me if I wouldn't mind letting him have the envelope. That brought me to earth with a bump and I began to realise just what I was missing through my d—d bad luck for the fourth time. I didn't curse or say a word, I simply sat there and thought and realised what it was to be the unluckiest creature on the earth or I imagined I was. Well, it really is enough to drive anyone mad, this kind of thing. Oh! Phyl, I don't know how I am going to carry on. I simply hate everything and everybody about me out here.

Well, after writing a note to Wenley to ask him to let you know what had happened to me, and one to the Major to tell him where I was going, the ambulance arrived at about one o'clock. This place is No. 7 General Hospital; it is in the grounds belonging to a monastery, as well as in the greater part of the monastery itself. The part I am in is for infectious diseases, of which there are only a few cases of measles and about thirty or forty of German measles. There are, I suppose, thirty or forty large tents in this part, each holding eight officers or fourteen men. We mess and sleep in the same tent and they are very comfortable. The floor is boarded, and mats on top; the beds are placed down either side from one end of the tent, and at the other, where I am writing, is a space occupied by chairs, one large and two small tables, and a little bookcase. By each bed is a little cupboard to keep one's things in. The whole of the interior of the tent itself is made of some thick pale yellow stuff, and looks remarkably cosy. But all the time I keep thinking that I would have been at home now and going across on Tuesday to you, my darling; whenever shall I get away?

On Friday I was in bed all day after going to bed after tea on Thursday. I felt jolly rotten all that day, and stayed in bed till lunchtime yesterday. Today I don't feel at all bad, except that I have a bit of a cold.

Well, now, sweetheart, I am going to stop. I haven't had a letter since Monday and I do so wish one would come. Don't address any letters here because I shall only be here till next Saturday; then I go back to the Battery.

Bye-bye, my own dear Lady Love. Forever and ever, your Englishman

My sweetheart

I have got two letters today. I was so glad to see them this morning; one was written on the fifth and one on the ninth – what ages and ages it seems since then. I wonder if you have found out anything more about how things are in the way of getting to you. I do hope by now they are more or less normal and that I will be able to arrive in time for breakfast when I do come. I go back to the Battery on Saturday and I really hope that I get away as soon or nearly as soon as I get back. Oh! Phyl, I am longing to get away. Do you know, I am beginning to get superstitious, because you know last leave was my third, and they say, 'The third time always does it' – I wonder.

Yes, isn't it an awful mess that Dublin is in. I have seen the pictures in the papers; I'll bet the — Huns are laughing up their sleeves about it all, the brutes. I am glad your family are all safe, but you seem jolly worried about your dad again. Surely he is getting better now. He hasn't had any collapses just lately, has he? I wish I had known it was his birthday the other day, the eighth of May; I would like to have written a short letter to him. Letters do take such a dreadful age to come and go.

Phyl, I do wish your brother had not been moved away from Churchtown. It means that I shan't see him, and do you know, Dad took an awful fancy to him. He said he thought he was a right down good chap with his head screwed on the right way, and he wished very much he could see more of him. I do want to see him so badly, just because he's your brother and I know I shall like him.

I must go to bed like a good lad now as it's 9 pm, and we have to be in bed by 9.30 here. I forgot I wanted to tell you that you are a naughty, naughty lady for staying up so late every night; you should go to bed and have a really long sleep each night, and then it might help you to forget some of your worries, and I shall be very cross if I find you white when I come to you, because then I shall know it is because you don't get enough sleep.

Night-night, you darling

Forever your lover, Eric

16 May	*Walked into flying ground with Davies (a Terrier). Went into St Omer after tea with Davies.*

FRIDAY 19 MAY

My sweetheart

What a glorious day it is, and how I wish you were one of the sisters here; then I could spend the whole long day with you. Well, today is my last day, and as I said to one of the men, we shall start again on the high road to 'Kingdom Come' after a rest of ten days. This morning I was rooted out of bed by the orderly at the unearthly hour of 6.15 and made to wash and shave, because he wanted to clear the washing arrangements away before the day orderly came on duty. Then I returned to my couch until breakfast time, which I ate in state in a dressing gown. I wonder when I shall have my next breakfast in pyjamas and a dressing gown. How do you like this writing paper? I got the orderly to buy it for me in St Omer. It is quite nice to write on.

Phyl, I have just finished reading *Sam's Sweetheart*. I would never have been able to have come back home to marry someone I didn't love because I thought it was my duty. Of course, it all turned out for the best, but then it never does in human life, or very rarely. My dear, how I long to be with you, and if I hadn't caught this beastly, silly, kids' disease, I would have been in my heaven on earth. If you were getting ready to go out, I would have been waiting for you in the garden, sitting on a camp chair, as I am now. It's simply glorious weather, and how lovely it would have been at your home again. Will I ever get there? It's enough to make anybody desperate, this continual stopped, stopped, stopped.

Yesterday afternoon, a machine-gunner and I went up to the flying ground near here to have a look round. We saw about fifteen machines start off and as many land. It is fascinating, and I felt I wanted to join the Flying Corps straight away and make a start. This place here is a school and they have every kind and description of machine. By Jove, I wish they would take us home on leave in an aeroplane – think how quickly the journey would be done in. In the evening, just before tea, I was sitting in this same place just by the door of the tent, in the shade, when Sister came along with a captain behind her. I said good afternoon, in a casual way, and then seemed to know his face. It was a man I was at school with and also at the university as well. He is a captain in the RAMC and had got German measles. He's only the second fellow I have met out here from home, so we had a long talk together last night.

And now, bye-bye, my Lady, until I am back at the Battery.
Your Eric

SATURDAY 20 MAY

My dear, dear love
I got back here at about twelve noon this morning after getting up at 6 am, having a disinfecting bath and then breakfast at 7.30. I left the Hospital at 8 am and caught the 8.50 train from St Omer. I had to walk from the nearest station, a matter of four miles, and oh! it was hot. I had my saddlebags and oilskin to carry and it just poured out of me. But, sweetheart, when I got here, what do you think I found: two letters from you, and one from Mum. I was so glad to see them, and as everybody was out, I sat down and had a good read all to myself. I am so pleased about your brother getting his second star, but heavens, I feel horribly jealous of him. What an ass I was to enlist in the SR instead of as a Temporary – I should have had my second star two months ago if I had.

No, love, it was nothing worse than German measles – not even proper measles. With the latter, one is in hospital three weeks and then you are sent to a seaside place in France for a week, but they won't let you take your seven days at home, no fear. I was only in hospital ten days and shouldn't really have come back till tomorrow; however, I was afraid the next leave would be due this weekend, so came back today. Now that I am back, I find Wenley went on leave on Thursday. Oh! Phyl, honestly, I shall go dotty if this kind of thing goes on much longer. I've just about come to the end of my tether and I shall apply for a transfer if things don't improve jolly soon.

What a beastly shame it is that your dear daydream can't come true, about sick leave. When I come on leave, each time I go to bed seems hours, precious hours wasted in sleep. I'd give anything to be able to stay up with you, and if we felt tired then we could just go to sleep in each other's arms in a big chair or on the sofa. It almost makes me want to get wounded so that I can be with you for more than a few days. When all is said and done, what is leave? Just a drop in the ocean of love, but how beautiful that drop is. It's the only thing that makes life worth living. Phyl, honestly, I want to come to Athlone this leave most terribly. I think it is a lot of good time wasted in a way, so far as the number of days go, but somehow I have a feeling that it must be your house in which I am to have you with me this time. I think the thought of our love for one another starting there will make up for the extra days which we would have if you came to my home. Besides, it's such an awful expense for you, and not too safe, to come across each time. Then again, I ought to get two leaves bang on top of one another now.

Sweetheart, it's simply gorgeous weather here; it would be heaven to have weather like this while I'm on leave. Then we could go, as you say, a long way up the lake, just you and I, and forget everything but our love. You must think of all the nice, secluded 'no-one-ever-comes-near' spots that you can and then we can pick and choose when the time comes. At the end of your letter, you say, 'Because if you get leave now after this I am going to be with you for it somehow.' You dear, dear person, how I want you always. But why do you go and doubt me in the very next sentence, after saying the dearest thing you could: 'That is, of course, if you want me !' Will you ever learn not to doubt the least little bit?

Your lover, yes, Phyl, your lover,
Eric

Sweetheart

I wonder when the next letter is coming; it seems an age since Sunday. I do want another so very badly and I hope it has another daydream in it. Why, Phyl, that was just what I had thought of, a whole day alone with my Lady up the lake. How beautiful it would be, but surely we could go up by boat, couldn't we now? How far is it to row? Three miles, or perhaps four, not more, I should think. I could manage that even in my present condition, I think. Sweetheart, wouldn't we make it a dear love day. We would have to take our lunch and tea with us, and start straight after breakfast, which would have to be jolly early. Then we would pinch plenty of cushions and a good rug. Of course, it would have to be a lovely day. When we got to Hare Island, we could beach the boat, and then trot off together to find the nicest, cosiest corner possible. Then we would see the sights of Hare Island and return to our corner and get lunch ready. What a pity it is you don't like champagne – we might each have drunk the other's health out of the same vessel. I would clear the lunch away while you lay on your cushions and talked to me. Then I would come to my Lady and want her to give me all the love she had and I would give her all mine, and we would forget all about the world and just love one another and try to make up for five months of life absolutely lost, gone and nothing gained, except a beastly temper and an awful aching heart. Oh! when will it all end.

I am going to have a long talk, when I go on leave, with Dad, about what I shall do after the war is over. I really don't know what will become of me. Phyl, do you know it will ten to one mean I shall go to some godforsaken place for years and not see you, perhaps, again. I feel absolutely desperate sometimes when I think of what is going to happen to us both after this horrible business is over. I couldn't stay on in the army because I hate the life. Sweetheart, your lover is so very miserable that I don't know what I'm doing half the time and I honestly feel I don't care what happens just at present. It's simply and solely this eternal waiting, and hating this present. There's nothing but bad news for me. My name has gone in again for leave, and do you know what I have discovered today? I shall only get six days clear at most, instead of seven. The division we are attached to for leave only gives seven days leave, instead of eight, as our division does. These leaves, if we get them, will be the first lot from this division, and of course it had to fall to me, and as we go into action again in a week or so, it will be the last lot as well. Fancy, after nearly five months and being stopped four times this is going to happen. It's hopeless having bad luck like mine.

The work here is very like a rest camp, only we are on duty every other day, owing to there being only two at present, as Wenley's on leave. I must turn in now, darling. The love of your f-e-d u-p lover,

Eric

FRIDAY 26 MAY

My Lady

I am going to start a letter now and send it off, so that it will reach you by the first, I hope. Do you remember the last first of June? I do. We arrived in the salient four days before and on the first I moved back to the Battery, after being in position just in front of the huge seventeen-inch hole. Heavens, to think that it is twelve long, dreary months ago, and I wonder if I shall say the same and be in the same country twelve months hence, God forbid. I've had my fill of this war, but at the same time, the beastly Hun has to be thoroughly licked. I sent off 'Phyl' to you that day and in two days I shall have had the two 'Phyls' a year. They are both in front of me now; one is looking straight at me and is trying very hard to smile at me. I wanted them to welcome me when I came into the room and to watch me when I went out, as the serious one of the two always does. Why can't they both come to life and talk to me and tell me what they have seen all the time they have been with me? They have been in some funny places out here.

Today has been a lovely day and we have had the Battery sports: mounted events in the morning and dismounted events in the afternoon. The jumping was quite good this morning: three men came down – one we all were certain was half-killed when he fell right under the horse at the water jump. But no, he got up all right, only getting a bruise on the thigh; it is marvellous what escapes people have. There was no event for officers at all. This evening I had a jump on the new charger I have got, a black called 'Darky'. He was one of Robinson's horses when he was captain, and was always going lame; he is all right now, though. I came an awful smack over the bar or pole jump. The horse fell and I came off and landed right on my head, and somehow only scraped my cheekbone a wee bit. The horse was quite all right, and so was I at once; he jumped rather well afterwards.

Oh! sweetheart, I can't help thinking what hard lines it is about my leave. After waiting five solid months, I shall only get a seven days' leave. We shall just have one leave before going back to our own division. It really is enough to break one's heart. I know I shall get it, though, just because it is so, and my first day will be your birthday. It ought to be a good omen after this long wait. I shall not refuse the leave either, although it's a day short. I don't know how I shall get through the days; the only thing I want on this earth is my Lady, and that's what she is going to be when I come, because she has said so long since. The 'catty' part will all have to go.

On Thursday I went into town near here and tried to get some Lancashire roses, but there wasn't a rose of any kind to be had and so I had to come away disappointed. I did so want to send you some so that you could have worn them on Thursday.

I must finish this this morning or it will not reach you in time for the first. It took me nearly an hour to dress this morning; my left arm and right hand were so stiff that I could hardly move them. It is another simply glorious day here and I wonder if it is the same with you. I expect you will have just gone to church, looking far lovelier than any other lady. I am going to our church service in a little while – we have had one each Sunday since we came. The Major is a strong believer in trying to make Sunday as different as possible for the men, and it's a jolly good thing.

So Joan Robinson has arrived after all. I wonder what she is like; I don't think I ever saw her, except perhaps when she was a little girl – I believe I did then. Sweetheart, I sent some of those books back to you yesterday. I hope they arrive safely because I only had a little brown paper to wrap them in. Oh! Phyl, how I long to be able to give you your first birthday kiss and wish you many happy returns, as I do by this letter with all my heart and soul. Will you do something for me? Will you put 'my' shoes on when you are dressing for dinner and let 'Eric' see you, and then I can think I was there and put them on for you.

And now, sweetheart mine, I must fly off to church; we have it in a field in the open air. Simply all, all your lover's love to you, and many, many very happy returns of the day when it comes. God bless you, Phyl,

Eric

25 May   *On duty. Went to Abele for material for lights (gun) on bike. Fearfully hot. Went to Bailleul for pay.*

28 May   *Had an argument tonight with the Major about my leave. Damn him.*

29 May   *On duty. Driving drill in morning. My leave form came before stables, left after. Rode nearly to Hazebrouck, then got a lift. Caught 8.33 train to Boulogne.*

TUESDAY 30 MAY
TELEGRAM TO PHYLLIS IN ATHLONE, FROM EUSTON

London at last cheers, Eric

175

Dear lady mine

Here I am at home at last – how funny it seems to be able to say that, and how lovely. The thought that I am on my way to my Lady at last is almost too good to believe. There, I have had to change my pen and I can't say I like this one. It is so funny writing with a pen after using nothing but a pencil.

Sweetheart, I must wish you all the happiest returns possible for tomorrow, again. Your birthday, oh! I would love to be with you, but there, I can't have everything, I suppose. Saturday, oh! Phyl, think, one, two and a half more days from now and I shall be with you, with you, my God, how wonderful. Phyl, do you realise I shall have five days with you? *Five*, my darling. I cross on Friday night, arrive Saturday morning, and, if you will have me, stay with you till Wednesday evening. After all my waiting I have been rewarded by getting a ten days' leave instead of only seven as I expected or nine as in our own division. This of course means eight days clear.

Did you get my telegram last night from Euston? I hadn't time from Folkestone or Victoria, as I wanted to get to Euston as soon as I could. However, I had two hours to wait there, so I made off straightaway and made desperate efforts to try and get you some red roses. I went to six different places and couldn't get one anywhere. So I returned to Euston, sent off the telegram, had some tea and then went to the train, and eventually arrived home at 10.45 pm and found only Dad in. Mum had gone into town to the theatre and started off before my telegram arrived. So Mum didn't know anything about my coming until I went and opened the door; she nearly fell down with astonishment. Oh! Phyl, you can't possibly realise how wonderful it seems to be here, really here, after five whole long months, and still more because I'm on my way to you.

AFTER TEA

Alex, my friend, came here this afternoon; he has a new

motorbike and sidecar, so I had to go for a run with him. We went to Southport and back in just about record time. It was splendid !

I had an awful rush on Monday. My leave form arrived just before stables, and I waited till stables were over and then asked the Major if he would mind me making a start straightaway because there was a train from Hazebrouck at 3.15. He let me go, so away I flew to my billet and did a quick change, wash, pack up and got my horses and started off at 1.45. We (my groom and I) trotted a long way and finally got onto the main road to Haze. This I wanted to do as quickly as possible and then stop a motor ambulance or lorry and get a lift for the rest of the way. But not a car of any description passed us until we were only five kilometres from Haze. By then, of course, it was too late to catch the train even if I did get a lift. My gee (Tommy, I was riding) was getting rather tired because I had very heavy saddlebags on and it was awfully hot and we had ridden sixteen miles. Well, a lorry turned up and so I got a lift and sent the horses back. I arrived in Haze quarter of an hour late for the train which I had thought might have got into Boulogne in time to catch the leave boat that night. However, as I found out later, it didn't get in in time and so I missed nothing. I caught the 8.20 train and finally got to bed at Boulogne at 2 am. I caught the mail and leave boat across yesterday morning and got to London at four.

As I am writing this, Kim is lying on his back, a mass of fluffy hair at his feet. I do hope you have a very, very happy birthday, and Mum sends her love and very best wishes for tomorrow.

My sweetheart, I can hardly sit still when I think that in two days I shall see you, hold you very close and tight to me and kiss those dear, lovely lips, as I have been longing to do for five weary months. I wonder when I shall hear from you – I do hope there is just a wee short note at least tomorrow. I have brought all the letters, Phyl, and will bring them with me, when I come. You dear, dear lady, how my heart is just pounding away and I just feel as though I want to go about yelling out how much I l-o-v-e you, you darling. And now it's just on post time so I must buck up and finish, as this must go tonight.

Bye-bye now, every atom of love in me is for you, Phyl.

Your Englishman

Leave Lime Street 11.10 tonight. Eric

My very own dear lady

What do I feel like? Oh! my God, I don't know. What a terrible thing real love is at a time like this, and yet how wonderfully, wonderfully dear. But it's hard, so very, very hard to leave you. The boat is just moving off: bye-bye, dear old Ireland and all it holds for me. I couldn't write in the train because some people got in at Mullingar, and with them talking all sorts of small talk and gassing nineteen to the dozen. I looked out as the train passed your house, but I couldn't see anybody in any of the windows or in the garden. What a happy time I have had there. I learnt a lesson, too, Phyl. I learnt what hell life would be without your love. Sweetheart, I watched and watched to see if I could see you again, to catch one more glimpse of you as the train moved off. But you only turned round that once and then were swallowed up in the crowd.

I wonder how long it will be before I come to Athlone again – not fifteen months, if I can help it. It all seems so hallowed to me now. St Mark's, I think, above all. Sweetheart, that seemed the most wonderful thing that could possibly happen. Phyl, I thought it would be the other thing because I imagined the 'catty' one would take years to conquer before it could be bent and made to go to the background. I know how you hate the 'public' idea of engagement, and so, dear heart, your lover felt as though he was awaiting his 'death sentence.' It was only an hour or two earlier that I had got back the love that you had taken, from before we went to bed the night before. Then, when I managed to tell you that it had to be one thing or the other, and when you said yes, Oh! lady mine, I did just worship you. I thank God with all my heart for giving me the love of the dearest woman He ever made. May He keep her safe and bless her while I'm away, and make her happy, too. One thing that relieves the terrible empty ache that is nearly driving me mad is the thought that my Lady has beaten the other in one great fight.

I think you are thinking about someone who isn't there but who's loving you and yearning for his Lady. This must be posted at Holyhead, as I want you to get it as soon as you can. The boat is tossing a bit so I must say night-night, darling.

Forever and ever, your lover.
XXXXXX

THURSDAY 8 JUNE 1916
THE FREDERICK HOTELS LIMITED, ROYAL PAVILION HOTEL, FOLKESTONE

My Lady, my own dear, lovely sweetheart
Here I am, stuck in this place. What an awful, terrible waste of good time it seems: six and a half hours hanging about. I am going to send this off before I leave so that you will get it sooner. I was so glad I could post that other letter on the boat because the steward said it would get to you this morning. I am a rotten sailor; it was not a rough crossing last night but I didn't feel too well, but as soon as I lay down on my bunk, I felt better.

I got the steward to wake me just before we got into Holyhead and it was a glorious night, but it made me long and long for my Lady. I looked across the sea towards where I knew she was. Going back this time seems hundreds and hundreds of times harder than it has ever felt before. Why couldn't I have been with you when you have to tell the world that you're engaged?

I'm just going to write as often as I possibly can; although your lover can't be there himself, he is sending all his love to his Lady. I have been writing my diary up this morning and I can hardly remember anything but Tuesday and yesterday. Tuesday the sixth of June – did you ever think of this? It is exactly halfway between your birthday and mine, practically to the very hour you said 'Yes' at St Mark's. What a terrible lot can rest on the two words 'yes' and 'no'. Well, my whole life was in the balance then. I wonder what your dad thought when I went to say goodbye to him; somehow, I couldn't speak as I wanted. I would like to have told him how dearly I loved him, for he seems as much my dad as yours now. I wish I knew how your dad is now; he was so poorly yesterday – may God grant he is better.

I must go and have lunch now. I never came across such a funny idea in my life: everyone who is not a resident had to pay before they went into lunch and it really wasn't up to much. Well, I suppose it's all in the game. It is a simply lovely day here and I wonder what you are doing now – are you going out in the car or are you going to paint the boat? Why can't I be there? It is hard, this going away. I couldn't get a sleeping berth on the train at Holyhead so I had to share a compartment with a naval lieutenant. We managed to keep people out by shamming to be asleep, and so each had one side and I slept pretty well. I had breakfast on the train down but could hardly eat anything, just as last night I hardly touched a scrap at dinner.

Sweetheart, I left my haversack, map Hazebrouck 5A, and also my penknife behind me. The last, I think, is in the place where we bent the sixpence; the map, I think, is in the dining room and the haversack on the hat stand in the hall. I didn't tell Mum in my letter last night about our engagement because I hadn't time, but I am going to do so as soon as I can when I get back. Sweetheart, promise me you'll write to her: tell her just what you like about it; she will understand, I know.

Dear heart, I shall want a long letter at the end of the fortnight. I wonder what it will have to tell me. Please tell me everything, even about the times the 'catty part' gets the better of you. I would much, much rather know everything.

And now bye-bye, my own dear lady. How your lover loves and longs for you, now and always, Phyl.

Saturday 10 June
Posted from the Field Post Office on 11 June

My own very, very dear lady

Here I am, back again, just a little bit nearer the line than I showed you on the map, quite close to the road between B— [Brielen] and E— [Elverdinge] – you may be able to see a farm marked. I have only a short time, as I have to go up to the infantry. So now I must tell you what happened after finishing the letter at Folkestone. I went out and posted it, and the man said at the post office that it ought to get to Ireland next morning, so I do hope you got it yesterday. Then I walked round the town, and then it was time to go aboard. You could see the coast of France from Folkestone and when we got to Boulogne you could see the cliffs at Folkestone quite clearly.

The train left at seven, so we had only a short time to wait, and then we started on the weary, slow, snail-like journey up here. The crossing was lovely, perfectly calm and sunny, but I began to think of what we might have done if only the weather had been finer – but soon I found myself thinking of what we had done and how wonderfully dear those five days were. Soon after we had got clear of Boulogne, it started teeming and I don't remember anything more until a porter shouted P— [Poperinge] at us several times.

So we collected our gear and started in the pouring rain for the officers' rest place. When we got there, we had some hot tea and bread, butter and jam and then turned in at about 2.45 am. I felt just dead to the world and I didn't get up till 9.30 yesterday. After having breakfast there, I started off to find this place. I was walking along the main road when a motor ambulance came along. So I stopped it, and as luck would have it, discovered a captain I knew coming back from the hospital, so I got a lift as far as his Battery and had lunch with him. While there I found out where this place is and after lunch walked on here and finally got here at about 3 pm.

The Major is on leave at present, and Burrows, I believe, goes on the thirteenth. I ought to be the next to go in the Battery, but as I dare say you may have heard, the leaves have been cut down by more than half, and so it means we only get leave about once every four and a half months or something dreadful like that. However, Phyl, we must just hope for the best, yes, the very best this time. Sweetheart, I wrote a letter miles long to Mum and Dad last night, telling them about our engagement, and I'm just longing to hear from them both. I must write to your mum tomorrow; I don't like to think of what she would think of me if I don't. It's Burrows's birthday today; he's twenty-four.

I've got to go now, my darling. I would like to stay here (on my bed made out of a wooden frame and canvas stretched across) and write more to you. So bye-bye, my very, very, own Lady. Forever and for all time,

Your Englishman

SUNDAY 11 JUNE

My sweetheart

Today started very badly: it poured until about 5 am and then gradually cleared up and it is now quite nice and fine again. I was up all night – because at present there is nowhere to sleep – with the infantry. A dugout is being made, so I had to try and sleep on a form in the mess dugout. It was beastly hard and I woke up feeling as though I had been kicked all over. Except for machine-guns and some firing over on the right, the night was quiet and wet. I walked back here as soon as Beavis had got to the OS at about 4.15 am. It is a good hour's walk and so I got to bed about 6 am, feeling jolly tired. I slept till 12.15, then got up. This afternoon I have been tracing a map for Burrows.

Phyl, I have just been rereading the letter you sent to the hospital. Yes, wouldn't it have been heavenly to have got a month's leave, but do you think my Lady could have put up with her 'silly donkey of an Englishman' for that length of time? Do you think we would have got engaged? I do, because your dad has been troubled about us for a long time, I think, and I am sure that he had made up his mind to speak to me about it the next time he saw me. Phyl, I hope it would have been so and that everything would be as it is now.

I'm happy, so very happy right deep down, and this happiness seems to come to me when I feel as wretched as I do at times, in fact, often. Somehow, it seems to chase the empty, lonely feeling away and just makes me think of the dear lady who is waiting for me and wanting me to come back to her, just as much as I am longing to go to her.

Although I could hardly have got a letter from you yet, I didn't half-realise how awful it would be to have to go two weeks without a letter from you, Phyl; I seem just lost without them. Somehow, it doesn't seem a bit like my birthday because I know there would be a letter from you, but I'm just going to grin and bear it.

Burrows wants me to take over the mess when he goes on leave, but I'm not going to, because it means more work in my spare time and I want all that to write to my Lady.

You say in this letter that you were cleaning the car and suddenly found yourself thinking about what you would do if I got a long sick leave, and you wished my home was in the country. Phyl, I have often wished it was on some river where we could go by ourselves and get miles away from people, as we could at Athlone. I was thinking I would hire Alex's motorbike and sidecar and I could take you where ever I wanted. We would go to Tinkerfield, and be there quite by ourselves. Then we could go for picnics together on the moors or down by the River Ribble, and we could be together from morning till night. Phyl, it would be heaven there. I have always loved the place. I would show you where I fell in the brook and got soaked, and where I made a dam and used to sail my boats. I would show you the iron spring we found, and the plants Dad and I planted. I haven't been there for nearly four years now. How beautiful it would be to carry you off in the sidecar with me for miles and miles, and we would simply fly along, because you really are the bravest lady I have ever seen in a car. Several times when we were out together in 'Sadie' my heart jumped and yet you never turned a hair. Oh! I know I would drive like the devil, Phyl, I know I would, because I should be half-wild with delight.

Phyl, I must stop; Burrows wants me to go out and watch some work tonight.

Bye-bye, dear lady, for always your Englishman

MONDAY 12 JUNE

My sweetheart
What an absolutely heavenly surprise it was, getting a letter tonight. We get them awfully late now, and mine had gone by the time yours arrived. When I started it, I couldn't think what had happened to your birthday. Then I suddenly tumbled to it that you had written it long ago and had been sitting on it. I'm so glad you sent it and I had it to read yesterday, as I wanted one so very terribly. My Lady, why should you want to reward me for feeling miserable about the roses. You have given much, much more than a reward for it: how much happiness seems to rest on that little word 'yes' and how much misery I would have gone through had it been 'no'.

It's a simply pitch-black night and raining like the dickens. I hope it clears up for tomorrow. I have been working – or rather, supervising the work at the gun position we are making – practically all day, and Wenley is out there now. It has been a beastly day. I'll try to finish this letter tomorrow.

TUESDAY MORNING, IN THE OS
Good morning, my Lady. I hope you're feeling a great deal more comfortable than I am at present. It's simply teeming, and the place leaks like a sieve. There is a bitterly cold west wind blowing and it fairly whistles through this place. Shall I tell you what it's like? Well, to start off with, it's a bit of a trench on the

top of a high bank. The trench is about five feet deep, and as I sit at this kind of shelf-table at the far end from the door, my elbows are touching either side. The trench is blocked at the end where I am, and the sides are riveted with corrugated iron and stakes, which, by the way, are caving in in one or two places. The whole thing is about thirteen feet long and is covered by a low roof, and at this end I can't stand up straight.

The roof, unfortunately, is far from waterproof, and it's rather a case of dodging the drips; at any rate, I'm wearing my oilskin at present – it's safer. The far end turns towards the rear and west, and so, with there being a west wind, it is blowing right in at the door, and going out by the lookout slit which runs along the east side of the trench, level with the ground outside and just directly below the roof. Through this we look out with either glasses or a telescope. The place is about 2,000 yards from the Boche and so we can't see much. The only piece of furniture here is a broken chair, which I am sitting on at present. I had my breakfast at 9 o'clock: two fried eggs and some bread and butter. The tea has not arrived yet although it is now 11 o'clock. The fire went out and the telephonists had to go in search of wood.

So far, I have had no shelling. I hope it goes on like this. I'm having jam sandwiches for lunch – do you remember the last ones I had? I'd give anything if these could have been made by the same dear hands. For tea, I've got a big lump of lunch cake, and I get back to the fold in time for dinner about 8.30. Phyl, a little wee mouse has just popped out from behind some sandbags at the back of the table, and I've put down a trail of breadcrumbs for it. It's just taken the first. They – there goes the second – run down the table towards my writing pad, and the last one is on the pad. I wonder if – there goes the third – it will dare to come for it; here he is again. He's a wee bit scared. It's getting very close to my arm, and every time I move it along the page from side to side, he runs off. He was within two inches of my hand then – the fourth and fifth have both gone now. He's been very busy; he found the lid of the mess tin that I had my fried eggs in and he was fairly tucking in. He has darted back again now. I stopped writing to have a look round and Burrows arrived, so we fired a few rounds and discussed this place and the beastly weather. We had a good laugh over his misfortune last night. At some unearthly hour his bed subsided onto the floor, or rather the right-hand leg near his head got tired and gave way, and he woke up with a start, finding himself nearly standing on his head! Oh! I would have liked to have seen him; I'll bet the language was choice, to say the least! My hands are beastly cold; I wish it would shut up raining and be nice and warm. The Boche have just been making it unpleasant here, so I had to subside into the bombproof close to, until he had finished.

We all have to wear the 'tin hats' or steel helmets now whenever we are east of the guns. I've got mine on at present. They are beastly heavy things, but from all accounts are a great protection. Wenley is an absolute sight in his. He has a huge head, and consequently the hat perches right on the top: I couldn't help howling with laughter at him the first time I saw him with it on.

Phyl, you dear lady, how very good of you to send me a DA. It makes me feel such a beast for not giving you anything, and I wanted to so badly. Sweetheart, thank you very, very much; it will be another thing I can carry about with me that my Lady has given me. I'm awfully upset, Phyl, because it hasn't turned up yet. Phyl, how can I tell you how much I love you; you don't regret anything, not even deep down in you. You are 'proud to be (my) lady in the eyes of everyone'; you can't realise how much it means to me. I only can hope that my letters bring all, all the help and love that her lover can possibly give her by them.

I wrote a long letter to Mum and Dad telling them all about you and I asked them both to write to me. I am just longing to hear what they have to say to me and of course I will tell you, sweetheart; you have just as much right to hear as I have. But it was horrid, having to write and tell them; I would much rather have told them myself and have had a good talk to them both about it all.

Burrows has just rung up to say he goes on leave today and, as the Major won't be back till Friday, I shall be OC. Heavens,

I shall be jumpy. I must have my lunch now, sweetheart, and say bye-bye. Your Englishman sends every drop of love that is in him to you, Phyl, to be by you when you need it most.

God bless, my Lady, now and forever
Eric

WEDNESDAY 14 JUNE

Phyl

I am just worried to death tonight: I have got about five thousand things to remember and my head is just buzzing round. I am not allowed to say, but there are things happening, and all the bally arrangements have to be made by yours truly, and now, in order to improve matters, the light is going out. Tonight, the daylight-saving bill business comes into force over here. Here comes another beastly message, and there goes the light – I've just got a candle so can go on.

Phyl, the DA hasn't arrived yet. I do hope nothing has happened to it. And the haversack, map and penknife haven't come yet, just because I am wanting them, I suppose, and I am responsible for the map. I have hardly had a minute today, because we are most awfully short-handed with all the work that we have to do and only the three of us. I wonder if you know your lover is thinking of you and trying to imagine what you are doing now, and that he is feeling most horribly cross and grumpy and wants his Lady to cheer him up so badly. Oh! think of it, it's only a week tonight since I left you, and a week yesterday I spent the most wonderful day of my life. How terribly slowly it has gone.

Last night I had to leave the OS early in order to get down here before Wenley went up to the infantry as Beavis had not got back from the wagon line. On the way down I managed to give my knee a twinge and when I arrived here I felt as sick as a dog. I think it really was the beastly state of the ground I had to come over and the fact that I had a terrific weight on my shoulders. We have got new respirators and they each weigh about a ton. I had that, another ordinary respirator, a pair of glasses, and Beavis's haversack, which was full of stuff, and it was raining. On top of all this I had my steel helmet on, which alone seems to weigh nearly a ton. My eyes feel a bit groggy tonight so I'm going to bathe them before I turn in.

I suppose your brother will have gone back last night – did you go on any picnics with him in the car? I wonder where you went? I expect all the countryside knows about us going to Kilmuir Point that day. You remember all the people passing along the road, and we thought nobody would pass? How I wish I was there now; it does seem so heavenly, and to think that it all came about and I did do those things. How the time simply flew. Will this beastly business never end?

THURSDAY 15 JUNE
The Major came back this morning, so now everything in the garden is lovely in that direction. This morning I handed everything over to him and went through all the details. This afternoon I have been working hard at the gun pits. There is heaps and heaps to be done yet, and in so short a time too. Sweetheart, leaves have been cut down so much now that they might just as well be stopped altogether. Thank heaven I got away when I did. I hate to think what might have happened had I not.

I shall see Tommy and Darky in a few days' time now and I shall try and get as much riding as I can. Do you know, I still feel the wrist at times. The other day I was using a felling axe and it gave me gyp once or twice, using the muscles again. Sweetheart, I've got about twenty letters I must censor so I must stop and do them now. There, I've just finished them and the man is waiting for this, so bye-bye, my sweetheart.

Your Englishman

My Lady Phyl

It's quite a nice day, which is rather a remarkable thing because
it's been horrible lately. This morning we started work at 6 am.
The men are doing two fatigues a day, 9 to 12.30 and 2 to 4.30.
I can tell you, it's hard work, but it's got to be done. I was jolly
glad I was not here this morning, about 11 am, because the Huns
took it into their d—d heads to shell the road in front and
carefully put two or three beastly close to here. One landed in a
little outhouse – about two yards further and it would have gone
right into the bedroom where Beavis, Wenley and I sleep.
However, it didn't, and a miss is as good as a mile, isn't it? I have
to go up to the infantry tonight. It's a rotten long walk but won't
be so bad tonight because everywhere is drying up splendidly.

Lady mine, the DA came last night; hasn't it taken an age to
get here? It is a nice case and thank you very, very much for it,
you darling lady, and thank you very much too for the cigarettes.
I am going to have one of them now out of your case, and here's
to the lady that gave them to me. I'll tell you why the case was
late in coming – because it would take them some time to put
those dear wee initials on it. It just fits in my breast pocket.

Wenley and I are moving off from here tomorrow night and
so for a day or two I won't be able to write. The Colonel is here
now, and he and the Major are talking nineteen to the dozen.
As soon as we go back I am going to root round and find out
how I stand on the army list and then, if I'm eligible, I'm going
to speak to the Colonel about a second star. I think it is a shame
that people miles behind the line should get twice as many
leaves as we do, who are up here. I can't imagine when I shall
get leave again, as the Colonel says it's more or less a matter of
luck now.

There is another whole week before I can have a letter, but I
hope it will be a long one telling all about what has been
happening to you since I left and how you have felt. Phyl, I
don't think I ever told you that, as I was on my way to

Broadstones after leaving you, I followed what I thought was the road we went along in the car from Moate towards Mullingar. I am sure I could nearly see the place we turned round at, at that road junction. It was a nice afternoon that day, after the beastly wet day on Sunday and Monday morning. Do you remember how 'Sadie' wanted to jump all over the road, especially going down that bit of a hill outside Moate on the way back. I really thought at one moment it was going to be either the ditch or the hedge, but there was no cause for alarm because it would have meant a nice long leave, wouldn't it? But in that case, I, only, would have to have been hurt – if you had been injured in any way it would have been horrible. Do you remember the gentleman flying past us as we were going to give 'Sadie' a drink?

Sweetheart, how would you like me to go into the Flying Corps? A thing came round last night about it, but I didn't send my name in, although I had more than half a mind to do so. I'm only waiting till something comes round about anti-aircraft guns and then down goes my name for it. Wenley has just arrived in, breathless – they had to cut and run because the Huns put some shells unpleasantly close to where they were working.

Phyl, do you remember the foxtrot that I asked the band to play at the State Restaurant when we went to dinner on 'our love day', the leave before this last one. Well, the men have just got it going on the gramophone, and it has made me feel all funny inside and an awful longing for you, Phyl. I feel just terribly lonely, but you mustn't worry. Please give a little wee bit of my love to your mum and dad, and now all the remainder is sent to you with this, forever and ever.

Your Eric

MONDAY 19 JUNE

Lady mine
Here we are, out again. What a time I had the last three days; thank goodness it's over. I told you in my letter written on Friday what I had being doing that morning. I had to go up to

the infantry after tea, and as soon as we had had dinner up there, I was on the run until 1.30. I had to fire about fifteen times at machine-guns which were causing trouble all night. About every ten or twenty minutes I had to jump up and run to the telephone and get a couple of rounds fired at either one place or another where we knew the MGs were. Then about 12.30 am a terrific bombardment started on our right, and we thought the Boche were going to make an attack. The row was awful, and everybody was out and watching it. It did die down, but started again very hard at about 2 am. I thought there was going to be another gas attack because it was a perfect night for it. At any rate, I didn't get a wink of sleep until 4 am. Then I had to go to the OS at 5. The bombardment was a fine sight, but it must have been h—l to be in it. I was so sleepy when I got there, I sat down on the broken wicker-bottomed chair and dozed fitfully; every now and then, I got up and had a look round, and then sat down again and tried to sleep. After breakfast I had to do some firing, and was relieved by Beavis at one o'clock. Then I had to trek down to the Battery and get a wash and change, as I had to go down to the wagon line that night. About a thousand messages came in and people kept ringing up and, as the Major was not in, I had to answer the messages and speak on the telephone. After tea, I managed to get an hour's sleep and then had to bustle round making arrangements for moving off that night, which I eventually did with the wagons at 11 pm. I rode Tommy down and as I was with the wagons had to walk the whole way, about ten miles. Several times I nearly fell off my gee with going to sleep and was jolly glad when we finally arrived at the wagon line at 1.30. Then I had to find out where Wenley was sleeping and I found him in a farm some distance from the wagon line, and got to bed at 2.30 am. We got up at 8 yesterday morning and left the wagon line with the Battery at 11 am, with a march of twenty-two miles in front of us. Halfway we had to water and feed the horses and finally arrived here at 6.15 last evening. I had nothing since breakfast and had an awful headache. However, I felt better after having some dinner at 9 pm. I nearly jumped out of my skin on finding two letters on the mess table, one from Mum and one from Dad.

Sweetheart, what do you think they say in both of them? They both say we did quite the right thing, as long as we are sure that neither you nor I will ever regret it: well, as neither of us are ever going to think of such a thing, then we did do the right thing. Phyl, they are both awfully glad about it and said it didn't come as a shock to them, because if there was any shock at all, it had come long ago when I first told them about you. Mum said she was going to write to you and your mum and so I expect by now you will have heard from her. Phyl, they are both very fond of you and there was absolutely no need for you to think Mum thought differently, the last time you were at my home, because it was simply she was worried about my sister's ear, and also maids were troubling her.

Dad said there was no need at all to have any doubt about him and Mum being pleased, and that if we were quite sure that we could wait, as we would have to, before we could think of marrying, he felt quite certain we had done the right thing. He also said your father was quite justified in asking what he did of you and me, and that if he (Dad) had been in the same position he would have done so himself. Sweetheart, they both asked me if we had thought about religion. Dad said that we ought to understand exactly what one another thought, because it has led to trouble in many cases. Well I can't talk about it in a letter. My views are very simple and I will tell you them the next time I am with you and you must tell me yours. I don't know why, but I feel no fear in my mind about it. I always keep my worship of God absolutely to myself and don't allow any of the everyday business of this world to affect it. I just ask God for what I want and thank Him for what I've got. But there, I'm not going to talk about it in a letter; we will have a good talk the next time I am with you.

And now, sweetheart, I'm going to write the ending of Dad's letter, just the last few lines: 'Now, lad, I must close, I trust and hope you will come through this war to spend many years of life with your heart's choice. Be constant, be firm and be careful; think before you act.' It's just like him; I can just imagine him saying it. And so, my Lady, everybody is pleased about it, and I, well, I hardly think I can realise how dear and wonderful a thing has happened. I know the years that have to come will be just centuries to me, but wait, I have no other thought but that I will wait until my Lady will become my very, very own. That is what your lover wants. When two people get engaged they are going to marry one another sometime. He wants that wonderful time to come when his Lady can be with him for the remainder of his life, just you and I and our love.

The parcel of cheese straws, Vaseline, haversack, books, map and penknife arrived on Friday night and were packed away, so I did not get them until this morning. I am writing this in my room. Wenley and Beavis sleep here also. It is a nuisance, not being able to have a room to myself, but we can't get another for love or money round here. The cheese straws are in front of me; the Major is not going to have a chance of eating them all. I have been tucking in at them; they are simply luscious. Thank you very, very much, you dear and thoughtful lady, and for the Vaseline as well. I must hurry up and read *The Harvesters*. I will send it back as soon as I have finished it. When I opened the parcel today I fairly jumped for joy when I saw the note, and although it is only a wee note, it seems to tell me my Lady is thinking about me always. I am going to put the Vaseline on every night, and I'm sure my eyes will be much better each morning, because my Lady sent it for me.

Night-night now, you very dearest lady in all the world.

Forever and for all time,

Your Eric

THURSDAY 22 JUNE 1916

MY DEAR ONE

Sweetheart, it's a simply glorious day; why can't I be with you, my dear, dear lady? It's just the lovely kind of day we wanted so much for each day I was with you. Not a cloud to be seen, except two small wisps away to the south and a lovely clear blue sky.

Just the kind of day it makes one glad to be alive and well, and yet there is all the time the dreadful lonely ache in my heart for ones I have left behind. I wrote to Dad last night and told him about the awful sorrow that had fallen on you all. My darling, I know how dreadfully sorry they both will be for you all, but for your dad's sake they will be glad, because they know how terribly he had suffered. I wonder how your poor mum is; is she bearing up well, Phyl? Oh! this cruel war, how awful it is, being stuck out here, miles and miles away from you when I know you want me most, and I am wanting to be by you now to try and do all in my power to be a comfort to you. Will you tell me if you would like to hear what your dad told me, that Tuesday morning, when he spoke to me about you? There is no harm now, and I think it might comfort you as it did me and made me know I loved him with a great fond love.

I am going to try and write as much as I can today, but even if I don't get any more than this page written, I will send it off tonight because I know you will want all the letters I can possibly send. Now, my darling, I must stop for the present.

3.30 PM
Sweetheart, I just can't tell you in words how dreadfully the awful sorrow you must feel cuts my heart and makes me feel such a wretched being, not being able to do a hand's turn for you in any way. After this letter, I shall not speak about the sorrow you are suffering now; I shall try my best in my letters to make you think of our world. Because I think you would rather I did, and I hope I am helping you. I have given my life to help you, to guard you and to love you. Thank God that your dad died so quietly and peacefully; what a joy those last few moments must have been to him. Phyl, I know they were because he told me – but no, I must not say until you tell me whether I can or not. Imagine, after all the terrible pain which he has practically never been rid of for eight months, to have absolutely none and to die with his dear ones near him.

And now, dear heart, in this letter which you started the day I left, you ask me to forgive you for being as you were that

Monday night. Oh! Lady mine, I've nothing to forgive; it is you who must forgive me. It was my fault for saying what I did: I am such an awful idiot at saying something to you which you are likely to take in the wrong way. Darling, if there is anything for me to forgive, it is done a hundred thousand times over; how could it not be so when the very next day you consented to become my own Lady in the eyes of all the world. How I thank God now that I did the only thing your dear dad ever asked me, and I was and am rewarded now, first by the love which you have given me, and then by knowing that your dad was glad that we were engaged.

And now, dear lady mine, bye-bye for the present. If it makes it any easier for you to write to me, do so and tell me everything. Your lover, now and for all time,

Eric

22 June   *A beautiful day. Second Army commander General Franks came round lines this morning.*

23 June   *Rode to Wormhout this afternoon with Erilles, got nails for harness room. Burrows returned from leave.*

FRIDAY 23 JUNE

Sweetheart
I am going to send you what I have written down about our five days: just what happened and what I thought. I have only copied the first page out and so I am going to send it off with this. Oh! those five happy days; how wonderful they were and how very, very happy I was, except for one night, and how very awful that was. What agony there can be without my Lady's love, and what happiness, dear lovely happiness, when her love is with me.

195

FIVE SHORT DAYS WITH MY LADY

Arrived at Kingstown about 5.30 am. When I got to Kingsbridge, I found the train did not leave for Athlone until 9.30, so asked if I could go by Broadstones. The man said, 'Yes, but you'd better hurry up, as the train leaves in ten minutes, at seven.' I jumped on car, and man made bally old gee canter whole way. Train late so caught it by the skin of my teeth; never thought I would. Got to Athlone 9 am. She was there with her younger brother, Buzz, bless her. I didn't know he was there and kissed her. How glad I was to be with her again; she is the sweetest, dearest being on this earth and what an age it seems since we two were together last: five whole long dreary months, but now it's over and I am with my darling again. The car was waiting down below and I started it for her while Buzz backed a horse and bus out of the way for her to drive the car out into the road. How beautifully she did it, too, and no one could have done it better. I sat in the front alongside her and couldn't think what to say. I only wanted to watch her every movement. When we arrived at her house, Buzz and I collected the things and put them in the hall. How very wonderful it seemed to be back in the old house, where our love for one another had started. I took my things off and went into the dining room. It was nice to see her mum again, but she told me her husband was rather bad again. How hard it seems that he should have to suffer so much; I'm afraid it's only a matter of time, and really, for his own sake death would be a blessing. Then Buzz and I went upstairs and he told me where my room was – Oh! it was hers, my Lady's own room that I was put in. The very room she writes to me in and thinks about me in, all by herself; how dear it seemed that I should be allowed to sleep there. I opened my suitcase, got out my things, brushed my hair and then went down to breakfast.

Dodo and Joan Robinson were in the dining room when I got there. Dodo's just the same quiet person, but she can be lively in her quiet way. Joan seemed very merry and a good friend, I should think. After breakfast everybody left except Phyl and me. How wonderful it was to take her in my arms again and kiss her, after all these weary months. She told me Buzz was shocked when I kissed her on the station, but I couldn't help it, I just had to. Phyl, Buzz and I went for a walk round the garden after a little while.

Afterwards I was allowed to see her dad. He looks just the same as the last time I saw him in Dublin; how pleased I was, though, to see him again. We had a talk and he told me exactly how things stood. He has got cancer on the stomach and it is merely a matter of time before the end comes. How brave he is about it – no soldier could be braver than he – and how very dear. We talked about the war and the North Sea battle and then I left him. Phyl, Buzz and I put the car back and Phyl and I went round the garden. She showed me where she had watched from as I went away from Athlone, and then I was told where the rose 'Irish Elegance' grew. It was one of those she sent to me before I came home on leave the first time. I've got it in the case with her two photos now.

After lunch, Phyl asked her dad if she and I could go out in the car; he said we could. So we took our tea with us and off we went to Kilmuir Point. I remember every inch of the road and the things that had happened during those happy days when I was with her at Athlone. We went along the lower road to Glassan, by the lakeside and past the deer park. Then, when we got past Glassan, I remembered very well the last time we came along here in the other direction. How different it was then, as we were both sitting in the back of the car and I was grumpy. When we got to Kilmuir Point, we left the car near the cottage by the farm and carried the things with us, looking for a cosy spot out of the wind. We scrambled over a wall into a field; what fun it was, and when I wanted to lift her down from the top, she wouldn't let me, so she jumped herself. We went down by the lakeside in among the trees. After I had been told all about the part of the lake that we could see from there, we found at last a place free from rocks where we could sit down and have our tea. It was rather close to the road, but we thought no one would pass along it, so didn't bother our heads about it. She would eat hardly anything, and the chocolate cake she had made was so good, too. When we had finished, we cleared away, and then the time slipped away while we just held one another fast and poured out our love, after the long, long time during which we had nothing but letters.

We never noticed how fast the clock was going round until it was past seven, and then we had to fairly hurry in collecting the rugs and coats and in getting to the car. Several people came along the road behind us while we were lying behind the small boulder, but why should we care about them. We had to back the car about to get her round in the narrow road, but it was soon done by my clever lady and off we went for home. We got back at 8 pm and Phyl ran into the gatepost as she came into the drive. She just bent the off wing a bit, but did the car no damage. After dinner we went into the drawing room together and were there till very late. We talked about her dad and ourselves, and then I took her in my arms and was the happiest man on earth. How terribly short those hours were, though; they seemed more like as many minutes. Her mum came in about twelve and said she was going to bed, so that meant we ought to go. But oh! I didn't want to; it seems such awful waste of time sleeping when I might be with my Lady. We stayed together until I had to drag myself away and let my dear lady go to bed. And so, with her going, there ended the day, but it was not till we had taken off our shoes and walked as quietly as we could upstairs and had kissed goodnight at the head of the stairs, that the day was over. I know I shall sleep better than I have ever done because I am sleeping in the room where someone I love thinks very hard of me. Oh! God, I do love her, and how dear it is to know she loves me very dearly.

Now, dear heart, I must run off and post this. It's simply teeming thunder rain at present, and the heavenly artillery is rumbling away. Bye-bye, you darling, you dear, dear lady mine.

Your Englishman, now and for always.

Sunday 4 June

Not a thing did I dream last night; I slept until Lizzie came with my water at about 8.30. Then, as I woke, I realised I had slept in my Lady's room and had had the most beautiful sleep I could ever have. I didn't want to get up, but I began to think of the precious time I was wasting there. Lizzie brought me a cup of tea and some bread and butter and I was told breakfast was not till after church. I got up at about 9.15 am and it was simply teeming then. The service at the barracks was at ten, so I had to buck up. I arrived down just in time to go with the others as far as the corner of Northgate Street. I left them at the post office and walked to the barracks chapel. It fairly teemed, and my British Warm got pretty wet by the time I arrived there. The service had started, so I sat at the back, in among the Tommies, and enjoyed the service. I knew one man in the choir and the parson, and I left at the end of the service without speaking to anyone, because I came to Athlone to be with my Lady and nobody else. When I got back, I found the others there, and we had breakfast all together. Afterwards, Buzz and I went down to the garage and straightened the wing that Phyl bent last night. After we had finished, she came down and watched us cleaning the plugs for a long time. I saw her dad for a few minutes before lunch – I wanted to ask him something about the car and so just looked in. He seemed better, I think, then. How terribly worn out, though, he looks, and such an ill colour. What a horrid day it has been, blowing and raining for all it's fit, and I did want it to be fine.

After lunch, Phyl and I were together in the drawing room. I am always longing to be alone with her, and then when I am, I seem to forget everything I want to tell her about what has happened out at the front, and I can think of nothing but the wonderful love that is always raging in my heart. My Lady sat on the edge of a big armchair by the curio table until I went over to her and led her to the sofa. Then we sat together in the corner furthest away from the door with all the cushions in the world round about us. The wonderfulness of being with her again; it all seems like heaven on earth, she is so very dear. Every now and then she would start up, thinking she heard somebody outside in the drive, so after a time we went down to the garage and sat in the back seat of the car with the garage doors closed. Buzz came down to let us know tea was ready. We all had tea together in the drawing room, and Buzz and Dermot had a great feed of cake, which I carved. After tea, I went up and saw her dad. We talked about the naval battles in the North Sea and the war in general, and then my Lady began playing all sorts of things on the piano. When I got downstairs, I felt I wanted to sit down and listen. I knew the words of some of the songs and soon she began to sing some of her own songs. How lovely it is to hear her, and I can do nothing but watch and watch her. I never can even think of 'The Old Grey Hills of Home' without a big lump rising to my throat.

After she had finished, the lamp was brought in and the blinds lowered and curtains drawn. I arranged these last so that there was no chink through which the light could flow, and then we were together for a few hours, all to ourselves. How I am longing for many more hours and days like these I am having now. What heaven it would be to have my Lady with me for all my life. How I hate the time for going to bed; it seems so terribly hard to leave her. And now two of these precious short days have gone. Why can't time go slower when I'm with her? It simply runs away. Goodnight, you dear one, and may I dream a dear, dear dream of you who I love with my heart and soul, now and for all time.

Saturday 24 June

Phyl, sweetheart
I had to send off that one page only. I have been on duty today and hoped to get some time this morning to write to you, but it was just my luck that the Major told me there were baths for the

men today and I had to march them there, two and a half miles there and back to the baths, and waiting there about an hour. Twice today it has simply pelted, and this morning, early, when I got up at 5.30 am, it was teeming. Well, it's fine again now, thank heaven. The lines are still in a beastly state; I have just been having a look round the gees and slithered and slipped about like a drunk man.

I feel just wretched tonight. I don't seem to be able to get time to write, and yet Wenley and Beavis annoy me by telling me I am everlastingly writing. I do wish I had my own room. Then I could sit up till all hours and write, but I can't do that, as there are three of us in one room. Sweetheart, will there be a letter for me tomorrow? It's simply awful, this knowing you are in great trouble and not hearing a word. Will you try and tell me as much as you possibly can in your letters? It's two weeks tomorrow since my birthday – how many, many weeks it seems since I left you walking back along the platform at Athlone. Phyl, what a cruel world this is, and how very few and far between are the happy times. Oh! I want a letter, I do, I do; this waiting and knowing nothing is terrible. I'm dead sleepy, so I must turn in now.

SUNDAY – 11 PM
My darling, what an idiot I am. I wanted this letter to go tonight and now it can't.

I went to Dunkerque with the Major for the day and intended to come back by the afternoon train, but when we got there, we found there was no early train back, being Sunday, so we had to come by the 7.30.

Well, sweetheart, we had a very interesting day. We got there about eleven and walked along the docks and saw some submarines. We were very keen on having a look over one, and as luck would have it, a naval lieutenant that the Major knew rolled up and showed us over his boat. It was awfully interesting. I had never been down in one before. After we had been all over it, we went and had lunch with him at one of the hotels and then took the tram to Malo. It was a glorious day and we sat on the beach for a short time, watching the shipping and aeroplanes. Then we had a look at some more docks, and in doing so discovered the seaplane place, so went inside and asked if we could look round. The Commander came and told us we could, but that we must have some tea first, so off we went and had tea in their mess, and then looked round all the planes and watched one launched and start off. One came down at sea and was towed in. Then we walked back to the town and caught the train back. It has been a very pleasant change to get clean away from the Battery for a few hours, as well as most awfully interesting.

Sweetheart, will you pray very, very hard each night for your Englishman to get leave very, very soon, and I will do the same. Oh! Phyl, I want to be with you with such a terrible longing, I hardly know how the days pass. Will this cursed war never, never end?

Monday afternoon – 3.30 pm
My Lady, I have just come off parade – have been taking gun drill this morning and afternoon. It is practically my job now, and it does take time and patience with some of these new fellows that we got, but all the same, once they learn they are jolly good. One of the gees has been ill with colic for four days now; she has suffered most terribly but has hung on to her life simply marvellously, and I honestly think she is getting better. She seems almost human, and pushes her nose into my hand when I go to her. This afternoon I was stroking her neck and she looked round at me and rested her head on my shoulder. One of my mares had a foal the other day; there was great excitement in the Battery about it. The little foal is a fine little fellow and has been called Billy. I'm afraid we shall lose both, though, because we are not allowed to keep a mare on active service when she has foaled. The little joker scampers all over the field that the mare is in, but never leaves its mother.

Oh! sweetheart, please send me just a note, however short it is, just to tell me you are all right.

Bye-bye, my own dear lady. Your lover forever,

Eric

Monday 26 June

My own dear, dear lady
I'm just going to write a bit before the others come to bed. It's simply teeming cats and dogs at present, although it has been beautiful all afternoon and evening. Just these last few days I have been wearing the pair of socks that you gave me while I was at your home. They are beautifully soft and very precious to me. Now I must write about Monday 5 June and our third day together at your home.

Monday 5 June

What an unkind thing the weather is: it rained in showers all morning, and was blowing hard down from the lake. I felt awfully sleepy again this morning, and the bed was so wonderfully comfy, I just slept like a clock. After brekker, Phyl and I stayed in the dining room. She began writing with the typewriter. Phyl started by writing, 'Eric is an ass' – she seemed to want to tease me. Then I wrote, 'What do you think it is going to do today; will it allow us to go away all by ourselves and forget everything but our LOVE.' There was no answer to that, but she asked me a question: 'Why did you go down the garden?' Answer: 'Because I wanted to get some forget-me-nots for my LADY. See?' It was fun; she kept pointing out which key I had to press next and tried to press it before I spotted which one I wanted. We were 'silly' with it for a long time until Buzz came in for it. We went into the study, where Buzz had been doing his lessons. He wanted to write for stamps or something.

So we went into the garden and down to the garage. Phyl took her knitting down, but I don't think she did very much. Why do the dear hours fly away so quickly and the awful ones drag? I don't know how long we stayed there – and time didn't seem to matter – until it was time to go to lunch. Then Phyl asked her dad if she and I could go in the car for a short run. So off we went to Moate and on along the Mullingar road. It was a lovely afternoon, but 'Sadie' didn't go very well. About halfway to Moate we stopped to look how the oil was, and discovered one of the back tyres needed pumping. That was soon done and off we went again.

We went about three miles beyond Moate and started off back. We had only got a short way when 'Sadie' stopped altogether, after making three or four weak explosions. We looked at the petrol tank and found it was bone dry, so put in another tin of petrol at once and started off again. Everything went well until we got well out of Moate. Then 'Sadie' began careering from one side of the road to the other, and I must say I was afeared it was going to be either the ditch or the hedge. But no, my Lady quietened her down and she was all right again soon. I felt I wanted to go miles and miles away and not bother about having to come back, just go on and on and on. We got back in time for tea and afterwards I went up to see her dad. When I came down, I found Dodo and Joan mowing the lawn and they told us we ought to take some exercise, so I started mowing and had my photo taken by Dodo and am sure must have cracked the camera. The others ran away and left Phyl and me to finish off the lawn. Then I started rolling while Phyl went on mowing. How nice it was to see her. She is able to do just anything: it doesn't matter what it is, she'll try, and nearly always does a thing, too. When we had finished, we took the machine down to the stable and put it away. Then we went up into the loft and had a look at some papers that were scattered about and belong to a Major Somebody, now long since dead. Then we sat and talked, and Phyl said I had quite enough kisses and that she wasn't going to have any more, so I said I was, and she ran away from me down the ladder and into the house. I didn't try to catch her because I was cross with her, although if I had used my sense it was only teasing. Well, I was just as grumpy as I could be, and hardly said a word at dinner. Afterwards, when I went into the drawing room, I found both Phyl and Joan. I got most fiendishly cross because I knew she had asked Joan to come in. Phyl asked me one or two questions which I answered in monosyllables, and tried to pay attention to Joan but failed hopelessly because I was simply wild. I couldn't help thinking how the precious minutes were going. Joan made some excuse and went out of the room.

Now, sweetheart, I must stop and take this to be posted or I shall be late. I had a letter from Mum today and she says she had a very dear letter from you, saying you were going to let the house and go away for some time. I wonder where you are going to. My Lady, I can't help telling you I do want a letter most terribly badly. Will you try and write one for me? It's just awful, this not knowing what's happening.

Oh! Phyl, I send you all the love a human being can have with this. God bless you, my own darling.

Your lover forever

27 June   *Got parcel with revolver in it. Tried new Browning pistol.*

TUESDAY 27 JUNE

Lady mine
I am just going to write a little tonight before I turn in, as it's my turn to be up early tomorrow. It has been a beastly day, raining nearly the whole time and as grey as grey; really, it doesn't help to make things better out here, and I think it might have a try. Oh! God, when will we get away from this cursed country? Fifteen solid weary months gone, and the best part of one's life. Well, I've one greatest blessing of my life to thank the war for. Phyl, your love is worth everything else I could have, and may I be spared to have it for many, many years of life on this earth. I am going on now where I left off this afternoon.

MONDAY 5 JUNE
After Joan had left, Phyl went on with knitting a pair of socks for me. She was sitting on the big chair by the fire. For what seemed an awful age I sat in the corner of the sofa. I said to myself, 'Don't be a sulky brute; talk to her', but I turned my eyes away as soon as she looked up at me. Then she asked me what

was the matter with me and God knows what I snapped out. Then I asked her why she had brought Joan into there. She said because she wanted to – it froze me and I felt all hard inside. Then we didn't speak for what seemed like another age: precious minutes, never to come back. The sensible part of me was getting stronger and I wanted to go to her. Then she said, 'Eric, come here', and looked at me. She asked me again and said, 'I'm sorry, Eric, it's my fault'. I couldn't stand it any longer and I went to her. I told her why I had been like that, and what a brute I felt when I found out she was only teasing me and she had intended having a jolly evening all together. Then the time flew by and I loved her. Her mum came in and said she was going to bed, and would I have a drink. I said I would like one very much, and so she got it for me. Then she went out and I was with my love again, but oh! my God, I didn't know then what had to come. The most unutterably miserable night I have ever had in my life and all because I was again a — fool. Just before we were going to say goodnight, Phyl teased me; I can't remember what she said. Thoughtless brute that I was, I told her that at times she almost seemed like a —. My God, how she recoiled from me. I knew I had stabbed the love she had for me and she hated me. Then when I tried to explain that I didn't mean what I said, she wouldn't hear a single word and she got up and was gone, and I had killed her love, and how I had hurt her. I don't know how long I stayed there with my face buried in my arms, and over and over again I prayed. The agony I went through then was hell. I knew how much her love meant to me then. I had killed the love with not thinking what I was saying.

I got up and went into the passage. The candle was burning there, so I could see my way, I managed to get to my room somehow, then I just gave way. How cruel she was, I had seen on my way upstairs. There on a stool were 'my' shoes, the ones that had never been left like that for one minute before. She couldn't even bear to take those with her, and I knew how Phyl hated me then. What a hell I went through that night. I lay awake for what seemed like hours and hours until I must have fallen asleep, praying to God to give me back the love that was worth much more than my own life to me. So ended the third day with my Lady, in the most awful misery for us both. Never shall I forget the horror that was written on that dear face after I had said that word. What a terrible lesson that was; God grant that I may never see her like that again.

WEDNESDAY 28 – AFTERNOON

Phyl, my darling, I got a letter today; thank you, dear, for writing. I began to think such horrible things had happened. I am so very glad your mum is keeping up so splendidly; she really is wonderfully brave about it all. Life would have meant more pain and suffering, except that he was with his dear ones. I wonder if my letters will be any help to you. I have sent a letter off each day. Isn't it really scandalous how people are treated at times in the service? They were heartless devils for muddling everything they attempted to do. Poor Eddie, how awful it must have been for him, especially when he did get back and found your dad gone.

And now, my Lady, I must take this across to the mess for the post. Will you give my very dear love to your mum, and please, dear, write and tell whether I can write to her or not.

My very fondest, deepest and best love is all for you, Phyl.

Your lover,

Eric

THURSDAY 29 JUNE

My Lady, the very dearest that ever lived

Here it is, night again, and I never sent any letter off today. I was so tired last night after sloshing about in the mud all day, so I went straight to bed, and I think if a thunderbolt had come it would not have wakened me. Today has been nice and fine, thank heaven, and this afternoon we had an equipment inspection, and afterwards I went through all the gun stores in one of my subsections. The whole thing took me from 2 till 4.30.

This evening I gave Tommy a little training in jumping. Up to tonight, he would never go over unless there was another horse in front of him. We started by bringing him quietly. Then we took him to a jump, bringing him over with a long rope. He went first shot, and continued to do so each time. Then we gave him a rest and put a saddle on and I tried him. He jumped awfully well first go, and after three or four more jumps I sent him back to his stable. He is looking fit now and is simply full of beans, although he is such a lazy little fellow at times. His coat is beautifully soft now. How many times I have sung 'The Old Grey Hills of Home' to him as we've gone along. It seems to fit in with the time of his walk so well. Sweetheart, I wonder if you and I will ever be able to go for long rides together in some faraway country, in the woods of Canada or New Zealand or South Africa. What heaven it would be to go out together and come back to our own little home when we liked. Will those happy days ever come? If only this war would end.

FRIDAY – 12.30 PM

Phyl, I shall have to send this as it is, because the Major and I are going to have a sail in 'the' boat we were over in on Sunday. By Jove, won't it be exciting. I hope it isn't too windy, though. We have got to ride there, as there is no train, so I must be off. I will try and write again tonight when I get back, but I must send this today, because I didn't send one at all yesterday.

Just all, all, all my dearest love to you, Phyl.

Forever, your Englishman

FRIDAY 30 JUNE

Sweetheart

Here I am, back again. I feel jolly sleepy after the long ride. The sail was rather a farce, owing to the heavy weather, or rather strong wind. The boat was not allowed to go outside the harbour so they took her into the middle of the dock and sank her there for us. It was awfully interesting, but not half as interesting as if we had actually gone outside into the open sea and dived. Somehow I thought it was rather too good a thing to ever come off, but it was beastly bad luck being stopped by the weather.

Phyl, I wonder how you and your dear mum are now. Have you been wanting your lover as badly as he has you? It's three long weeks since I got back, and seems like years. Phyl, will this business ever end and let me be free again? I think I will have done my share by the time it is over. I want to be sitting on the sofa in the drawing room with you and go to sleep there, instead of this beastly place separated from my Lady by miles and miles of sea and land.

SATURDAY AFTERNOON

My darling, I have just come over from the mess and I found this very dear wee note there for me. My Lady, how very glad your lover is that his letters are helping you. Phyl, I must tell you the honest truth about leave. The Colonel promised that he would let me go early to make up for the five months I had without one, and now it's all stopped. I really haven't any idea how long it's stopped for: perhaps for two weeks or a month or maybe for longer. I hope it will not be for two weeks even. How I wish I could tell you there is the smallest chance of one in sight, but there is not at present. Now I am going to start the 'fourth day with my Lady' – the most wonderful day of my life. First I felt the wretchedest being that ever lived, then the awful dread of uncertainty, then the feeling that my whole life was at stake, then a great happiness followed with confidence, and finally, heaven on earth, my Lady.

TUESDAY 6 JUNE

I woke at about 6 am. Was there a more wretched being living? What was I worth? Simply nothing. I was a noodle, a — fool. I had killed the love of the dearest, most wonderful woman; I had hurt her beyond all conception through the most utter — stupidity, and now I had got my deserts. I couldn't forget the thought of the awful loathing that I had seen in my Lady's face a few hours before.

Bed was unbearable, so I got up, hoping and hoping she would come down before breakfast so that I could speak to her alone. But there was no sign of her, so back I went upstairs, hoping I might meet her on the landing, but no. So down again to the dining room. I tried to read a newspaper, but every line seemed to say, 'You beast, you have hurt her most terribly.' Why don't I think properly and say what I mean? If only she would listen, I might be able to tell her it was not meant. If she wouldn't listen then I must go and leave her. I threw the paper down and went outside, down the garden, to think by myself. It was a lovely morning, but had it been pelting I shouldn't have cared, because I must go away, perhaps never to see her again. I must make her understand, how I prayed and prayed, and I grew calmer but the awful dread was still there. I went back into the dining room; the others were there but she had not come down. I must try and be cheerful but it is hard when one is feeling worse than hopeless. Then she came in. I pulled her chair out for her as I always did, there was a kind of 'Thank you' said, and my heart sank.

Afterwards, they all went out except Buzz, and he asked me what was the matter with Phyllis. I had to tell him I didn't know. We went into the passage and towards the hall door. As I got near the window, Phyl came from the hall. It was my only chance. 'Phyl, may I speak to you,' I said, very quietly. 'Of course you may,' she said, still in that same voice. We went into the drawing room. What was I to say, how could I make her understand? 'I want to speak to you about last night,' I said. 'Oh! don't, you'd only make it worse.' I said, 'I must, Phyl. I didn't mean that word. Oh! I didn't, I didn't.' The agony I felt was too much to bear, and I don't know what happened then, until I heard her say, 'Eric, your Lady was a beast last night.' And I found my head against her breast and her arms around me. Oh! Thank God, she had listened. I was happy now, because she had given me back her love.

After a little while we thought of what we might do, I wanted to go away and not come back till late, so that I could be alone with her. What a terrible lesson I had learnt, and how terribly dear her love was to me. So we decided to go to St Mark's in the car and take our lunch with us. While Phyl was getting the food ready, I was to go up and see her dad.

So off I went in high spirits and thought he looked considerably brighter. We had a chat about the news and then he said to me, 'Eric, I want to talk to you about Phyllis.' I listened very carefully. He said, 'I don't think it's right or fair to either you or Phyllis that you two should go on meeting as you do at present and being together. It is not fair to Phyllis to have herself made food for the scandal of the people round here, nor is it fair to her mother or the others. Now, Eric, I blame myself entirely for anything that has happened up to now, because I should have stopped you coming here at first, if I had not wanted this to happen. But, lad, I took a great fancy for you at the beginning, and now it is too late to do anything even if I would. Now I want you to settle between you what you are going to do: are you going to be engaged to each other, or let it be just as it was before you met.' How my heart sank and I felt wretched. Only the night before we had been talking about marriage and Phyl had said, 'I don't think I ever will marry.' Only a few minutes before, I had got her love back after it had been taken away from me for a whole long night, and now I must ask her this, ask her to become my wife some day. How hopeless my chance seemed. And I said, 'Phyllis and I never gave being engaged a thought. It has never troubled either of us what others thought. But I do see now that it is not right to go on as we are, for the sake of you both and the others. I will tell Phyllis what you say and ask her, but she has very decided opinions of her own about marriage and she doesn't believe in it.'

'I am very surprised indeed to hear what you say, Eric. Of course, I knew she had all sorts of sentimental stage ideas in her head, but I didn't know how much her mind was biased by them. I always objected to her doing this public singing because I knew it might cause silly ideas to get into her head. Now, Eric, I don't want to force you either way; you can please yourself which you do, and I know you'll understand, I'm doing it for the best. I

211

don't know whether you are well off or not; if you are not, then I expect it will be many years before you can provide a home like this for your wife. I have never wished to marry either of my girls to a rich man: it's more a curse than a blessing. I don't mind whether they live in a palace or a cottage as long as they can keep themselves respectable and have a good husband to look after them and protect them. I know you would be that, because you are a level-headed lad, and an honest fellow, I know.'

I took his hand – that poor hand, wasted away to skin and bone – in both mine and knelt beside the bed; a great big lump was in my throat. To hear his deep-down thoughts was wonderful and I loved him dearly and kissed his hand. 'Oh!' I said, 'thank you for what you've said. I would be very very good to her; I would take care of her with my life.' Then that dear man said, 'Eric, lad, I love you; take care of my little girl when I'm gone.' 'You're not going yet,' I said. 'Yes, lad, I am. I shall not last much longer, thank God. I have only lived for my wife and the kids, but it's been torture. Go now, lad, and tell her all about it.' 'Will you be glad if she says yes?' 'I will, lad, indeed I will, because I know you're an honest, good lad. Come, let me kiss you, and then go.' He kissed me on the brow and then I left him, that brave, brave man who should have been a soldier. The torture he must have suffered, and yet hardly a murmur. Why should he be stricken with an illness like that? I loved him dearly, he was so very kind and he loved me.

I went downstairs feeling unhappy, because I thought Phyl would not consent to us being engaged and have it shouted about. But if she wouldn't, I knew what hell life would be without her. Why can't two people love one another without everybody having to know and talk about it. I went down to the garage and got 'Sadie' ready, feeling all the time that what I had to tell my sweetheart would spoil our day and perhaps be the last time I would be with her forever, on this earth. Then I went back into the house and collected rugs and coats and then Phyl came along with the food. She was so happy, and looked so very dear; how cruel it seemed to make her feel miserable again, but it had to be done. Well, I would not tell her until I had to.

There now, sweetheart, I must stop, and take this to the post. Bye-bye for the present, my own darling,
Your lover

My darling
Sweetheart, I'm afraid this won't be very long because I have barely an hour and it takes me ages to write to you. I suddenly find myself miles and miles away, thinking about what you are doing or something we have done together. We all felt pretty rotten last night; I think it must have been a touch of the sun. It was baking hot in the afternoon.

Oh! Lady mine, I have got a dear long letter from you today. You were not certain as to whether it would get to me or not for some time. Yes, I heard a rumour that only postcards were to be written from the front after 1 July. I was frightened it might be true, as the horrid rumours so often are – it would have been awful. This last letter has come quickly and arrived here this morning in just over two days. Forgive me for writing as I did; I imagined all sorts of dreadful things were happening to you and yours. How very wonderfully dear your letters are to me. Sweetheart, you simply can't tell how glad I am that my letters have helped you; I wish I could go on writing every day, but I will write to you whenever I possibly can. I am very glad to hear about your mum – she is a dear brave lady. You are all so wonderful, and the more I see of you, the more I thank God for bringing me to Athlone.

This morning and afternoon we have been practising for the horse-jumping competition, which is coming off on Friday. I managed to get Tommy over two jumps after a lot of trouble; he is a stubborn little devil, though.

And now, I've got to go. Bye-bye, love of mine, for a little while.
Your own Englishman

Lady mine

I am so sleepy tonight; what shall I talk to you about? When will the day come for me to be able to say, 'There, sweetheart, I've done my bit for my country and for my Lady.' Yes, it is a happy thought that I am out here to protect you and yours against these brutes, beastly as it is out here, in every sense of the word. What I would give for it all to be over and done with, that I might start my work for my Lady. Oh! I pray that our men down south may beat the devils to their knees, and so they may do as they have been done by. The news seems good tonight – good luck to them; we shall do something to help them soon.

It is much the best thing you can do to go away from your house. It will do you all no end of good, but why go away to the wild west? You ought to go to Trehaddur Bay near Holyhead. If you go to the same place as you used to go, it will only bring back memories and make you sad, but you know best, and I don't know the west at all.

I am not going to write about 'The Five Days' tonight. But how very dear it has been, going all through it again, and I have put it down as I felt then at the time. How do you like my new writing paper? I bought it in D— [Dunkirk] the last time I was there. Has anyone said anything to you about our engagement? I told Mum she could tell anyone she liked about it, and, Phyl, I often feel so happy about it that I want to write and tell everybody. It is wonderful to think of my own dearest lady.

Night-night now, Phyl. I love you for all time,

Eric

WEDNESDAY 5 JULY

My Lady

This afternoon I went into a place [Wormhout] near here with Wenley, Miller and Burrows. We had some tea there, and then I went to buy some lace for you, but I couldn't get any that I liked very much so I'm going to wait until I go in again. They make all kinds of lace. One is very fine and usually forms a narrow border, another is less fine and is to make up into collars, and another is the brocade kind: it is lovely and is made for the top of the bodice. The only one they had of this last kind was not dainty enough for my liking.

Now I must go on with 'The Five Days with My Lady'.

TUESDAY 6 JUNE

We put all the grub in the back of the car. Then I started 'Sadie' and off we went. 'Sadie' was a bit stupid at first but went all right after we had got clear of all the corners and on the road to Glassan. We had got about half a mile along the road when it started to rain in sheets, so we stopped and put up the hood. By the time we had done that, it had stopped. It was beautifully fine by now, and kept so, all the way. We went by the lower road and Phyl took the corner just out of Glassan at a fine pace; thank heaven, there was nothing in the way. We nearly ran over a silly old dog which was too lazy to get out of the way: right bang in the middle of the road and it stayed there until we were about two yards from it. Then it jumped up and bolted. Then we came to the entrance to St Mark's. How pretty it looked, with all the trees fully out and everywhere covered in buttercups. We had to go through three gates, then down a long drive, very overgrown with weeds.

We drew up at the back of the house. The view is lovely from there; you look right out over the lake and can see all the islands dotted about. The house is absolutely in ruins – what a shame it seems; it is such a lovely spot, just fitting for the happiness I found there. Although when I got there I was feeling far from happy. Then Phyl and I walked down the steps. The grass was very long and damp. How wonderful it all seemed to be there alone with her – a regular fairyland. We wandered about while she told me how they had camped out there and about the white lady and fairy cobbler who sits at the top of a flight of stone steps gazing down, and about the haunted tree. Also how her dad fired into the bushes one night when he heard noises in them.

We wandered down to the boathouse and onto the jetty, where they used to bathe from, and we found a place where we could have lunch. The sun was lovely and everything seemed to be so happy; even the birds sang extra hard. Phyl was happy, I think, too, but her lover felt very sad because of what he had to tell her in a very short while. And all the loveliness and happiness of the place seemed to just mock me, all the time.

After I had spread out the rugs, Phyl brought out the things for lunch. First came a cloth, then plates, glasses, knives and forks. By Jove, it was lovely: a daydream realised, and soon I got baked in the sun. When we had finished eating, I cleared the things away. Then I lay down beside my Lady and so the moments went on while we loved one another, and then I had to tell her. I told her what her dad had said and that I had promised to ask her whether she was willing to be engaged to me or not. Suddenly she said, 'Oh! Eric, I can't, I can't!' I thought of how I would have to go away and leave her altogether; I thought of what hell it would be like out there. I tried hard to let her make her own decision, but I couldn't help saying how much it would mean to me, because her love means everything to her lover. Then I held my breath for her to say which it was to be. I wonder what the little Peggy Whitethroat thought of it all, as she hopped from branch to branch and chirped away. Suddenly – oh! God, my ears could hardly believe it – she said, 'Yes, yes, yes, I will.' Sweetheart, did ever a man love a woman as I loved you then? I was so very, very happy. We talked of what it meant, and found that apart from it being yelled from the housetops, it would not make any difference to us both. Yet somehow, when I look back, it has made a great difference to me. How the time flew while I held my Lady close and kissed her, trying to pour out all the pent-up love that I felt in me.

I must stop, Phyl, it's post-time – I don't think I shall have time to reread it all, as it is.

Bye-bye, sweetheart mine forever,

Your lover

Oh! my darling

How very terribly your lover longs to be with you now. This letter that I have got this afternoon is the very saddest I have ever had, and I know what utter misery you felt when you wrote it. You must try to be the brave lady you have always been, the dearest and best in all the world. Sweetheart, I thought of what would happen to you if your dear dad did die after I had that talk with him about you: he told me how you would be. I thought of how you had been brought up by the side of that lovely river and lake with the motor boat and car, and I knew how very hard it would be for you when he was gone. Why haven't I tons of money to help you with now, instead of having practically nothing, as I have at present?

Sweetheart, what are you doing in connection with the house-letting? I suppose you are advertising in papers; don't forget, there are any number of people in England who would jump at a house like yours. You must not lose heart yet, and you must remember it is a bad time for letting, on account of the war. The best thing you can do is to take your mum to the seaside for two weeks, or a month if possible. Try and get her to go out as much as possible, for walks or short rides in the car, and love her more than you have ever done. Lady mine, there is no need at all to talk about not having been allowed to find your feet – you've done that long ago. All the same, it is a great pity that you were not allowed to make more use of your singing before. Think what it would be like to be singing to hundreds of people and holding them till after the last note had been played, before the whole place rocked with clapping.

It must be dreadfully hard when you think of those happy days that are gone. Your dad knew the lake like a book. How I would have loved to have gone with him in the motor boat up the lake. But you are going to be very happy in the future, and your mum will be too, when she sees that all her children are happy.

Yesterday we were all in the highest of spirits because we

217

thought we were going south, but also we were all down in the dumps by bedtime. I do wish they would take us away from up here; we have been kept here far too long as it is and yet there seems to be no chance of going now – it is rotten luck. The jumping took place in the afternoon and was not good on the whole. As usual, the whole competition was altered at the last minute and taken out of our hands.

It's nearly post-time now. So bye-bye, and remember always how very dearly your Englishman loves his Lady.

SUNDAY 9 JULY

My darling

I got another letter today, and how it cheered your lover up. You said I could write to your mum, so I did so at once. Why should you be ashamed of that sad, sad letter; didn't you promise to write just as you felt? Please tell me all your troubles, so that I may share them with, and for, the one Lady in the world. I know you are not a coward; you can never be that to me. No human being could stand the awful torment you have been through without giving way to it a little bit. How it made your lover love you when he thought that you had poured out your own thoughts to him. Remember our family motto: 'Prepared for good or bad'. Your joys are my joys, and your sorrows, mine.

MONDAY 10 JULY

We were out all morning on a drill order, doing a march round the roads. Everything went well until we were about three-quarters of a mile from home. Then three of my teams had to stop, with something wrong with the harness in each case. Some managed to catch up, but some came in some distance behind. The major made sarcastic remarks to Miller about it.

I'll write a bit about our 'Five Days':

Everything was changed by the little word 'yes', because I was so very happy I hadn't to go away. What a dreadful nightmare seemed to have passed, and I had wakened to find the lady I had loved so dearly still far more dear. So dear that I felt and knew she never could be loved enough, and I was her lover, her slave, her knight for always and for always. I wondered what the little Peggy Whitethroat thought of the whole affair; she kept chirping away in a tree quite close to us. All the other birds seemed glad and the whole place seemed far more beautiful than it had done before.

But the time flew away: teatime passed – my Lady and I did not think of that – and seven o'clock drew nearer and nearer. Those precious minutes, they seemed like seconds. It was 6.30 – heavens, could we get back in half an hour? We collected all the things and ran off, away from that happy spot, away from the lake and the lovely trees. I wonder when I shall see it again? I hope it won't be very long before I shall be there with the lady I love with all my heart and soul.

'Sadie' had waited patiently in front of the house. She must have wondered what a very long time we were, and yet to me it seemed only a few short minutes. I started her up after we had lowered the hood, and then came the turning business. It was soon done, though, and away we went, up the drive. 'Sadie' seemed worried, and stopped twice on the hill, so I got out and helped her by pushing. We soon left dear old St Mark's behind, and charged along the road for home.

Two officers from another Battery have just been here, and so I had to stop, confound them. I shall have to stop now, sweetheart.

Your Englishman

[This entry from Eric's diary completes the story of their five days together.]

7 June

Up at 7.30. Phyl's dad very ill. Phyl, Buzz and I went to meet Eddie coming by the mail. Had a long talk with Eddie. Packed my bag. Phyl and I went to the motor-garage, then broke the sixpence. After lunch, we sat together in the drawing room. She doesn't want an engagement ring but the other will have to be made of rubies and sapphires set in silver or platinum, the rubies to take the shape of a rose. Promised to bathe my eyes.

TUESDAY 11 JULY 1916

Sweetheart
Just a line to tell you not to expect a letter for a few days. I will write as soon as ever I possibly can. Bye-bye for the present, my own darling,
   Your Englishman

WEDNESDAY 12 JULY
FIELD SERVICE POSTCARD, POSTED 14 JULY

I am quite well.
Letter follows at first opportunity.
I have received a letter from you lately.

FRIDAY 14 JULY

Oh! You dear, dear lady mine
I got a letter miles long last night and I want to simply kiss you

220

and kiss you away for it. I can't thank you enough for it, sweetheart. I hadn't a moment to sit down and write, and even now it's 12.30. We are back in the same part as we were in last August, and are living in a cellar. I have been up at the OS every day since we came here, and I'm feeling dead sleepy tonight. I wish I could tell you the whys and wherefores of what has really happened lately, but I can't, so news is practically nil. As usual, we only got about two-thirds of our full time out, this time.

Phyl, I have already dozed off twice since I started this. Will you please forgive your lover if he goes to bed? He's so tired. This is a rotten place; we live in one small cramped-up place and I can never get away by myself to write.

Night-night, dear, dear lady.

Your very tired Englishman

11 July   *Marched to new wagon line outside Poperinge. Got motor buses up here just in front of Ramparts Menen gates.*

SATURDAY 15 JULY

Phyl, sweetheart

It is now twelve midnight: isn't it awful, starting to write now? I have been down at the wagon line all day, and then, when I got back, I had to do several jobs. The mail has only come in a few minutes ago. I got a wee note from Mum and she says she got a letter from you. She says, 'But from what she says, she does not see her way to coming over to us when you get your next leave, so of course, love, you must do the same as before. Would you rather go right through to Athlone?' I wonder when that next leave is going to come, and what you will be doing by then. But isn't my mum a dear, always thinking of what I would like to do. But it may be a long time before I do get my leave, and perhaps by then your mum would come over to my home with you. I do so want her to meet my mum and dad. If only this business

221

would show signs of ending it would help, but I can't see any.

I can't finish off 'June 6' at present. You will have to forgive your Englishman if his letters don't come so often now. But after we have settled down properly I may get more time – there is always an awful lot of work to do for some days after we come into action.

Perhaps your plan about staying on for the summer is the best for your mum after all, and she is so fond of the garden. Buzz's house in the garden is a cosy place; I was down there with him on the Sunday evening. I wonder which corner you sat in. If you are going to make use of your singing, you will have to be in Dublin for that.

Did I tell you we have a new addition to the family here, in the form of a small puppy. He is a fine little joker and quite a nice little mongrel, something like a foxhound but lighter in colour. He is called Trousers!

Have you heard from Eddie again, and if so, is he back in England? I know you will tell me just everything that happens. Sweetheart, this is a rotten kind of letter, not half the kind I want to write to you. I must stop now, Phyl.

Bye-bye, dear lady mine. Always and always,
Your Englishman

TUESDAY 18 JULY

My Lady

I got another lovely long letter last night and I went straight to bed and read it. I am so very proud of my Lady because she has found the way out of a big difficulty. I hope your mum can bear perfect strangers in the house. My Lady thought of it and it only proves to me that she is the wisest lady God ever made. Has this Major Savage come to the barracks recently? I hope they are really nice people, because although you will not be actually with them all the time, you are bound to see an awful lot of them. How awfully sad for them, losing their only son.

Sweetheart, the idea of the houseboat is the very loveliest

idea in my mind. How I would love to spend my leave like that with you, just you and I alone in the bay in St Mark's. Please tell me all about the boat, what it is like inside and outside and how many rooms there are.

And now, about the lace! If I get the edging for you, what length do you want it? Would two yards be sufficient? I shall have to wait until we go out again, now. And now, madame, about my eyes and yours. This letter has worried me, because you said about me giving this beastly conjunctivitis to you. So I asked the doctor about it, and he said mine was not at all contagious, so I hope I haven't given it to you. My eyes here are very bad, and the doctor has written away about me. He has suggested I undergo a treatment for them, as he considered they were getting worse. But the awful part about it is, I shall not be allowed to read or write. I really don't know how long I could go on for like that.

I go up to the infantry tonight. It's a lively job here. Bye-bye, and God bless you.

Your lover

FRIDAY 21 JULY

My very, very own darling

Phyl, what a dear letter this is that I have got today. I have been down to the wagon line today, and I got it while I was there. It took me a lovely long time to read, and I shall read it over and over again. I can see you are worrying about what your dad said to me about your having got 'stage ideas' into your head. By it, he evidently meant that you had got hold of romantic ideas: at least, I took it to mean that. I really am beginning to dread writing letters when I have anything hard to explain to you. I do wish I could be with you to tell you properly and see that you understood.

Now listen, lady mine. I'm going to hospital tonight about my eyes. I don't know how long I shall be there, and what I shall or shall not have to do there, but I will try and write as much as

I possibly can. I am also trying to get a transfer to the anti-aircraft corps. I don't know whether the Major will allow me to go, but I'm going to speak to him about it. I think it's more in my line than this game. At any rate, one has more of a command – I mean, the guns are always under one's own control.

Now, sweetheart, I must finish off because I have got to start off in a few minutes now.

Bye-bye, Phyl, for the present. I send just all, all my love to you, you wonderfully dear lady.

Eric

SUNDAY 23 JULY

Sweetheart

Here I am in hospital again. This place – 12 Casualty Clearing Station, Hazebrouck – is solely for officers, and there are quite a decent lot here. But I feel an awful fraud, having so little wrong with me, but at the same time I do want to get this thing put right once and for all. One feels very much like a boy at school, because there are all sorts of regulations and rules to obey. For instance, we all have to be in bed at 9.30 pm. Then the water for washing and shaving comes at 6 am, and you have to get up then, but you can get back to bed again, and breakfast comes in at 8 am.

Here, we are in a house on one of the main streets. There is another gunner in my ward, and four others: three infantrymen and one engineer. One of the infantrymen talks from the moment he wakes up till he goes to sleep again at night – luckily, he's a most amusing chap.

MONDAY MORNING

One man who is going away today found some stinging nettles in his bed, and someone made him an apple-pie bed and tied tight knots in his pyjamas. Well, I must go to see the eye man in a minute or two. I wonder what he will do. I hope to goodness he can put an end to the whole business. I will let you know what is going to happen, and then I will answer that dear, long letter I got on Friday.

MONDAY AFTERNOON
I can hardly see what I am writing, as he dropped some beastly stuff into my eyes and told me to come back in half an hour, and when I returned, he put some more drops in. He said I was to go to him tomorrow, and he would see if glasses would help me at all. I'm quite sure they won't – it's not the sight, it's the lids, in my mind. Sweetheart, I don't know whether you can read this. The whole lot is blurred, so I'm going to stop.

Bye-bye, my own very dear lady,
Your lover

MONDAY 24 JULY

Phyl
Here I am, sitting writing this in the window of this place; it faces right onto one of the main streets of the town. It is quite busy at present with all sorts of traffic; I think the majority is military, though. This afternoon I went into town and had my hair cut. The blurredness has passed off now, but my eyes feel awfully sore and the pupils are fearfully large.

I feel as homesick as I can be. I think it's seeing decent people about. When we're in action, we see nobody that reminds us of those at home. Oh! Phyl, why can't this ghastly game end? Whatever we do seems to go wrong somewhere.

Tell me, how are the Savages getting on: is everything running smoothly? Phyl, how very often I go back and try to live the happy times I have spent with you over again. But there is one thing that comes to me now more than anything else and that is that afternoon at St Mark's. It was heaven, just heaven, and it was my Lady that made it so.

I have just been round to the eye man. He has given me a prescription for a pair of glasses which I use for long-distance work. He said there was no need to use them when I was using the telescope or glasses, so I told him I used one or the other for all observing and that they would therefore be practically useless. Well, I will try them and see if they do any good. At any rate, it is not contagious, so what have you to say about those dear lovely eyes of yours? Just you be quite certain they are quite all right, because my Lady has not to have red-rimmed eyes, even if her lover has.

Well now, I shall most probably go back tomorrow. There are all sorts of rumours here that we are moving. I wonder if it's true. At any rate, I want to be back if we are. Now, my darling, I'm sending something with this and the other DA, which I am posting today. I send just all my love of every kind. I chose it out of a whole crowd and yet it isn't nearly half-lovely enough for my Lady, but it was the nicest I could find.

Bye-bye now, sweetheart.

Your lover

---

25 July   *Canadian with shell-shock in ward today, awful.*
Bought lace collar for Phyl, finished letter to her
and sent lace. Eye man said I had to have a pair
of glasses for long-distance work.

THURSDAY 27 JULY

Lady mine

Here I am, back at the Battery. There were two letters from you waiting for me. We are out again – for how long, we don't know, and where we shall go, we don't know. Things are very unsettled now, and everybody gets excited. I hope to goodness this is the big push, and something is going to bring the end more in sight. I didn't get here until about 8.30 last night, as I had a ride of about eight miles. The others got here in the afternoon.

Oh ! Lady mine, you are so very dear to your lover in these letters. Each one that comes has something in it which makes me tremble all over because I love you so much. I am awfully glad the Savages are nice, and I do hope they will go on being so. They must feel most dreadfully the death of their son – was he really only seventeen? It really is scandalous that they allow kids of that age to go in for anything of that kind, because they can't possibly be up to all the tricks of the trade that a man is. Phyl, I got the dearest letter from your mum in answer to my last two to her. I'm glad she goes into the garden a lot; fresh air will help her so very much.

The Major has been telling us about this Battery's history. It was out in India before the South African war – in fact, it went from there to South Africa. The whole brigade was right through the Siege of Ladysmith, and particularly distinguished themselves the day before the siege started. Then it was in Picton's brigade, I believe, at Waterloo.

What a funny thing it was that you opened the book of the Army List. The last time I looked, I was about thirty-sixth, but that was for Jan this year, so I must now be about forty-first. Also, I have to be recommended again, and the Colonel who did so last time has left us, so altogether it still seems a long way off. Why the dickens won't this — thing finish altogether. I get that fed up.

FRIDAY MORNING
I am just waiting for my breakfast. As I am on duty today, I go out at 9 am on exercise for about an hour. Then the horses are watered. There is no parade until 11.30 stables, but all the officers attend at the office and may be there until time for stables.

Bye-bye now, lady mine. All my love to you forever,
Your Englishman

Phyl

It's a simply glorious morning. I'm sitting out in the field in front of our farm [at Droogland near Houtkerque aerodrome] with my back against an apple tree. There are a whole crowd of our planes buzzing about overhead, and little wee spiders occasionally walk over the page as I write. Burrows and Miller are sitting close by, writing letters as well. The night before last, one of the planes got lost owing to the ground mist. It was getting late, too, and he needed petrol. He had to land somewhere, so came down in this field. Luckily he only damaged his machine slightly. It was an awful shame he didn't know he was so close to home. However, he – this observer – came into the mess with us and had a talk. Funnily enough, the observer comes from quite near home, and I have seen him somewhere in Liverpool before the war: he recognised me, too. Wenley and I went to dinner with them last night and I met another man, who told me my friend Colin was killed – he was a really decent fellow. The sooner this war is over the better; so very many good people seem to be going now, and the worst of it is, there are hundreds, thousands more that will have to go before it's all over. I have just been looking through the casualty lists.

Now, about the letters. I wonder if you got the letter I had written to your dad the night before I got your letter, telling me he had died. I could not stop it because it had gone during the morning. I wrote telling him how pleased Mum and Dad were about our engagement. I wrote to you that night. I had to send my servant with it, as I missed the man taking the letters. It must have gone astray, but my servant was sure he had posted it. What did you think of your lover for not writing at once when he heard? And if you didn't get this first letter, you'd think I took mighty little interest in the news. I was trying to draw your attention away from your dad's death, if only for a short time, so I gradually said less and less about it. You also say, 'By the way, I don't quite see why it should have been up to you to find a way out of our difficulties, or that there is anything to be proud of in the way I have found.' It was up to me to try and help you, and there was a lot to be proud of too: it was my Lady that thought of the way out. I just want to have you with me, to try and chase away the 'catty part' with all my might and love.

Just before we went into action last time I had to sort out my surplus kit and had the old soft cap thrown away. I had kept the badge from it, and was sending it to my Lady, but I am still waiting for a box for it. I must admit, the eyes are feeling much better since I came back from hospital, and yes, thank you, lady mine, the Vaseline does make them easier to open in the morning. Yes, the pair of socks was in the parcel you sent. Surely I thanked you for them. If not, I do thank you very much indeed. All yours fit me beautifully – other people's are always too large.

And now I must stop, as it's getting near post time. Just every atom of my love to you, darling, from your lover.

Tuesday 1 August
Examined by Base Censor, Posted 6 August

Sweetheart
I got a letter today posted on Saturday – that *is* quick. I wish they all came as quickly as that. I don't know when this will reach you because the last post went today from this place, and heaven only knows when the next one will be sent.

I went to bed on Sunday night and stayed there until this afternoon at 8 pm. I had an awful night on Sunday, or rather at 2 am Monday morning. I started by having a most awful stomach-ache and then was violently sick. Even cold water would not stay down, and of course, I was left just like a limp rag. The doctor said he thought it was either the water here or the heat. Beavis is down with the same thing and has been sent off to hospital tonight.

3 August   *Up at 5.30. Train journey from Pop. took from*
             1 to 7.45 pm. When we arrived at Doullens we
             had dinner in a restaurant. Rode into this place,
             Louvencourt, slept in a very dingy house.

SATURDAY 5 AUGUST

Sweetheart, it's nearly four days since I started this letter. Well, I was afraid I wouldn't have a chance of sending it to you for some time. I started this off a long way off from where I am now. The country is lovely here, plenty of low hills about, and lots of trees and woods. The roads are fiendishly dusty. Burrows and I went for a short ride on bikes last night, and came back white from head to foot. It's simply glorious weather. We have all had our hair clipped short on account of the heat and look just like Boche. The horses are quite fit. Phyl, there's an absolutely lovely little stream not very far away from this place. Burrows and I went there last night. I thought what a very dear thing it would be to be in a canoe with my Lady on it. The trees hang right over, and meet, and the banks are covered in thick bushes and hazel saplings. It is only quite narrow – just about room for two canoes to pass. It is a real chalk stream and as clear as crystal. Well, perhaps we'll come and see it together sometime.

I got a note from Mum, saying I had said that she might not care for me to come to Athlone, but she says I can come any time I want, so that even if you can't come to my home, next leave I get I might be able to come to yours again. It would be just awful going home on leave and knowing all the time that I would have to come back again out here without even seeing you for a minute. I am very glad you like the lace, Phyl. I wish I could be with you to be 'thanked properly'. I wonder when a letter is going to come. I'm just longing for one.

Just all my real, real love,

Your Englishman

Phyl

I got the first letter I have had for a whole long week. I have been wanting one so very badly, because I haven't been able to write. We have been on the move such a lot. Sweetheart, this letter was written on the thirty-first, and I have only got it today – they are taking an awfully long time, and I do wish they wouldn't.

Yes, you told me about Buzz going to Portlick. How lovely it must be there now. He keeps the larder supplied. I wouldn't mind being able to help him to shoot rabbits and fowl. I'm getting rather tired of this big game hunting. I only hope to God that the 'game' are still more tired of it.

Phyl, your idea about the houseboat would have been nice. It's just the holiday Mum and Dad would love, and the boys would go nearly mad with delight. Oh! I don't think there could be a nicer holiday than that. I know what an absolutely glorious time I had up at Windermere before this cursed war started. Five of us from the university had a houseboat up there, and we did have a fine time.

There is a continuous roar of fire going on all the time to the south. We hear it in the distance at present. The flies here are awful; there are millions and millions of them, and they persist in crawling over my head and make me simply wild because they tickle so! I have got my glasses: a pair of rimless ones, just like Dad's. They are as light as a feather, but all the same I hate the — things. I shall have a chance of testing them now, soon, I think. There are some lovely roses round here, Phyl, but I can't find one real Lancashire rose for you. I have been on the watch since I left hospital for one. They are all either pink ones or tea roses, or else ramblers. We are all getting quite used to sleeping on stone floors and brick floors again. At present, four of us – Wenley, Miller, Burrows and myself – sleep in one large room here, on a brick floor. But it is a treat to see some country which is more or less hilly. Rudkin, our adjutant, spoke to me about my second star a few days after I got back from hospital. He said he

231

was going to get the Colonel to recommend me again for it. I do hope he does – why, Buckley, who came from Athlone with me, has had his nearly six months, but of course, he is a temporary and I'm not. I was an ass to be an SR. We have another man as captain now. He was in charge of the school when we were there. Burrows was, of course, only acting captain, and is now senior sub. again. The other man, Hog, is quite young too.

And now it's high time I went to stables. You dear lady mine, your lover sends just every morsel of his love to you, for always,

Your Englishman

7 August   *Up at 5.30 am. Moved off from Louvencourt at 7.40 to Bertrancourt. Searched for billets. Four sleeping in one room on the floor. Lots of shelling going on down south.*

WEDNESDAY 9 AUGUST

Lady mine

It has been a scorcher today, and the dust on the roads is something awful. I seem to have done nothing but water horses all day. We have to go four times a day during this hot weather and it is a mile and a quarter to the water from here: that means nearly an hour each time we go. Wenley and I are taking duty turn about here, at present, as the other two are busy elsewhere, digging. There are innumerable bugs of all kinds, sorts and description flying about me while I am writing here in the mess, a room in a farmhouse [at Bertrancourt] They come in in droves, being evidently attracted by the lamp.

It's a lovely night. How I wish I was with you, just walking round the garden. I'd just want to be by you, close to you, with your hand in mine. Has the new doctor come yet, and if so, does he want a house? Did you finally decide where you would go if you did let your house? Well, I must go round the gees and then to bed.

It has been cooler today, so this afternoon I rode up to the place where Burrows and Miller are. I got back about an hour ago and am fairly sweating now.

At long last, I got letters from home. Dad is taking the boys down to stay with one of the uncles. Mum doesn't say whether she and Dad are going away or not. Last night I think I must have wakened up sixty times. Bradley, my servant, had not arranged the things in my valise (which I use as a mattress) nicely, and the bumps came all in the wrong places. With lying on a brick floor, it is rather necessary to have them in the right ones, too!

You are a dear lady to think about the books for me. I brought back some of my old notebooks and engineering books with me off leave, and I haven't tackled them yet. We have been shifted about so much since I came back, and last rest, I spent all my spare time writing.

How is 'Sadie' going now, and how did the soldiers varnish your boat? Do you go for any rows? I wish I was there to take you. It's jolly near post time and I want to send a letter, however short it is, tonight.

Bye-bye now, sweetheart, always your Eric

10 August   Went to gun position between Mailly Maillet and Vitremont.

Saturday 12 August

My own dear lady
I seem to be much, much further away from my Lady now, and the letters are few and far between. But then, you have got the Savages to look after now, and your mum, so I must try and be satisfied, but, lady mine, it's not an easy thing. We are not sure what is going to happen at present – first we hear one thing and then another.

I got a letter; I was so very, very glad when I saw it there for me. I do pity you if you are having it as hot as we are here. At present, I'm as hot as can be. Beavis came back last night and is at present lying exhausted on the bed.

Phyl, do you mean in this letter that you can't get any petrol at all? I knew it was pretty bad, but I thought you could get a certain small allowance at any time by putting in for it. If it is not so, it will mean that you might just as well not have the car at all. Really, although I can understand how absolutely enormous the supply for the army must be, still, seeing the awful waste that goes on out here, I can't help thinking the supply necessary could be cut down with careful using. None of the lorries ever think of stopping their engines when they are in a line.

AFTER TEA

I feel more stewed up than ever now. Thank heaven I'm not in the infantry; it must be absolute — marching this weather, especially on these roads, here, where the dust is simply terrible. On Thursday night, I had dinner with Buckley. It was awfully nice; we had it just outside his tent in an orchard. He is living here at his wagon line by himself. We talked about nearly everything under the sun, starting with Athlone and all that happened to us there, and finishing up with what was going to happen out here and the people out here. Oh! Phyl, it is nice to find someone out here who I can talk to about Athlone. It always seems the very dearest place in all the world. Hog went today to command the Battery that Buckley belongs to, so we are the same family as before once again.

SUNDAY MORNING

I have just come back from church [at Bertrancourt]; the padre gave us one of the best sermons I have ever heard. He is absolutely splendid with the men – no high-flown language, just simple and straightforward. The padre was talking about 'God is love' this morning, and I knew I loved you with all my heart and soul.

It's simply lovely now, just a cool wind and not too hot. I am sitting out in the little orchard and kitchen garden outside our mess. The Major is lying on the grass about two yards away. What lovely country this is, and how awfully glad we all are to get out of that other ghastly place. The flies in the house are awful, but it's quite free out here. The old woman was telling me that they grow all their vegetables in this little garden, and this year she complains of a lot of stuff having been damaged by the soldiers. There are strawberries, cabbages, potatoes, peas, turnips, onions, gooseberries and apples, with plants of stock dotted here and there and grass all over the place. Surrounding the garden on three sides are the 21st Battery horse lines, and ours are next to them. There are any quantity of apples about, but they are all cider apples and taste just like wood.

I sent the badge off on Friday night; it went by letter post. I hope it arrives safely. Did you see any of the racing the other day? Don't they start miles away, up the lake, and finish somewhere near St Mark's? It must be fine, yacht racing and motor-boat racing. I have always wanted to do some, but never have had the chance.

Bye-bye now, lady mine. For always,

Your Englishman

WEDNESDAY 16TH AUGUST
POSTED 17 AUGUST, ARRIVED ATHLONE 20 AUGUST

My Lady

What a lot of news I could tell you, if only I was allowed, but we have got stricter orders still about censorship now, and so I must keep my mouth shut, I suppose. I don't know what has happened to my letters. I get practically none now from anyone. Miller gets frantic if he doesn't get one for three days, but heavens, I've gone four already this time, and I hadn't one for a whole long week when we first came here, and when I do get them they are days old.

There are five of us sleeping in one room at present. We are packed rather like sardines in a tin. I wish to goodness I could get a place to myself, but with all these moves it isn't worth bothering about, because we never know how long we are going to be in one place. Miller ricked his back while he was up digging and I'm afraid we might lose him. I do hope not, he is such a nice fellow. Worth all the others put together.

Lady mine, wouldn't this world be a happy place if all the things that happen in books happened in life. I like *The Harvester*. There are some books I have read which really make me feel I am living through what the people in them did; I forget it is only a book while I am reading. Will you tell me what you think of it? Wouldn't it be a lovely kind of life? And what a beautiful log cabin it must have been.

On Monday I had to go up to the place where Miller and Burrows were digging, to fetch some ammunition. It had been a dull, grey day all morning, and when I started out without the wagons, it looked rather threatening. Well, we got about a quarter of a mile and it started to rain; it got worse and worse until it was simply coming down cats and dogs. Some of the men had not got coats, and got simply sopped through. Then it cleared up and nearly baked us, so they got dry. Just as we started back, it came down again and blew a regular gale – this time it came right through to my skin. So you may imagine what the men without coats were like when we arrived back. We had to come down a steep hill on the way back. The road was a new mud one, with a big crown on it, and two pairs of horses came down – their feet simply shot from under them. Of course, the drivers and horses got covered in mud from head to foot. I really think the mud is as bad here as it was at the other place, but there is no doubt about which is the nicest country.

The other day, I watched a cock pigeon making love to a hen pigeon: it was awfully pretty to watch him. He talked to her for a long time, and then stroked her wing, then her neck and head. Then he evidently asked her to let him kiss her and she wouldn't at first. So he began all over again, and this time she let him kiss her. After a lot of kissing, he stopped and looked

round until she made a funny little noise, as much as to say
'You're neglecting me', then he kissed her over and over again
and stroked her head and neck with his beak. Suddenly, off she
flew, and he after her.

Well, sweetheart, we are off again tomorrow – heaven knows
where; I'm sure I don't. Here comes tea, so I must shut up. Bye-
bye, lady mine.

Always and always,
Your lover

18 AUGUST 1916
FIELD SERVICE POSTCARD, POSTED 20 AUGUST

I am quite well.
I have received your letter dated 7 August.
Letter follows at first opportunity.

17 August   *Left Bertrancourt 11 am, marched all morning.
Got to Camesmil about 3 pm. Had lunch under
the trees. Slept five in a barn.*

18 August   *Left Camesmil 11.15 am. Very slow march to
Doullens. Arrived Meillard 5 pm. Fine chateau
for billet and a piano. Law, what a row.*

19 August   *Left Le Meillard 10 am. Rained hard all day. Got
to wagon lines near Amiens at about 5 pm. Slept
in a barn. Twenty-fourth came alongside us on
the march.*

SUNDAY 20 AUGUST

Phyl
I've got a short time before we move off, so here goes. My dear,

what a time we are having. The night before last, we had a large house for a mess. It was a lovely place in a little village. The owners were not there, only a caretaker and his wife: they were awfully good to us. There was a lovely drawing room with a piano in it. We made an awful row and had a dance – at least, three of us had: Wenley, Burrows and I. Wenley and Miller played. We all wanted Beavis to sing, but couldn't get him to! Miller and I slept in a farm in the village. The night before, we all slept in a barn together, and last night we did the same. Really, I am getting quite used to sleeping anywhere and am always jolly ready for it.

Yesterday it rained in buckets-full nearly the whole time we were marching. I had a Burberry, and an oilskin underneath and also a pair of Burberry pants on. So I kept fairly dry, except for the drops which kept falling off my cap down my neck. The men got soaked during the night – those that slept out all night were wet through in the morning; the others managed to keep drier.

Like an owl, I managed to give my knee a twist yesterday and it kept waking me up all night with aching. It's pretty stiff this morning but I hope it will wear off. At any rate, it looks like being fine today. It is rotten, we don't get any mail at all these days.

I must stop now, lady mine. All my love to you.

Your Englishman

20 August   *Did not move off till 1.45 pm from wagon lines. Then went via Bertangles and Allonville to Vecquemont. We camped by the canal, out in the open; it was a lovely night.*

21 August   *Had a bathe in the canal this morning. Marched off at 9.30 am to near Bray, via Corbie.*

23 August   *Up at 5.30 am. Went into action this morning. Putting up gun lights all day. Firing tonight.*

23 AUGUST
FIELD SERVICE POSTCARD, POSTED 24 AUGUST

I am quite well.
I have received your letter dated 13/8/16.
Letter follows at first opportunity.

WEDNESDAY 23 AUGUST 1916

My love
There is an appalling row going on. It has never ceased all day;
it's just as though hell had been let loose, and I'm sure it is, up
in front. I've just sat down, have been on the run since 5.30 this
morning, except for a few minutes this evening. The others are
in bed as it's midnight, so I'm going to try and be with my Lady
for a few minutes and then I shall turn in and think of her until
I go to sleep. Oh! Phyl, I wonder if all this is ever going to end
– it seems as though I've done nothing else all my life. Two years
ago, on the fifth of this month, I left home for Dunree; I never
thought then where I should be in two years' time. They've kept
us on the move lately; we've hardly had a minute to ourselves.
Thank heaven, we have had more or less fine weather since the
beginning of the month.

   Now listen, Phyl, there is something wrong altogether. In the
last letter there were several things that told me so. Lady mine,
I just want all the dearest letters I can possibly have now,
because I am really, really in it. I have tried to think over and
over again for the last three weeks that it was owing to your dad
going, and yet it was not only that which had caused the
difference in your dear, dear letters. So I just have to ask you
what it is. Oh! sweetheart, they seem all so cold now: just an
ordinary kind of a letter, with none of your own wonderfully
dear thoughts in at all.

FRIDAY AFTERNOON
Sweetheart, I've just got to look alive, as I am stealing time.

Yesterday we were hard at it all day, digging and strengthening pits and firing – from 5.30 to 10.30 solid we fired hard. There was the most colossal row going on that I have ever heard. I saw one of our planes get hit full in the centre with one of our own shells – it was simply crumpled up. The sky was black with them, and a large number were flying very low. I wonder more were not hit. It's very much quieter today. Thank heaven, none of us were hit at all yesterday. Now I must run off and put up electric lights. I have it all to do myself and it does take an age.

When will another letter come, lady mine; you don't know how I just long and long for them. My love to your mum, but all the very deepest and best is for you, Phyl.

XX Your Englishman

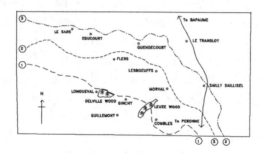

The Allied lines
1. 15 September 1916
2. 1 October 1916
3. 30 November 1916

SUNDAY 27TH AUGUST

Oh! my Lady

I don't quite know what I feel like today – we have just buried dear old Burrows. He died last night about 5.50 from a shrapnel wound in the back, and Miller was slightly wounded in the hand by the same shell. We had finished tea and were all talking together in the mess. Then we decided we would go and see what ought to be done to the new mess we were making. Miller went out first, then Burrows, then me. Just as I had got outside, there was a bang, and a shrapnel shell burst about fifty yards away from us. Miller and Burrows fell flat and I made a headlong dive for the mess. Miller said, 'I've got it in the hand, are you all right?' Burrows said, 'I'm hit in the stomach', and lay on his side, moaning a little. We were both not more than a yard from him and went to him. The Major came out, and he and I began to undo his clothes, but he asked the Major to leave him at present. That was the last thing he ever said, because he lost consciousness. Miller ran off for a doctor and we got him on a stretcher straightaway. The doctor came and looked at him and immediately said he could do nothing, that he was dying. Then he looked at him again and he was gone. Oh! Phyl, how very, very dreadfully sad it is; somehow I hardly realise yet that he has gone. It somehow was all over so very terribly quickly and now there is a big, big blank, because he was a real good soul. He and Miller were far and away the nicest of the lot, and Miller has gone away as well.

Oh! Phyl, it's awful to think of his fiancée, an Irish girl from Dublin. They were to be married next month, or as soon as Burrows could get leave. I had to write to her and tell her about his death, as he asked me once if I would do so, should anything happen to him. I just don't know how I wrote the short note to her, and God knows, I'm a poor enough hand at that kind of thing at the best of times. He was always so cheery, and we were just as happy as we could be when he was in command and the other person out of the way, and now he's gone.

LATER

I got a letter from Mum this evening; she said that things in Ireland were still unsettled and I pray to God that you are safe. It's a whole week yesterday since I had a letter from you: please, please write to me if you possibly can. It's nearly three months now since I was with you. When will another leave come along? I can't see any sign of it at present. Oh! Lady mine, the times and times I have looked at and kissed that dear, dear photo, and I've asked it all sorts of things it could never answer, yet I've almost thought it had done so by a change in look.

Tomorrow morning I am going up to a signal station for

twenty-four hours. The officers of four Batteries take it in turn and I'm going tomorrow. Dear old Burrows was up for us last time; he said there was a good strong deep dugout there, so I'm feeling fairly happy, as long as they don't bomb me on the way up. Yet I can't and won't see the point of worrying about that kind of thing after seeing Burrows killed yesterday: it's just God's will and nothing else, and neither I – or anybody else – can alter it. I wonder where old Miller is now – he deserves to get home, and our doctor said he is sure he will at a time like this, because they push nearly everybody straightaway, even if they are only slightly wounded. Well, good luck to him. I don't think anyone could meet a nicer fellow anywhere.

Now I must go to bed. Every atom of my real, real love to you, sweetheart.

Your Englishman

27 August   Burrows was buried today at about 1 pm, just near the Maricourt Road. Beavis came up today.

WEDNESDAY 30 AUGUST

Sweetheart
There's a simply ghastly din going on, but we are quiet ourselves for a short time and so I'm going to try and write a few lines. Oh! Lady mine, I scarcely know what I'm doing these days – it's just one continual run, the whole time. Yesterday and today it has rained incessantly, and at times it has come down cats and dogs. The mud is awful and we just can't keep dry: my dugout is soaking wet. Still, I'm so scarcely in it that it doesn't matter much. I've heard people talk about 'sunny France', but by Jove, if they came to this part they would have something else to say.

This ghastly din goes on day in and day out, and on top of it all, I haven't had a letter from you for eleven whole days. Oh! lady mine, if only I knew why, it might help a bit. I hope you are safe and all right – I imagine such dreadful things that may happen to you. Please, please Phyl, if you are all right and can write, do so for the sake of the love I have given you, now and for always. I've got to go and do some firing now at 12.25 am. Night-night, dear heart.

THURSDAY AFTERNOON
I shall have to send this as it is, as it's post time and we have been firing all afternoon. Thank heaven, it's a glorious day, and we can get our things dry a bit.

Bye-bye for the present, Phyl. All my love to you now and forever,

Your Eric

AUGUST 31 1916
FIELD SERVICE POSTCARD, POSTED 1 SEPTEMBER

I am quite well.
Letter follows at first opportunity.
I have received no letter from you for a long time.
Eric

2 SEPTEMBER
FIELD SERVICE POSTCARD, POSTED 3 SEPTEMBER

I am quite well.
Letter follows at first opportunity.
I have received no letter from you for a long time.
Eric

31 August   Boche put over stink shells all day.

1 September Relieved Collins. Quiet day. Gassed by stink shells all night, 8.30 pm to 4.45 am.

You dear, dear lady mine

What a selfish brute I have been in my last letters – instead of seeing there was something wrong, which I could have tried to put right, I whine because you haven't written. Oh! sweetheart, you can't ever know how terribly glad I was to see that letter yesterday afternoon; thank God you are all right. It has just been the most miserable fortnight I've ever had. When will I drive that nasty little devil in you away? Your love 'is a poor thing' when it is just worth everything in this wide world to your Englishman. Oh! Phyl, you don't understand what it means to this human being. I've just felt as dead and dull and grumpy and brainless and utterly stupid, forgetting all sorts of things I should have remembered, wading through each day with just a spark of hope each afternoon before the mail came in. I wanted your dear love letters again to know that my Lady was thinking of me and loving me hard all the time. I haven't had one real chance to write a long letter for a month now.

We were firing hard when the post came yesterday and had been all morning and afternoon. When the rate of fire had slackened a bit, I ran across to the mess from the guns and took a peep to see if there were any letters for me. What a great big jump my heart gave when I saw the dear old blue envelope with your handwriting on it; I just seized the letter and rushed back to the guns with it. I opened it and sat on the top step of a dugout and started to read it. At first I was so afraid it might have bad news for me, on top of everything. Why didn't you tell me truly about the Savages at first? I was so glad when you told me that you had liked them. I know so very well from the present life what it is to have to live with people you don't like. Oh! Lady mine, it must have been h— for you with all the other trouble on top. I wish I could have been with you to try and make things happier for you.

LATER – 7.15 PM

I couldn't send this today because I went for a long tramp up towards the line with the Major this afternoon. What a hellish spot it is round here: everything blown to blazes. There is not a sign of anything standing in the village of G— [Guillemont] except two or three tree stumps. Every brick and stone is overturned – it's awful. I got a Boche respirator for a souvenir; it's a jolly good one too. We saw a crowd of prisoners come past here this evening, earlier. Oh! I should have lots to tell you about all this, next time I come to you. I must remember it all.

I had a letter from Miller today. He says he doesn't think he will get across home now: he is at present at Boulogne. He said that he had had a long talk to Burrows only the night before he was killed. He had told him his fiancée had said that God would take care of him. Isn't it a sad, sad world – poor dear old Burrows, what good fun we had with him at times. Yesterday we turfed his grave and put some railings round it and are having a nice wooden cross made. It looks so nice and tidy compared with the others.

Oh! Lady mine, I want you so very terribly badly, I want to take you in my arms and press you so hard against me that neither you nor I can breathe without the other feeling each breath. I want to give you endless kisses – long, long very gentle ones. God grant that I may try my hardest to fill up the big gap that your dad's death has made, and make me unselfish and always think of the dear lady whose love He has given me.

TUESDAY AFTERNOON
I shall have to send this as it is, Phyl. I haven't had a moment all day and I did want to write more. I've just got two letters, hurrah! Jove, how lovely, I will try and write again tonight.

Just all the love in the world to you, my own, own darling, from your Englishman.
XXXXXXXX

TUESDAY 5 SEPTEMBER

Well, my darling, they've all gone to bed and left me to write in peace for a little while, before I go out to these blessed guns. You see, we shoot night and day and take the night watches in turn. I'm on from 12.30 to 2.30 – not a particularly nice time, either, as I'm feeling sleepy already.

The letter that was lost with the bag turned up tonight. It had been opened – heavens, what inquisitive beasts there are in this world. It took me just lovely ages to read the two letters and I don't know how and where to start to answer them, so I'll just ramble on and say things as I think of them. My darling, it is simply wonderful what a change seems to have taken place since these dear letters have started coming again. Oh! I do want them; I do indeed. Oh! Phyl, I love you more and more as the time is going on, I do indeed. I want just the 'silliest' letters that you can write, and just when you feel you can write them, lady mine. And now I must run out to these bally guns. Goodnight, you darling, you dear, wonderful darling.

WEDNESDAY AFTERNOON

It was simply pitch black last night and the ground was beginning to dry up a bit after the rain earlier on. You would have laughed if you had seen me floundering along with about ten pounds of sticky mud on each foot. I was simply dead tired when I turned in at 2.30. This morning I took all the electric light fittings off the guns and packed them all up. It is a job, and I only finished about half an hour ago. Beavis has gone to hospital again today; he has never really been right since he came back, and his temperature went up to 103 this morning. I got a letter from Burrows's fiancée yesterday; it was a very nice one. She asked me one or two things and I was thankful that I could tell her. I wrote back last night.

Oh! Lady mine, I'm so glad you are doing the sailing – it's just the best thing for you because you get the really fresh, clean air, and also if there is a good breeze it makes it exciting, and it's fine to think that your mum loves it. But please be very careful of treacherous rocks about. Oh! I am glad about the petrol being fine again, but it's a beastly nuisance about it getting stolen. Have you informed the authorities? You may have to pay a small sum for the second, but only a shilling or two.

I've got to go up to that beastly signalling station place tonight for some stupid reason.

Lady mine, always and always your devoted lover.

SATURDAY 9 SEPTEMBER
EXAMINED BY BASE CENSOR

Lady mine

I have just got a few minutes before stables, so I'm going to make the best of time. Thank heaven we are out of that ghastly row for a bit – how long, of course, we don't know, but the longer the better. Though it was only such a short time in, it has been the worst we have had by a long chalk. We are having a few horse races tomorrow – officers only. I am riding one of Burrows's horses, a light bay gelding. He's pretty fast but can't do the pace for very long; however, he's got a lightweight riding him. Each race is a mile flat. This afternoon, Wenley and I are going to a small race meeting near here. One of the Yeomanry squadrons are holding it and there are some professional jockeys riding. Jack Anthony is riding; it ought to be quite good. Hurrah! The Major has let us go early, so we shall be off in a minute or two now. This morning I was up early with Wenley and we had a good gallop round the course.

In my last letter, I told you I had to go up to the signalling place for the night. I expected to get back next morning, but I got a message to say I had to stay up there all day. Then the Boche began shelling us. However, they did no damage to us, because the dugout was at least twenty feet under the ground. Then I should have been relieved at 5 pm and the man did not turn up until 7.15 pm. So I finally arrived down here at 9.30 pm after a good hard ride.

I'm afraid this is only a newsy kind of letter, Phyl. Bye-bye, sweetheart. I'll write again just as soon as ever I can. All my love to you for always,

Eric

7 September   Up at RD all day. Boche shelled amm. wagon on the road behind Bernafay Wood this morning. Got horses down to wagon line at Meaulte.

9 September   Mem. The attack of Sun. 3 Sept. Infantry got through Guillemont and reached final objective, but had to retire a little owing to infantry not getting Ginchy, also machine-gun fire from left. We supported 16th Div. Infantry. They fell back a little to sunken road in front of Guillemont. On 5 Sept. a part of Leuze Wood was taken.

10 September   Heard we had to move wagon line. Made sight boards. Trekked off at 8.30. New wagon line near Barnoil on hillside.

12 September   Up to old position this morning. Went up to new position just below Guillemont and Leuze Wood this afternoon with Wenley and Stubbington.

MONDAY 11 SEPTEMBER

My darling

I got two letters today and they are both so very, very dear and wonderful that I hardly know whether I am standing on my head or my feet. They just make my Lady seem as though she was with me, if ever a letter could do that. Oh! Lady mine, why can't I be with you? When will I get back to you? Phyl, I feel nearly mad with longing for you tonight. Just all the love that I can ever feel seems to be for you, no one but you. Only this afternoon, though, Wenley was saying he thought it must be awful for those we love at home – worse than for ourselves out here. Although we out here have all sorts of little and big unpleasantness which make it like h— on earth, I know it can't be as bad as what you have to go through, because we have nearly always plenty to do and life can't be so monotonous.

I've hardly sat down all day, except when I read the two dear letters. I haven't had a think for three days now. I was just dog-tired on Saturday night when we got back from that race meeting, and as stiff as the dickens after the thirty-mile ride we had. Yesterday we moved again and I was like a piece of limp cotton when I turned in last night. Heaven knows what is going to happen. I'm getting now that I feel always so utterly fed up and tired and sick to death of everything. Why won't things show just a glimmer of the end, why won't they? I'm afraid, lady mine, that I'm the one that is losing all the bravery I ever had in me. Poor old Burrows's death has knocked every atom of that out of me, and I simply dread the thought of going into action again, and it's not far off. That poor girl, the awful, terrible lonely feeling she must have in her heart now that her lover has gone. Oh! Phyl, I got such a nice letter from her, thanking me for writing and telling her so soon after it had happened. I'm going to send it to you, I think, because she said something very dear about you and I. They were going to be married as soon as he could get home; it's terribly sad. All his kit was packed up and sent to his home. I told her every little detail I could think of about his death and his grave. Please forgive my letters, but I can't help thinking about dear old Burrows's death; it makes everything so much worse out here and I keep feeling so utterly miserable. The awful longing for you comes on so very badly. What years and years it seems since that time in Athlone when you made me feel just the happiest being God ever made, at St Mark's.

TUESDAY AFTERNOON
I had to stop last night and go round the lines as I was on duty yesterday and didn't get back till 12.30. Wenley and I have just got back from the new place we are going to. Oh! Lady mine, it's just awful: the dead are lying all over the place; it's a simply ghastly sight. There are Boche and our own men all mixed up – God knows why the poor devils have never been buried.

Sweetheart, I got two more dear letters today, one written on the fourth and the other on the seventh. Really, I don't know what has happened to the post now. I suppose it's this beastly push. Your lover doesn't know how to thank you for these letters, they are just worth everything in the world to me at present. I keep thinking of all the horrible business out here and I can't see any end in sight – oh! God, will it ever come? This morning I went up to the old position we left a few days since to collect some material for the new one, and while I was there I made a rough sketch of Burrows's grave, as his fiancée asked if I could get a photo taken of it but no one has a camera.

No, Phyl, I'm not a wee bit tired of your telling me that you love me, why these letters you have sent me are just the very dearest I have ever had. I can hardly believe that my Lady is longing and longing for me, and that there is just heaven on earth waiting for me when I get back.

Just all, all, all my love to you, dear heart, now and for always and always.

Your Englishman,
Eric

SATURDAY 16 SEPTEMBER

My dearest
Thank you, darling, for the lovely plums. They have carried perfectly. I can only write a few hurried lines, but I must tell you about the wonderful letters that have come. Oh! Phyl, you don't know how wonderfully real they make your love for me, while I'm in this cursed place. I feel almost happy because my Lady is loving me with all her heart and soul, just as I am loving her. I got a letter today and one yesterday, two on Wednesday, two on Tuesday and two on Monday. Would to God I could get home to you: when will this end? Oh! when, when, when?

Lady mine, the things we have got all round us are absolutely the most revolting sights I have ever seen in my life. There are bits of poor wretches lying unburied all over the place. They are in such a state, no one can face the job of burying them, even if they had the time. We have covered up seven already and they are the least decomposed of the lot. The ground is literally ploughed up with old shell holes, in many places so close together that it is impossible to walk on the top; one has to walk in and out again to get along.

We started early in the morning yesterday, and fired all day long up to eleven o'clock at night, and we had to make our position at the same time. The night before last, I got to bed at one o'clock when we finished firing, and the night before at 5.45 am and I was up again at 8.30. On Wednesday I was up here all day digging. When I got back to the wagon line at night, I heard we had to come into action the same night, so I had another journey up here. They have guessed at home where I am.

Oh! Phyl, I do long to be with you, to go on all the expeditions up the lake and to bathe. Why, it seems almost too good to ever happen, to have a bathe in the lake – we can hardly get a scrap of water to wash one's hands and face, let alone have a bath. Well, what else can we expect at such a time? Thank heaven, so far the Boche has left us alone. It will be hell if he starts his games here.

I am glad that Eddie got home again, and I know how very glad your mum would be. When does Buzz go back to school? You must have had a long row back after you got becalmed off Winning. Well, lady mine, we must just hope that very soon I shall be able to come and stop with you for a long, long time. Then we can really do all our daydreams. I think the lady ought to be kissed and hugged till she can't breathe and all this should be done by her lover,

Eric

15 September Started bombardment at 2 am; at it all day long. Guns behaved very well. Our attack failed twice.

Sweetheart

What a happy (????) life this is, it's raining in absolute bucketsfull, just spilling as hard as it bally well can. This place is just one mass of slippery mud and it has never ceased since it started early this morning. Lady mine, the Major and I had an exciting time dodging shells yesterday afternoon. We started off with the intention of registering. We got about three-quarters of the way to the place we were going to. It was just our side of a wood [Leuze]. There we stopped for two hours, sitting behind the concrete wall of an old Boche dugout, while the devils plugged all round us with 5.9s, 4.2s and Little – I had to stop here, as all of a sudden a stream of water from the roof came right on the centre of my head and onto the paper. To continue – Willies. While we were there, one landed two yards on the other side of the dugout and one plumb on the roof of it. Each time we got dirt rained on us but no one was damaged. The whole time wee splinters were dropping close to us.

They quietened down for a few moments, so off we went through the wood, the telephonists laying out a wire as we went. Hardly had we got halfway through when they started pounding it everywhere, as hard as they could go. The place was black with smoke and we couldn't hear them coming for the noise of the bursts. The earth was flying in all directions and bits of trees were hurtling about. Still, we couldn't stop, or rather it was better to go on. So on we went, as quickly as we could walk, stumbling, tripping over broken branches, jumping over shell holes and falling into them, ducking when one burst too close to us. Well, we got to the front of the wood and then found we could see absolutely nix for shell smoke. The only thing we could just make out was the broken tower of a church. So we fired a few rounds and found the guns were all right. Thank heaven we did, what with the Boche banging right behind us and on one side, and our own heavies pumping it in not far ahead. We came back across the open, running for all we were fit, because we were in view of the Boche trenches, but they didn't worry us with their machine-guns. Our heavies were keeping their — heads down and they were not shelling that part. I told the Major on the way up that that was our best route but he was afraid of the machine-guns and so we went through that cursed wood.

Well, sweetheart, it has not rained quite so much this morning but I am afraid it is going to start again. Bradley, my servant, reconstructed my dugout this morning. I hope to goodness it works all right now. I got your letter written on Monday and, do you know, I was fiendishly jealous of Harold. How dare you let any man take you for a walk. I feel just so very selfish of you in that way. But I am so very glad you enjoyed yourself there and I only wish you could go to places like that oftener. The plums are fine – we ate all the firmest ones and have had the others cooked. The apples are also very good but haven't carried as well as the plums.

Oh! sweetheart, I wonder when I shall get home to you again. It's just awful, this longing and waiting for the dear wonderful time to come. I suppose it will be winter again – nearly, at any rate. It's bitterly cold at nights now. What it will be later on I hate to think.

Thank God, it's a lovely afternoon. All my wet things are out drying. What a mess everything is in, though. We did very well yesterday; that is something to be thankful for. I am sending you a souvenir. It's the shoulder title off the greatcoat of a dead Boche with the number of his regiment on it. I cut it off myself the other day. It's quite all right, because the coat was well clear of the corpse. The mud on it I have not removed, as you see.

Last night I had a lovely dream about you. You and I were staying at a hotel in Dublin. We were in the lounge and you were playing for me and singing some songs. Suddenly I was called by someone in the hotel to speak to one of the men in the Battery about rations. I remember I asked him how many loaves of bread he had brought and what weight of meat. You see, I can't keep away from this business even in my dreams, and only a day or two ago I kicked up about short rations up here. When

253

I returned, you were still singing, and a lady asked me who you were and said you had the nicest voice she had ever heard. I told her you were my fiancée and I remember feeling just very proud of my Lady. She said she hoped we would be very happy always. When I was wakened I was so cross, because the Sergeant had brought me back to this hellish place, away from my Lady.

Just all the very dearest love you can think of is for you, my darling,

Your lover

XXXXX

FRIDAY 22 SEPTEMBER

Sweetheart

It's just a glorious day today, how I hope it keeps fine. The rain has been simply awful; you have no idea, I am sure, just what it can be like when it really is wet here. Try and imagine yourself walking across a freshly ploughed field in a heavy rainstorm, and it will give you some idea of what it's like, walking about this cursed country in wet weather. The day before yesterday I spent up in a trench observing. It was raining cats and dogs nearly the whole time, and blowing a bitterly cold wind as well. I had a Burberry with me but it was soon wet through, and then I began to shiver, both with cold and the shelling. The brutes shelled rounders all day long with 4.2 and Little Willies. Five times we got showered with dirt, and one brute landed on the side of the trench, not ten yards from us. It shook up my inside and sent my tin hat all askew (just the concussion) and of course nearly buried us.

In the evening, shortly before I came down, I had to watch a trench because it had been reported that there were a large number of Boche gathering in it. Well, imagine my delight when I was told I had to watch closely, for just at that time they were banging us with Little Willies. You don't hear the shells coming at all. The first thing you realise is that there is a — bang and a horrible smell of high explosive. These beastly things were falling just on the side of the trench over which I had to look. I waited till one had arrived, then jumped up and had a quick look round, and down again undercover before the next one came. This I did over and over again, but it was jumpy work and I was so very glad to leave the place.

On the way back, two telephonists and myself came across two poor infantry machine-gunners, absolutely stuck in the bottom of the trench. They were standing up to their knees in mud and it was literally like glue. Well, try as we would to get them out, we couldn't do it, so I sent my two men back along the trench to get two shovels that we had passed, and not until we had dug the mud away all round their legs could we get them free. You see, the more they struggled, the deeper they went and without help they couldn't possibly have got free.

And now I have some good news to give you. Miller has come back to us. I am so very glad he has, and although I was feeling absolutely fed up and tired, it made all the difference when I saw him. His hand is quite better, and as a matter of fact, the bullet had never actually gone into his hand but had simply grazed the bone near the knuckle, and he found it in his pocket.

Of course, we had a long talk about poor old Burrows and I think it did us both good. He is up in the OS today. I have been writing this in the mess and everybody in the neighbourhood has been in there this afternoon. So I kept getting stopped every two minutes.

I'm in my wee dugout now. It's really quite a cosy little place as long as it does not rain too hard. The walls are sandbagged and some ammunition boxes are let in for shelves etc. My Lady is on the wall on my right-hand side, just by the little shelf for the candle. The other photo is on the wall just on my left. My bed is my valise and it rests on ammunition boxes along the left-hand side of the dugout. At the end, just outside is my washing place. The roof consists of two sheets of corrugated iron and is consequently not bulletproof.

Lady mine, I got something else the other night when I came in here: there were two letters waiting for me. One is so very, very dear and one is a newsy one. Now I must stop, love,

Your Englishman for always

My darling

Two more letters arrived last night, Phyl. Dear lady, they are so wonderful, these that I am getting now. I wonder why they always come in twos. It must be that the mail comes over every other day, or something. But we get a mail each night. I don't understand it. Stubbington and Martin were the two new men who came after Burrows's death. Stubbington was wounded, but Martin is still with us – quite a nice fellow, too. I am sorry to hear about Eddie. I do hope they will give him leave at any rate before he goes. Honestly, I am jolly glad he's not coming out here at any rate, because the casualties are something terrible every day now – at least according to the papers – owing to this push.

Lady mine, will you please promise me to be very careful what you do when you go for your sail on the lake, and also in 'Sadie'. I should go mad if anything were to happen to you. How I wish I could go with you; we would have a real good time. It's simply glorious here today, and it was yesterday. I do hope you are having this kind of weather: it does everyone so much good.

I was up in the OS all yesterday. I had so much observing to do that I didn't get a chance to write to you. Think, dear, it's nearly four months now since I was with you. Oh! I wonder when I will get home again. What would you like to do when I do come? Would you rather come over to my home and bring your mum with you, or shall I come to you, as I did last time? What do you think?

I got a note from Burrows's fiancée, telling me that she was sending out some rosemary to put on Burrows's grave; it's so dreadfully sad for that poor girl. Mrs Burrows wrote to me a few days ago and said his brother was near here and had been looking for the grave, but couldn't find it. So she asked me if I would try and find him. I wrote to him, but will have to wait until we go out again before I can look him up. We have been firing all day and Miller has been doing a spell for me this afternoon, but now I must go and relieve him.

Sweetheart, please, I want lots and lots of these dear, wonderful letters, they help so very, very much and make my heart just thump and thump for the only lady in all the world.

All, all, all my love to you, Phyl, now and forever,

Your lover

TUESDAY 26 SEPTEMBER 1916

My own darling Lady

Just a few lines to let you know all's well so far after yesterday. It was a great day for us here and you must read about it in the papers. But I foresee a week's very hard work again, now that our people have gone forward again so much – as though we haven't had enough to last us for many a week. As usual, we have all horrible thoughts of the spots we are going to. Well, it's no use worrying about it, because it doesn't do any good. My God, I shall be glad to get out of this, though.

Sweetheart, I have heard a real good rumour about the first of October. I wonder can you guess what it is? Oh! Lady mine, I pray to God that it may come true. I got another dear letter last night. I'm so sorry about the letters not coming, and I am a thoughtless owl not to send postcards. I must get hold of some and send one off every day. Thank heaven, I'm all right so far, and Miller came back safely this morning. We were both up forward yesterday. He was out all day, though, and I was only out until lunchtime. Then the Major went up and came back with a Boche prisoner. He was a little worm, but poor devil, I bet he had had a time. At any rate, he was as pleased as punch to be out of it all and I don't wonder.

My sweetheart, how I just long to be able to go down with you to clean 'Sadie'. We would do it real well. Bless the old thing, how very happy I have been when I've been in her. Would we do the cleaning though, do you think? I'm afraid I should say to — with the cleaning! Why can't I be with you for always? Oh! I'd just go all out if you were with me in the sidecar of a motorbike and I'd take you miles and miles away from anybody: I want to have you all to myself.

Now, sweetheart, I must say bye-bye. God bless you, you dear precious lady. All the love in me is for you, you, you.

Your Englishman

THURSDAY 28 SEPTEMBER
FIELD SERVICE POSTCARD, POSTED 30 SEPTEMBER

I am quite well.
I have received your letter dated 22nd September.
Letter follows at first opportunity.
Eric

26 September *Miller back early this morning. Heard we have to move up forward tonight. Went up with Miller to new position and working party. My God, what a place. Started digging and went on till 3 am. Everybody dead tired. Got message to return to Battery. Hell, what a walk, found ourselves going W instead of SW. Got back at 5.10 am.*

27 September *Card from Phyl and photo, also large cake. Parcel from Mum: revolver, toothbrush etc. Went to position close to Ginchy tonight.*

28 September *Dear letter from Phyl and parcel from Mum. Laid out lines of fire – awful job. Got to IB for mess; good place.*

29 September *Went up as Liaison Officer to French tonight. Found myself in front-line trenches. It was packed with Frogs. Stayed at Gunnery HQ behind Morval. Slept with Bradley on mound of chalk. It rained hard all night. Got guide alone*

> 9.30 to Batt. HQ in front of Morval. Stayed there till 4 pm. Returned to quarry and on to Battery. Found them leaving for wagon line, so had to trek on down. Very dead tired tonight.

30 September Heard we had to move today to Ville-Sur-Ancre. Left wagon line at 2.30 pm. Got here about 5 pm. Got letter from Phyl and Mum. Very peaceful here, thank God. Mem. 28 September. Sent rosemary down to Wenley to plant on Burrows's grave.

1 October A glorious day today. Wrote a long letter to Phyl. Heard we probably have to go into action on Tuesday. Oh! damn everything.

SUNDAY 1 OCTOBER

Sitting with my back resting on the side of a bell tent and using two of the ropes as arms to my chair. Sweetheart mine, it's a day which makes one feel it's good to be alive and how I thank God that I am after these last horrible weeks in action. We got here last night and of course don't know how long we shall be left in peace. Oh! Lady mine, I do hope they'll take us away from this dreadful 'push'! They've given us too much of it already, and as you can see from the papers, the casualties are awful. What will you think of your lover when you don't hear for two days, after he promised to send a postcard each day at least. Well, I must tell you what happened. The last letter I wrote was in the last position but one.

That evening, Miller and I had to go to another place with a working party, to dig a new position. I got there at 5.30 and Miller arrived with the men at 6 pm. We started to work straightaway, and with the exception of two rests of an hour each, dug hard until 3 am. Neither did the Boche leave us alone. When the men arrived, they were shelling, and several times

259

during the night they put Little Willies very, very close to us – shrapnel as well. The last is much the worst when one is in the open. That place was quite close to the southernmost of the two last places we attacked here. As soon as we left off working, we had to trek right back to the old place, leaving a guard over the new one. We arrived back at 5 am and lady mine, every one of us was dead tired out. My feet ached so that I could hardly stand. Well, we went to bed and slept until 10.30 am, then got up and had the usual duties of the Battery work to do.

At lunchtime the Major came in and said we had to go into another position (not the one we had dug at all night) that night. So off we trekked to have a look at it, and later, when we had come back and had some tea, we started off for it. Well, it meant another late night, and after messing around in the dark we finally got to bed at midnight. The next day we had to get the lines laid out for the guns to fire on and everything ready at the Battery for shooting, while Martin and the Major went forward to observe. That afternoon I sent off postcards to you and Mum, and generally got things straightened up. I was on duty all day. After dinner, I went out to start the guns firing. It was an inky-black night. When I came back into the mess dugout, the Major said, 'I've got a very pleasant job for you tonight.' My heart went down with a bump, because I knew it was something extra rotten by the way he said it. Well, I had to go as Liaison Officer to a French battalion.

It was pitch black and I had to walk to a place I didn't know and had never been near, over country I didn't know which was absolutely riddled with shell holes. Only two nights before, when we were coming back from the digging, we had found ourselves walking in a north-easterly direction when we should have really been going SW. Well, I had to go with another officer who was staying at the Regimental HQ while I went forward to the battalion. We found his place all right, and then I had to wait about half an hour until I was sent on with a guide, the time then being 1.30 am. On I trekked until I was handed over by this guide to another guide, then on again, scrambling out of shell holes and nearly overbalancing every time I took a stop. This guide soon got tired of me and handed me over to a party of 'Croix Rouge' men who were supposed to be going my way. On and on we went, slipping, slithering and scrambling about, with it raining like the dickens. In two places we had to run as fast as we could over the ground, because of the Boche shelling it. It was jolly exciting; the beastly things were dropping so horribly close. Two men got wounded on the way up – Frenchies, of course. Lady mine, I eventually found myself in the front-line trench, which was absolutely jammed with Frenchies and not an officer anywhere to tell me where I had to go. I didn't know and I had no guide. Well, it was no use there, and after shouting several times in French for an officer and getting no reply, I decided to go back to where I had started from and demand a proper guide. Luckily, I struck a party of French infantry who had been relieved and were on their way back to the very place I wanted to get to. So off I went with them, truly thankful to leave the front line behind me. Back I went over the same ground as I had just come, running across the same stretches of ground while the Boche plugged away on the off chance of hitting some wanderer. But, thank heaven, he didn't get me. I finally arrived back at the Regimental HQ at 3.45 am, absolutely weary, and although it was raining hard, I just scrambled up onto a bank of chalk and fell asleep in the open. But I wasn't to remain asleep for long, because I woke up cold and stiff in less than an hour. After three hours of sleeping and waking, I went to the French Colonel and told him what had happened and asked to be guided to the place properly. This time I was taken the whole way by one man, over nearly all the same ground that I had walked the night before, only this time I got to the Battalion HQ and not the front line. It was still raining like the — and oh! lady mine, the sights I saw on that horrible ground were simply horrible beyond words. I stayed there until I was called back to the Battery at 4 pm. Thank heaven, it was a good deep dugout, very deep down in the earth, made by the Boche. But the flies were dreadful in it – simply one seething mass of the brutes on the ceiling and walls. Well, love, I finally got back to the Battery at 6 am and oh! I was so very thankful. I got stopped twice on the way back by the Boche artillery barrages. Then I found everyone was getting ready to move to the wagon line.

Sweetheart, that is enough about all the beastliness out here, isn't it? Yes, dear, I got the cake quite safely, and what a lovely one it is, and the photo is very nice too. Why can't I be having an afternoon like the one on which it was taken, with my Lady? I got another dear letter yesterday and read it while I was jogging along on Tommy. No dear, Martin got Burrows's horse, as he is much heavier, and he is the man that came in poor Burrows's place. He is senior to me by about two months. You don't know how I longed to be with you while you wrote this last letter. I can just hear you say 'I won't be long, Englishman' when you went to shut the greenhouse door. So the Savages are going; well, I'm very glad. I do hope you will get someone who is nice, or let the house altogether to some nice people.

Now, darling, I must really shut up. I will write just as much as ever I can.

All my love to you,
Your Englishman

2 October   *On duty today, up early, started to rain again and kept it up all day. Major started for Amiens but did not get there. Major back for stables. Took men to baths this afternoon. Got oh such a dear letter from Phyl. Had champagne for dinner; it was good.*

3 October   *Started off in front of Battery with Major. Raining like the very devil. Got up here in the Morval Valley about 1.15. Battery not here till 11.40, blast them. Nowhere to sleep.*

My darling
Here I am in the blue once more. God knows where the Battery
is; I'm sure I don't. They ought to have been here two and a half
hours since. This morning it was raining hard again, after a
soaker all yesterday, and I trekked off with the Major up here.
Then he went back and told me to wait until they came. Then
I came to this Battery when it got dark, and was truly thankful
when they asked me to have a drink and dinner. You see, I had
left my water and coat on my horse, a way behind. What a life
this is, honestly. Tonight I have no place to lay my head, and in
fact I don't expect I shall get a wink because we shall have to dig
as hard as we can. The ground is simply cruel, the mud is awful.

Oh! Lady mine, I got a very dear letter from you yesterday
and it came just at the very time I wanted it most, because we
had just heard that we had to come back to this cursed place and
we had thought we had finished here. For my lunch today I had
some potted-meat sandwiches and a large hunk of your cake. I
will write to Buzz just as soon as ever I can. I do hope he won't
feel going to school too much. I'll bet he was glad when your
mum was able to stay the weekend with him.

Yesterday I had to take the men to the baths in the
afternoon. It rained in sheets all day and was beastly cold. Now
I must say bye-bye, darling. I'm quite well but very, very fed up
with this beastly life, and I'm just longing and longing always for
my Lady.

Night-night, dear one, for always, your Englishman

Sweetheart
I had to stop writing yesterday as a man suddenly turned up
telling me to come back to the wagon line owing to certain

orders. Well, love, here I am now, but I can't get away from this eternal mud. It is an extraordinary sight to see the wagons simply stuck fast in the mud, up to their axles, and even twelve horses couldn't shift them. Some of the roads have ruts over two feet deep in them and I honestly don't know how loaded wagons get along. Do you know, I was almost sorry to leave my tiny dugout because it was really such a cosy place. It was quite waterproof after the construction, but Miller said I was not wise to have no earth on the top of the corrugated iron, because it wasn't even shrapnel-proof. But if I had earth on top, the blooming thing leaked, so I preferred to chance the shrapnel and sleep in comfort.

Phyl, what would you have liked to have done had I been with you that weekend that your mum was away? I'm afraid in my present state I would have wanted to stay at home all the time. But if I had been feeling energetic, what would you have wanted to do, and where should we have gone? In good sooth, my Lady, that was a deed worthy of a gallant lady, that thou didst for the sake of thy lover, and verily thou mayest rest assured that he feels very greatly indebted unto thee. But apart from joking, it is just the dear kind of thing my Lady would do, and it's those kind of things that make me love her, and the hundreds of other things that she does. I'm sorry to say my two photos are suffering from the damp but they are still very dear, and how they make me long and long for the real one.

Now, my darling, I'm going to turn in. Just all the love in the world to you, you dear, dear lady.

FRIDAY 6 OCTOBER
FIELD SERVICE POSTCARD, POSTED 8 OCTOBER

I am quite well.
I have received your letter dated 28 September.
Letter follows at first opportunity.
Eric

I am quite well.
I have received your letter dated 29 September.
Letter follows at first opportunity.
Eric

5 October   Martin came up here to dig. I left wagon line to
reconnoitre roads up here. Met Major where the
wagons were parked. Came up here by the
cavalry track. Got a wagon stuck but shifted it
with ten horses. All slept together in mess. Hell,
how damnably uncomfortable, all cramped up.
Got a dear letter from Phyl.

6 October   Up at 7.45 this morning. Tested sights. Went up
to ridge between Morval and Lesboeufs. Sat in a
hole and registered Battery. Put some shrapnel
damned close to us. Worked at my dugout all
afternoon. Sent FSPCs to Phyl and Mum.

7 October   Slept in mess and was wakened at 3.45 am by a
torrent of water on my shoulders and feet. Had
to move my bed out of the way. Oh! the Devil,
what a life this is. Tested sights and fired all
morning. Zero hour for first Transloy show 1.45
pm. Infantry got held up by machine-guns,
gained very little. Got a letter from Phyl.

8 October   Raining like hell this morning. Everything
soaking. Miller's rheumatism bad. Relieved
Major after church. Was up for the second attack
this afternoon. No letters this evening. Wrote to
Phyl and Mum.

My darling
At last I've got just a few minutes to write. There – someone's just shouted 'Wagon's up.' Oh! I do hope there is a letter for me – no, none. I do want one so very badly, 'cause, lady mine, I'm just as fed up as I can stick and have been all day. It has rained like the very dickens all day and I have been soaked. My bed was all wet last night and the night before as well, though yesterday was fine. Just as though everything wasn't bad enough out here without the beastly rain. Poor Miller has gone back to the wagon line with bad rheumatism. It's simply through this continuous damp out here. He is much older than I am; thirty-three, I think. He is tall and slim and has a large nose. He is not really handsome, but has a very kind face, and is just what he looks: a kind, strong-minded fellow. I've got to run off and fire the guns now, Phyl.

11.45 PM
Well, lady mine, I've got them going properly now, so here goes for a bit more before something else happens – the Boche has suddenly started shelling just close to. Oh! sweetheart, how dreadfully you were wanting your dad when you wrote this last letter, but the terrible part is that the longing can never be made up for by those who are left. I remember when my granny died, and my mum was very fond of her and said she wanted to talk to her most dreadfully. I remember thinking at the time that my granny was very near to us then, and, lady mine, I still think it is so, when one feels that awful longing. I think it is the same with you and me – when we are both thinking of one another very hard and that dreadful longing comes. I wonder whether you think this is so? You dear lady, I haven't had any trouble with my eyes for a long time now. The doctor said they would recover after a time.

At present I am sitting in the mess dugout, which consists of a bit of an old front-line British trench with a sandbag wall across it from one end, and a roof of corrugated iron about one sixth of an inch thick. My dugout in this position is the wee-est thing you could imagine. I can just lie full length and no more. It is about a foot deep and three feet wide, and my bed consists of two mackintosh sheets, a flea bag with a pair of saddlebags and your silk muffler as a pillow; also a British Warm for counterpane. The sides are lined with sandbags and the roof is corrugated iron with some earth on top. I left my valise and most of my things down in the wagon line this time, and really, I couldn't get everything into this wee place. I slept in it for the first time last night and of course it had to rain cats and dogs and blow right into the door so that my bed got wet. The night before, I slept in the mess and again it rained like the devil and managed to pour onto me in two places: one on my shoulders and the other onto my feet.

Lady mine, of course I won't ask you to come to my home if you don't want to, next leave. What is it, though, dear one, that makes you not want to go? Will you tell me, sweetheart, please? You seemed so dreadfully frightened for some reason, but whatever it may be, I will come to you.

MONDAY AFTERNOON

Sweetheart, I got two letters today: in one you had the blues dreadfully badly, and it makes me long to be with you, to try and be a comfort, at any rate. You know, I get just the same way out here, and then I honestly wonder what is the good of going on living. But listen, Phyl, you are not to get that way, because the dear wonderful happy days are coming sometime – yes, very soon, dear. The other is just as cheery as the first is bluey, and it is so like my Lady to suddenly recover and be just the opposite.

It's high time I stopped because the post has to go. Bye-bye darling, just all my love, now and for all time.

Your Englishman

Lady mine

Here I am in the OS, a delightful spot consisting of a shell hole, dug out so as to be more or less comfortable. Thank heaven, it is a lovely day at present; the sun is quite hot. I am sitting on one of the steps, about four feet below ground level. My feet rest on another step from which we observe. By standing, I am just the right height to see through the periscope, which is stuck in the bank in front of me with its top just nicely above the level of the ground. The latter falls away in front, and there is a wide valley about three miles across in front with several small valleys in the bottom. I can see from here bits of a lot of villages, all surrounded by trees, but the nearest one is quite the largest of the lot. It looks almost untouched – at any rate, compared with those we have fought for and won.

Coming up here, two telephonists and myself had an exciting moment. I noticed one of our planes was flying very low. All at once, it turned and came down at an angle, straight for us. I stood stock-still, absolutely glued to the spot, and watched the thing come dead at me. It was no use running, because it was coming towards us at such a pace. I thought of throwing myself flat on the ground and would have done had I not seen that he straightened his machine and flew just over us, landing about 300 yards beyond us. The wheels touched the ground and the machine bounced, then touched again and turned completely over with its nose down and tail sticking up at an angle. The pilot got free and ran away about twenty yards, then saw some men from nearby running towards him, so went back. Soon there was a collection all round the machine. Apparently the observer did not get clear and was under the machine, but we couldn't see, there was such a crowd round in no time. I'm afraid he would get badly smashed up, though, from the look of things. The other day, I saw a machine fall from a great height and it was simply one sheet of flame the whole way down – what a horrible death. We couldn't see whether it was one of ours or a Boche.

Now I must have a look round, sweetheart.

It's after lunch now. I had a long look round because the light was so good, and I did some firing. I'm sitting down in the hole now because the Boche put a few shrapnel a bit close a minute or two since. I'm about six feet down. I wonder what my Lady is doing now. It will be just a week since the Savages left – I wonder did you dance on the doorstep when they had departed. I do hope things are better – it's cruel to know that my Lady is having an awful time and that I can't be with her to try and make things better. Oh! darling, when will the time come again when I shall watch hard out of the carriage window for your house and garden, the river and then for the one dear wonderful lady to whom I've given every atom of my love. Well, lady mine, I honestly felt I didn't care who I shocked when I kissed you; all I could think of was that I was with you, you, you. Well, the first of October seems to have slid past, and as yet there is no sign of it for us poor blighters who do all the fighting, although there are hundreds going who have never seen the line, except on the cinematograph or on paper. But then, grousing does no good. Poor Buzz – what a brute that fellow was, playing his dirty trick. But I'm jolly glad his lip is getting better and it didn't damage his teeth. That chap wants a d— good lambasting and I would take the greatest pleasure in doing it.

Last night there was an extraordinary sight: the Boche got the 'wind up' and he started firing for all he was fit, all along the line, and sent up flares by the thousand and rockets by the hundred. It really was a fine firework display. The rockets were signals, of course, to the artillery and troops in the rear. The flare lights were of course to light up the surrounding country, which they did effectively for miles round. I must have another look round now.

BACK AT THE BATTERY – 9.25 PM

Here I am back, love. I never started again, I got so interested in the aeroplanes; there were thirty-five that I counted in the air at once, and I'm sure I didn't count all even then; it was impossible to do so. I saw one of our poor fellows brought down by a brute of a Boche. The machine was in flames and the two men fell out – I was watching with a telescope. It was a horrible sight. Before the machine had fallen halfway to the ground, it was practically burnt up.

The Major came up this afternoon and, while he was there, Mr Boche put a Little Willie only a yard away from the edge of the crater of the shell hole in which we were sitting. It simply smothered us in dirt and knocked my glasses off the side of the bank into the hole. Of course, I must go and put my foot on them and break one of the glasses. I wonder what you would think of your lover when he wears his glasses. The pilot was wounded in that machine this morning and died when he got to hospital. The observer took control of the machine and brought it down; it was very little damaged.

I saw Wenham somewhere out here soon after I came out. Lucky blighter. I wouldn't mind getting a wound that would take me home and keep me there, or rather with you, for a long, long time. Oh! Lady mine, think: it's nearly nineteen long months since I came out here. I seem to have lived this kind of life all my days, and everything that came before seems like a dream. When will the nightmare end? I want to be with my Lady for always and always.

Just all my love, sweetheart.

Your Eric

Friday 13 October
Posted 14 October

My Lady

I wasn't able to write last night because I had to do some night firing and I was more than ready for bed after getting up at five yesterday morning. The postcards arrived with your letter, written on the fourth, last night, and do you know, they caused me rather a disappointment, because I thought when I saw the great big flat envelope that there was a lovely long letter inside, after not getting one for two whole days. But as soon as I felt it I guessed it was not all letter. I think, though, I must be getting spoilt with getting a letter nearly every day, as I have been doing lately. But it's so very nice to get them like this and they do help so. Even the bluey ones do, 'cause they make me realise that I'm not the only person that is having a bad time, and so make me pull myself together when I get fed up.

Yesterday I was in the OS all day. We did a lot of work all morning, strengthening a new shell hole which we have occupied, as we can see better from it than from the old one. All afternoon I was observing, the row was awful from our guns. I saw our infantry start off and disappear into the cloud of shell smoke in front of the next place, north of the one you mention in this letter – the one you were reading about, you know. Yes, we were firing there. The maps in *The Times* are quite fairly correct. Now and then they get a bit optimistic, but are usually pretty good. The weather has been more or less reasonable lately, thank heaven, but has fits of nastiness now and then. For some unearthly reason, I've got a beastly, runny kind of cold – adds to the pleasure of life out here, of course!

Oh! sweetheart, what an awful age it seems since those five dear wonderful days; so much has happened since then, and it all begins to get blurred. But still, I've got my wee diary, so I shall remember lots and lots of things to tell you by it, when I come. I wonder how much longer it will be before then. I'm so glad you heard from Burrows's fiancée, and I'm so glad I succeeded in helping her a little. I must tell her the plant of rosemary that she sent is in full life. There are a very big number of new graves in the cemetery since dear old Burrows was buried there. Several of them have railings round them now, but still none of them are as neat as his.

It's after lunch, and we are going to fire in a minute, and now it's nearly post time, so I must send this off. Bye-bye, dear one, again. Just all my love to you forever,

Your lover

My darling

I got two letters this evening. What an age it takes for a letter to come back from the time I send one off: it means a good fortnight. Why, we have been back from the so-called 'rest' nearly ten days now. Sweetheart, when those postcards arrived last night I wrote on one, and was going to send it today, but this morning I thought exactly the same as you, that I didn't like anything of ours being public property, so I tore it up and luckily managed to write a bit of a letter instead. Do you know what I long to be doing now? I want to be lounging on the sofa in front of a big fire and you playing to me and singing 'The Old Grey Hills of Home.' Oh! God, would that I could be listening to you now.

Mr Boche must have suddenly got a new lot of ammunition up 'cause he started throwing it about quite hard tonight and appears to be still at it on the left.

After dinner – 9.35

Blow! The Major kept me doing a job with him for half an hour and I might have been writing to you. Well, sweetheart, just to show you the joy of this cursed life: I've got to be up at 1.15 am again, until 3.30 am for night firing. It really means that we never get a whole night's rest, as Martin and I take it in turns. There was an awful *cr-r-ash*, a beastly 4-inch gun is firing all round here. It comes at a terrible pace and gives one no time to get undercover if you're outside.

I'm writing this in my wee dugout; I can just lie full-length in it. I am sitting on my bed with my feet in the doorway. The candle is stuck on a piece of wood which is jammed in between two sandbags. There are five pegs on which I hang my towels, gas bags, clothes etc. There is a shelf just above my head, made of the lid of an ammunition box, with collars, handkerchiefs and socks on it. Just outside the door (covered by two sheets of corrugated iron) is my washbasin, on a little ledge cut out of the clay, with an ammunition box on its side forming a cupboard just above the basin, with my shaving tackle and wash things in it. A narrow trench about four yards long and two yards deep runs at right angles to the entrance into the old German front-line trench in which the mess is.

Lady mine, I feel dreadfully sleepy – there's that beastly gun again. This time a bit of shell landed on the corrugated iron over my washing place. I wish the beastly thing would cease firing.

2.50 AM

Sweetheart, your Englishman feels horribly sleepy and wishes that he was in bed, fast asleep. How glad I shall be when I can have a whole night's rest for a week on end. Sweetheart, I've been sitting thinking how very much I shall miss your dear dad when I come again, thinking of the first time I ever saw him, that afternoon I came to tea, and then of the last time I saw him, how terribly worn and haggard, but how very, very dear he was to me then. What an awful feeling there was in my heart when I went to say goodbye. I knew it was the last time I should see him here on earth, and I couldn't say a word, my tongue seemed to be tied. But this isn't being very cheerful, is it? There's that cursed Boche gun still firing. What an awful pace the shell comes at. I do hate the thing.

I've got to go up to the OS today and so I must stop writing now and leave this to go by the post today. Night-night, my own darling.

Your Englishman

10 October   *Glorious morning. Woke up with a beastly throat and cold. Came up to the OS. Saw plane come down, thought it was going to land right on me. Saw one brought down in flames, counted thirty-five in air at once and lots more.*

12 October   *Up in OS all day. Saw infantry 'go over' to gain pushing-off point for the Transloy show on the*

14th. Got parcel and apples from Mum and wee note, also letter and pcs from Phyl.

14 October   *A choice day's work. Up at 5 am night firing. Got word to go to register brigade, had to cross 300 to 400 yards bang in the open and Boche shelled us with 4.2s; my God, it was unpleasant. Got to support line Shamrock trench, then on to front line. Wire cut twice while observing, ground and men difficult to observe. Finally finished registering at 5 pm. Came back through Lesboeufs across sunken road at level fifteen feet deep. Got a lovely chocolate cake from Phyl.*

SUNDAY 15 OCTOBER

My own darling

Thank heaven I'm here to write this after yesterday. I had a beastly job to do. I had to go down to the front line and register a place the Boche were holding, only 200 yards in front of our trench. The worst of it was I had to go 300 to 400 yards bang in full view of the Boche, with three telephonists and two other officers. Lady mine, your lover is not a funk, but by Jove, my heart was in my mouth about a hundred times. They spotted us, naturally, and fired at us with 4.2s. One landed three yards from us. Oh! lady mine, it was a horrible, horrible moment as the thing came towards me. Imagine, three yards only and I would have gone into smoke. Thank God, though, it was not to be. We arrived at the support line just dead beat and flopped into it, thanking our lucky stars we were undercover. The telephonists were simply splendid, as they always are, just real stout fellows – every one of them deserves a reward. Yet we are told that so many telephonists are recommended that gunners don't get remembered. But the gunners are not half as stout as the telephonists, and don't have one quarter as bad a time.

After we all had a breather, we went on down the trench, on

and on until we got to the place where I could observe from. The Boche bumped 5.9s and Little Willies all round us, so much so that I had to move to another part of the trench three times. Of course, the wire got cut twice, and we had to wait an awful time while it was mended by the two linesmen I had with me. I started registering at about 1.30 pm and finally finished three Batteries at 5 pm. By then it was nearly dark so we got back more or less safely. Do you know, a Little Willie landed absolutely dead behind where I had been observing in the first place. Luckily, we had moved away from the place two or three minutes before. It landed just on the edge of the parapet and knocked it all in. Honestly, I wouldn't be an infantry officer for a million pounds out here, the life must be absolute h—.

Well, I'm quite safe and sound, dear, once more, so there's no need to worry. I must shut up now, as it's nearly post time and I've got to inspect gas bags! The cake arrived yesterday: what a beauty it is. Thank you so very, very much for it.

All my love to you, lady mine, forever,
Eric

TUESDAY 17 OCTOBER
FIELD SERVICE POSTCARD, POSTED 18 OCTOBER

I am quite well.
I have received your letter dated 9 October.
Letter follows at first opportunity.
Eric

TUESDAY 17 OCTOBER

My darling
Oh! I got the very dearest lovely letter from you yesterday. The one about the weekend we would have on our own in your house, and what we would do with it. Really, lady mine, I can forget all about this beastliness while I read this letter, and how

I long to be able to do everything just as you say we would have done. I'm afraid, though, I would have been turned out of the kitchen for trying to make love, because the whole letter makes me just ache and ache with love for my Lady.

I have never eaten a flapjack, as far as I know. Don't they consist of flour, baking powder, suet or butter and water, or something of that kind? However, I know they would be luscious as long as you made them. I feel just as though I would want to dance round all over the place, and I'm sure I would pick you up (much against your wishes) and whisk you from the kitchen. Yes, perhaps I would sit and sulk when you teased me because I wanted loving very badly, but oh! sweetheart, I can just imagine how very wonderfully dear you would be when you melted and came to me.

And now for our evening. Well, first we would get ready for dinner, and you would put on – what? – that sweet grey dress with the sticky-up Elizabethan collar and my shoes. Then we'd have a nice dinner all to ourselves, and afterwards, when everything was cleared away and the curtains drawn and the chairs close to the fire, then we'd put out the lamp and make a good blaze. You would do that, as I'm not allowed to touch the fire. You'd kneel down and poke away at the fire till it blazed up. Then you would perhaps take your knitting, while I would gaze into the fire and think of how wonderful it was in 'heaven on earth', away from all this horribleness. Then you would have got tired of sitting curled up, and I would put my arms around you and lift you towards me. Then I would draw your head back ever so gently until you looked full up into my face as I bent down. Then a wonderful love quiver would run through me and I would bend down further and kiss you full on the lips. I can almost see those dear hands holding the knitting drop to your lap when I took your head in my hands, and I can feel the wonderful thrill of real love go through me as my lips touch yours. The minutes would slip away and the hours would fly, and still we would forget all time. What would it matter; we could stay where we were because then our world could go on without us having to think of going to bed. Perhaps we would go to bed, though, very, very late, and we would give each other a final goodnight kiss. Then we'd creep off to our rooms and dream lovely, happy dreams, to be told the next day.

Now, sweetheart, I must turn in; it's 10.30 and I've got to do night-firing at 1.15. Every atom of my love to you, dear one forever,

Your Englishman

15 October   *Up at 5.15 for a small bombardment, to bed again at 6 until 7.30. Tested sights and censored letters. Told Phyl about yesterday. Firing most of afternoon, a lot of Boche aeroplanes and balloons up. Sent Wenley 125 francs and asked him to buy 100 cigs for me.*

16 October   *Up in OS all day. Heavy bombardment of Dewdrop, Hazy, Sleet, Hail and Rainy trenches. Watched aeroplane flights, counted twenty-seven of our machines up at once. Got a dear letter from Phyl.*

17 October   *Testing sights and firing nearly all morning. Valley shelled with Little Willies. Gunner hit legs and arms. Sent FSPCs to Mum and Phyl. Wrote to Phyl about weekend by ourselves.*

18 October   *Zero hour 3.40 am. Attempted to get brown line in front of Le Transloy, attempt failed. Sniped Boche in the open near Dewdrop trench. French plane flew over line barely twenty feet up, daring fellow. Major came up in afternoon. Got letter from Dad and Phyl.*

19 October   *Started raining like the devil this morning. My dugout lasted until I was dressed, then it came in in a torrent from under the bottom sandbags.*

Rained all day, everywhere awful. Tested sights, promulgated orders. Night firing 12 to 2. Slept in mess. Wrote to Phyl.

THURSDAY 19 OCTOBER
RAINING LIKE — !

My dearest

The rain started early this morning and, heavens, how it came down in sheets. Everybody is soaked. The Major got a bath in the early morning from the roof of his dugout. Thank heaven, mine held until I was just finished dressing. I had told my servant to roll up my bed in case the roof began to drip on to it. Before I came into breakfast I did so myself, and as I turned back the foot, horrors, there was the whole floor flooded. I mopped a lot up with my sponge and filled my basin twice, then discovered it was running in fast under the bottom sandbag at the end. So I yelled for Bradley (my servant) and told him to take my bed into the mess, as this is the only semi-dry place now. When I returned after breakfast, I found the whole dugout flooded, nearly nine inches of water on the floor and about eighteen inches where I wash, just by the entrance. So I'm afraid my wee dugout is really 'done in' this time. Wasn't it kind of it to let me have a whole night's rest and not disturb me until I could cope with it. I hate to think of the joyful time I would have had if it had suddenly started when I was in bed.

Our mess cook, Bombardier Smithers, is too funny for words. The wet weather seems to raise his spirits – he is mud from head to foot, yet he's always joking about something and roaring with laughter. He is an old fellow, fat as you make 'em, with a big, rosy, dirty face: a splendid cook, too.

Now I've got to go to the guns, so bye-bye, dear heart, just all my love to you for always,

Your Englishman

My darling

Here it is, 10.30, and I'm just starting to write. I must thank you
so very much for this last letter, the one written on Wednesday
the eleventh, the same day that the missing one of mine turned
up. It is a dear, dear thing and helps so very much, especially
today when everything and everybody looks as miserable as it is
possible to be. Owing to my dugout being flooded this morning,
I am sleeping in the mess tonight; it is drier, at any rate.
Unfortunately, I shan't get to bed until 2 am because I have to
do the night-firing from midnight to then. We have another
sub. now. He's not a new fellow because he has been in the Div.
Ammunition Column for a long time. In fact, it's Arnold, one
of the three of us who were recommended for 2nd star – you
remember, he got it, and Lawrence was the other. It makes
things a good deal easier from a work point of view and for that
I'm jolly glad.

Yes, my darling, I do want reality so very badly. I want to be
by my Lady again; it seems a terrible age since I left you, so many
things have happened since then.

I stopped here and looked at my watch, found it had stopped,
so rang up the telephonist and asked him the correct time.
Heavens, what a shock I got when he said it was three minutes
past twelve. I rushed out to the guns – as quick as this d— mud
will allow, that is – and got them going. It must have been
11.30, not 10.30 when I started writing. Ugh! Sweetheart, it's
bitterly cold outside. Thank heaven, it's a lovely clear moonlit
night, so it may manage to be fine in the morning. When are we
going to be taken out of this show? It really is about time; eight
whole weeks and over now. The poor gees look dreadful and we
are all so weary of it. Martin had a lucky one the night before
last; a shell burst not two yards from him, just behind one of my
guns, and a wee bit just snicked his ear. Tonight, a shell landed
just in front of the other of my guns, and one man was slightly

bruised; it was a lucky thing.

What heaven it would be to be sitting in front of a good big fire with you right close to me, talking of all sorts of things and building castles in the air. We would just forget all about the war and talk about things in our world. Oh! I am so cold, lady mine, my feet are just like ice. Dear heart, this letter is so terribly dear; it makes me love my Lady with all my heart and soul, and it is the very greatest help I could possibly have out here. I know I shouldn't get the blues but really it is the horrible effect of this cursed climate, which in my mind is a million times worse than England.

FRIDAY, AFTER LUNCH – 2.30 PM
Sweetheart, you must forgive your lover for being a faint-hearted idiot in that letter. He is an owl, just because it rains and seems particularly nasty, to get a fit of the blues. Heavens, when I think of the poor infantry who have to stay for long hours or more in an open trench and get soaked, then have to sit all night in absolute freezing cold, well, all I can say is we gunners don't know how well we are off.

I had to stop last night because it was time to stop the guns firing, and then I turned in straightaway. I woke about fifty times, I think, because of the cold: ugh! it was awful. Now, I must say bye-bye, you darling; just every atom of love that is in me is for you now and for always.

Your lover

SATURDAY 22 OCTOBER, 1916
FIELD SERVICE POSTCARD, POSTED 24 OCTOBER
REDIRECTED FROM ATHLONE TO DUBLIN ON 28 OCTOBER

I am quite well.
I have received your letter dated Friday 13 October.
Letter follows at first opportunity.
Eric

20 October *Beautiful fine day; terribly cold, though. Tested sights, worked at dugout. Finished letter to Phyl. Got letters from Phyl and Dad.*

21 October *Frosty night, very cold, misty morning. Did some digging till mist lifted. Watched men bombard trenches. Saw two clinical barrages. Got shelled with lachrymatory shells. Had to walk down as Batt. started firing at 5 pm. Fired barrage again at 7 pm. Rations and water were overturned in mud. Went to bed early because of strafe at 5 am. No mail.*

22 October *Up at 5 am for clinical bombardment. Up again at 7.15 because team and water cart got stuck in trench by Battery. Major went to Sailly Sailisel. Lovely day. Fired salvos for Major. Did strafe at 4 pm, rehearsal for tomorrow's firing. Sent FSPCs to Phyl and Mum. Wrote to Mum tonight. To bed early for night firing.*

MONDAY 23 OCTOBER
POSTED 25 OCTOBER
REDIRECTED FROM ATHLONE TO PEMBROKE ROAD, DUBLIN
ENVELOPE DIRTY AND TORN

Lady mine

I'm not going to answer that last letter of yours written on Friday the thirteenth, just ten whole days since, because I have only a few minutes now, and also I haven't thought about it properly. This is just a note, instead of sending one of those beastly FSPCs.

It's simply brutally cold here now. Every morning the ground is caked hard on the surface and everywhere is white. During the day it is nearly impossible to keep warm unless one is doing some vigorous exercise. Even ten minutes after you stop, you are shivering again. At nights it's rotten; I can't keep warm, so I wake up at frequent intervals and then doze off again.

Yesterday morning we had a strenuous one and a quarter hours, hauling drivers and horses and a water cart out of the trench close by. For some reason, they managed to drop the water cart into the trench, and with it being full it dragged both the drivers (three) and the six horses drawing it in as well. One driver got pinned under three horses and all one could see was his face. Thank heaven, nobody was damaged and we got all the horses out. One was exhausted; otherwise they were all right. The roadway – a mud road – near here is simply terrible now. The mud is half-dried-up and the poor horses have to try and strain to get their feet out of it; I wonder half of them don't drop down and die with over-exertion.

Miller is still down at the wagon line. He is better, but is still not right. The pain has left his back and gone into his leg. Now, sweetheart, I must stop – duty calls, what!, what!

All my love to you, you darling.

Your lover Eric

THURSDAY 26 OCTOBER 1916
FIELD SERVICE POSTCARD POSTED 28 OCTOBER
REDIRECTED FROM ATHLONE TO DUBLIN, 1 NOVEMBER

I am quite well.
I have received your letter dated Friday 13 October.
Letter follows at first opportunity.
I have received no letter from you lately.
Eric

23 October   *Thick mist all morning. Zero hour for brown line and green line show postponed from 11.30 to 2.30 pm. Tested sights. Censored letters. Wrote to Phyl. Firing from 2.30 to 6 pm. Wrote to Miller. Battersby and Cornell went out early this*

morning to trenches and have never returned.
Wrote to Phyl about her plans.

24 October *Raining again as hard as the Devil, everything*
            —! Tested sights. Did firing. Got stuck in mud
            by No. 3 gun. Sent card to Mum. Finished letter
            to Phyl. Wrote for Primus stove repair and sent
            cheque for ten shillings. Nothing been heard of
            Mr B or Cornell.

SATURDAY 28 OCTOBER

TELEGRAM FROM LIVERPOOL
REDIRECTED FROM ATHLONE TO PEMBROKE ROAD, DUBLIN
COLLECT FEE ONE SHILLING AND FIVE PENCE HALFPENNY
TO PHYLLIS FROM JOSEPH (ERIC'S FATHER)

Eric reported by wire this morning dangerously wounded Oct 27 is in
casualty clearing station they cannot grant permission to visit.

My own darling Englishman

I wonder why I'm writing this, which you may never see – oh God, perhaps even now you have gone far away from your Lady – I wonder when another telegram will come; this knowing nothing is terrible, I don't know what to do. I simply have sat and shivered with such an awful clutching fear at my heart ever since your dad's wire came. It was forwarded from Athlone to Pembroke Road as that was the address we had given the post office, Mum brought it to Leeson Street. I was in my room unpacking and had just hung up 'Eric' over my bed, when the old maid came up to tell me Mum was downstairs and down I rushed. That anything was the matter never occurred to me until I saw her face. Oh my love, my love, what shall I do – but I must be brave and believe all will be well – dear one, surely God won't take you from me now. It will be the end of everything that matters because, oh Englishman, you are all the world and life to me. But I must be brave like you, dear, but the words of your dad's telegram will keep ringing in my head and squashing out hope. 'Dangerously wounded'. I say it over and over again till it doesn't seem to mean anything – when I came over to Pembroke Road with Mum, I tried very hard to pray but no words will come into my head, except 'Oh God, give him back to me.' This writing to you is the only thing that makes the waiting easier – everybody is very kind, I know, but I feel I would give anything to be just by myself – I think I will go to Leeson Street now to see if there is another wire.

SUNDAY 29 OCTOBER
TELEGRAM FROM LIVERPOOL TO LEESON STREET DUBLIN
TO PHYLLIS FROM ERIC'S FATHER

No further news have cabled clearing station.

TUESDAY 31 OCTOBER
TELEGRAM FROM LIVERPOOL TO LEESON STREET DUBLIN
TO PHYLLIS'S MOTHER FROM ERIC'S FATHER

Wire just received Eric died of wounds Saturday heard nothing more.

POSTSCRIPT

Eric was seriously wounded at Morval on Friday 27 October 1916, and was sent to the Casualty Clearing Station at Meaulte, where he died the next day, aged twenty-three. He was buried in Grovetown Cemetery at Meaulte near Albert.

Phyllis moved to London with her mother and became an opera singer. Eventually she returned to Ireland. She never married and always kept Eric's picture above her bed. She died in 1991, aged 99. She was cremated, and her ashes scattered on the River Shannon.

Jean and Tom Kelly visited Eric's grave at Grovetown Cemetery in 1998. They collected rose petals from it, which they later threw into the Shannon.

ERIC APPLEBY
1893 – 1916

PHYLLIS KELLY
1892 – 1991

Together at last.